Last Night in San Francisco

~

Tech's Lost Promise and the Killing of Bob Lee

Scott Alan Lucas

STEER
FORTH
PRESS

STEERFORTH PRESS
LEBANON, NEW HAMPSHIRE

For information about permission to reproduce
selections from this book, write to:
Steerforth Press, 31 Hanover Street, Suite 1
Lebanon, New Hampshire 03766

Cataloging-in-Publication Data is available from the Library of Congress

ISBN 978-1-58642-399-5

Printed in the United States of America

EU RP (for authorities only): eucomply OÜ, Pärnu mnt. 139b-14, 11317,
Tallinn, Estonia, hello@eucompliancepartner.com, +33757690241

1 3 5 7 9 10 8 6 4 2

For my family

CONTENTS

PART ONE

Someone Stabbed Me

Main Street was quiet at half past two in the morning on April 4, 2023. A scattering of cars, a figure sleeping by the trash. The Bay Bridge hung overhead, empty in the cold spring night. The ever-present security cameras watched as a man stumbled down the sidewalk.

The man, staggering and clearly in distress, called 911 on one of the two cell phones that he carried. "Help," the operator heard him say in a distraught, distant voice. "Help."

A driver sat in a Toyota Camry at the corner. The man saw its blinking hazard lights and moved toward it. What did he want? Was he looking for his Uber? Was he drunk? Was he high? The man lifted his shirt, and blood poured out from wounds to his chest. The Camry drove away.

Moments later, the man walked to the entrance of the Portside apartment building. He went to its call box, as if to summon someone upstairs. But before he could, he collapsed. His blood smeared the box and the pavement where he lay on his back.

All the while, his phone was still connected to 911. Calmly, the operator was trying to get him to say where he was. The man turned himself over and tried to talk again.

"Help!" he yelled. "Someone stabbed me."

Another car passed by. The man got up and moved toward it, but it had passed before the driver could see him. Then he collapsed again.

Using the data from his cell phone, the dispatcher sent police and EMTs to the man's estimated location, the 400 block of Main Street, a quiet part of San Francisco on the city's eastern shore, overlooking the dark waters of the bay.

"Advised he is bleeding out," said the dispatcher. "He's outside on the street."

In the emergency room at San Francisco General Hospital, physicians and nurses worked to save the man's life. The prospect was not good. He had been stabbed three times. Once in his right hip and twice in his chest — long horizontal wounds that sliced from one side of his torso to the other. One of the chest wounds was superficial, but the other had penetrated his heart, straight through and out the other side. Trying to save him, they pumped him full of blood and adrenaline. They performed a surgical incision — a thoracotomy — to access his damaged organ. Stapling his heart closed, they massaged it with their hands, desperately attempting to make it beat again.

At 6:49 A.M. — two minutes before sunrise — they pronounced him dead.

His name was Bob Lee.

Meden Agan

Two days later, I was home, planning a trip to Los Angeles for a story about artificial intelligence in Hollywood, when my editor at *The Information*, a tech news site, sent me an email.

"Any ideas how you might attack reporting around the Bob Lee murder?" he wrote. "I think that's a story we as a publication need to have a voice on."

I almost said no. I was busy with the other story, and I didn't cover crime. It felt like every other journalist in the world was writing about Bob Lee and like his death was the only topic of conversation in the city of San Francisco. Why bother? But I said yes.

Looking back, I'm not sure why. Maybe I wanted to join the other reporters working on the story. Maybe I wanted to solve the mystery of who had killed Bob Lee, and why. But to be honest, I think the real reason I said yes was that Lee had dragged himself to the Portside building. As it happened, I knew the building quite well. Growing up, my parents had close friends who lived there. We celebrated holidays there every year, my sister and I sneaking off during Passover to watch *Mrs. Doubtfire* on the VHS while the adults debated the Clinton impeachment and whether Barry Bonds was on steroids.

As a journalist, San Francisco has been my only real subject — a city that I love and resent in equal proportions. My career has taken me to the tops of its skyscrapers and to the bottoms of its basements. I've interviewed fishermen and billionaires, and I've written more about zoning than anyone should have to. For several years, I was an editor at *San Francisco* magazine, and as I had grown to understand the city, I felt more and more protective of it. Around the world, Bob Lee's death was being held up as an example of why my city was dangerous, deadly, and out of control by people who didn't know the Portside from Portola. Maybe it was that bad, but I thought that if our story was going to be told, it ought to be written by someone who actually knew it.

When I took the assignment, I thought I would work on it for two weeks. At most, two months. I had no idea where the job would lead. For the next two years, I would follow the life and death of Bob Lee wherever it led me — a world of life-changing technology, luxury condos, private clubs, and staggering wealth. It would also lead me in to a world of abuse, drug addiction, and crime. What I came to realize was that in telling the story of Bob Lee's life and death, I would be telling the story of the city that we had become: futuristic, optimistic, decadent, rich, important, powerful, and self-loathing.

But I didn't know that yet. All I knew when I started was that a man had died trying to get into a building in which people I had loved once lived.

The morning of April 4 came and went. The city went about its business. BART trains shot through the Transbay Tube. Cars packed the Bay Bridge, creating a traffic jam that stretched all the way to Emeryville. Coffee shops opened their doors, tourists rode the cable cars, and Elon Musk temporarily changed Twitter's bird icon to a Shiba Inu, an unfunny reference to an outdated meme. (Twitter is now known as X.)

On the other side of the country, once-and-future President Donald Trump was being arraigned on charges of paying hush money to porn star Stormy Daniels, and in Florida, Miami-Dade County announced a deal to rename its basketball arena, a necessary change ever since FTX, the cryptocurrency company that had previously held the rights, collapsed.

Among those who knew Lee, the phone calls, texts, emails, and DMs were already flying: *Have you heard about Crazy Bob? Do you know what happened? Wasn't he supposed to be in Miami? Doesn't he live there now? Who was he with? What was he doing? Why was he in San Francisco?*

There was one more question, too: *Where was that psycho bitch last night?*

Meden agan.

That was one of the maxims adorning the entrance to the Temple of Apollo at Delphi, advice for the ancient pilgrims who came looking for answers to life's problems. It means "nothing in excess." In other words, leave the party when the party's over.

By the time he was in his forties, Bob Lee had all the trappings of success that a twenty-first-century San Franciscan could ask for. He had tens of millions of dollars. He had worked at some of the world's most influential companies and invented an application used by millions of people every day. He had children who loved him, membership at the city's best clubs, and a new condo in Miami, where he had recently moved. Bob Lee was not famous. Unless you were in his field, it was unlikely you had ever heard of him, but the people you *had* heard of in tech, like Musk and Twitter cofounder Jack Dorsey, had all heard of him — and in many cases worked with him. Arriving in the Bay Area to work as a programmer for Google at the dawn of the century, Lee had worked on the Android operating system before moving to the financial services company Square (later renamed Block), where he created Cash App.

It had been a long climb from St. Louis, where Bob was born on December 20, 1979, to an Anheuser-Busch engineer and a newspaper reporter. Lee was one of many programmers who lived, worked, and flourished in San Francisco and the Bay Area. As the people who knew him best would tell me, Bob was extraordinary enough that his death became international news, but ordinary enough that his life could sum up his time and place.

The promises that Bob's life embodied could make you dizzy. Thanks to digital technology, authoritarian governments would fall, unimaginable fortunes would be created, and science and innovation would drive forward. Every great painting ever painted would be at your fingertips at a swipe. You could listen to any recorded song that was ever distributed. What couldn't you do with that capacity? Prior revolutions had just swapped one group of elites for another — but thanks to the internet, we would all join the new elect. Light was pouring out of San Francisco and remaking the world *ek gnosis* — rational, free, young, and rich.

Remember how cool your first smartphone felt? Remember how stupid it felt the most recent time you picked it up?

Today we know what actually happened: The world *has* been remade, and the results are sad and meager. Autocracies are as happy to use technology as democracies, and, thanks to ever-growing surveillance networks, it can be hard to tell the difference between the two. Giant unaccountable corporations have amassed incredible wealth and power, enriching a few while immiserating the rest. Down in the precariat, the gig workers, part-timers, and freelancers may lack traditional bosses, but they also lack living wages, job security, and control over their lives. Our culture is clogged with reboots, brand crossovers, and sequels. Everything is recognizable and nothing is interesting. At least the robber barons of old had the decency to act like robber barons. Ours want not only to rule but also for us to admire them.

At least, that's how it has felt in San Francisco.

Our city, like any, has always had its dispossessed and down-trodden. But between fentanyl, the coronavirus, and our stubbornly high rents, life in the city seemed worse than ever. There were people living in tents in almost every neighborhood. Downtown felt deserted. The streets were dirty — one survey found human feces on 50 percent of them. And a spike in hate crimes against Asian Americans made the streets feel not only at once barren and filthy but also dangerous. After our previous district attorney brushed one of the attacks off as a "temper tantrum," it felt to many residents as if the city's leaders were not interested in protecting them.

Nor did the rest of our leaders seem to be good stewards of the public trust. Members of our school board threw around racial slurs, broke the payroll system, tried to eliminate algebra, and wasted their time trying to rename schools. Dianne Feinstein, once our mayor and still one of our state's senators, seemed determined to die in office, which she finally did in September 2023. Nobody seemed to have the influence to prevent former Speaker of the House Nancy Pelosi from pursuing the same route. Our mayor seemed overwhelmed, and an FBI investigation revealed corruption throughout the bureaucracy.

Throughout it all ran a grim feeling of resignation: This was just what it was to live in the city. Expensive, miserable, and — on the wrong street on the wrong night — deadly.

3

Fuck San Francisco

Jake Shields was angry. But then again, Shields's profession was anger.

Shields grew up at the end of a dirt road in the Sierra Nevada, and San Francisco seemed like a different planet. But after earning a wrestling scholarship to San Francisco State, he made it his home. After college, he went pro, joining the Ultimate Fighting Championship. He earned a 31–9–1 record, enough to put him near, but not quite in, the top ranks of mixed martial arts. "He's never going to be the guy," said the head of the UFC when he let Shields go, but Jake kept fighting on Twitter, where he had half a million followers. He beefed with the rapper Cardi B, called for teachers who supported trans students to be "arrested, tried and then executed," and mockingly congratulated George Floyd on "three years of sobriety" on the third anniversary of the day that police in Minneapolis killed him.

On Twitter on the morning of April 5, Shields read an update from the San Francisco Police Department about Lee's death. Jake had already heard about it, even though this was the first public communication the department put out.

"#SFPD Homicide is investigating an early morning Homicide near Highrise Condos in the 400 block of Main at Harrison in SOMA," read the tweet. "A 43 y/o male from Mill Valley, CA was stabbed and died. Anyone that witnessed the crime or has information should contact us. We believe it occ around 2:30AM, if you have video or your parked vehicle captured video from time frame 2:10AM–2:35AM, from the general area."

From Miami, where he was living, Shields posted that he had just found out that "my good friend was killed last night while walking in San Francisco." Shields said that he was in the "good" part of the city and that the crime appeared to be a "random mugging/attack."

"Fuck San Francisco," he added.

Shields often inserted himself into events that he had nothing to do with, but in this case, it was different. Not only did he know Lee, but the two men had been planning to have dinner upon Lee's return to Miami. But, on April 3, Bob texted Jake that he was going to stay in San Francisco for one last night.

Soon after Shields sent his tweet, the television news revealed Bob Lee's name to the public.

The more Shields thought about it, the less his friend's death made sense. It wasn't just that Bob was Shields's friend, but he didn't have any enemies. He didn't get into fights. He was a positive guy. A peacemaker. Nobody would have wanted to kill him if they knew him. But while his death wasn't personal, it couldn't have been a robbery, either. When the police found him, Lee still had his wallet, his two iPhones, his watch, and his cash. What kind of mugger would leave all that? So if it wasn't personal, and it wasn't a robbery, what else could it have been?

Jake wouldn't be surprised if it was a street person, somebody crazy off drugs. The city was too weak to deal with them, and they were terrorizing people. He knew from personal experience — Shields had abandoned San Francisco after his girlfriend was mugged. But something else was bothering him — the Portside. Jake used to live there; Bob had been over. In his last moments, was Bob trying to find him? Would things have been different if Jake had been there? Could he have saved him?

"I didn't want to be the one to leak the name but now it's out," tweeted Shields. "Bob Lee is an extremely high profile tech guy so hopefully this will at least bring attention to these problems."

Even before Elon Musk bought it a year earlier, Twitter was no longer powering the news cycle the way it used to. But even if the site had declined further in relevance after the purchase, it could still throw a spotlight onto something — especially if Musk himself was operating that spotlight.

At 2:27 A.M. PST on April 5, Musk replied to Shields in a tweet seen at least seven million times. "Very sorry to hear that. Many people I know have been severely assaulted. Violent crime in SF is horrific and even if attackers are caught, they are often released immediately," he wrote, tagging San Francisco's new district attorney. "Is the city taking stronger action to incarcerate repeat violent offenders @BrookeJenkinsSF?"

"Yes it's extremely sad both the state of SF and this tragic death," Shields wrote back. "It's possible you even know Bob Lee because he's very big in the tech world and works closely with @jack." (Jack as in Jack Dorsey, the former CEO of Twitter and CEO of financial services company Square.)

Their mentions filled up with replies. One of Musk's employees linked to a story about Kathryn Steinle, a young woman shot to death in 2015 near where Lee was found, and wrote: "Where Bob was attacked is 'deemed' the good area. I lived on Lansing St in Rincon Hill in 2015 and loved the area. This was the downfall right here." The conservative activist Christopher Rufo said, "You should consider moving Twitter HQ to Miami." A pseudonymous account replied with a picture of the Bat-Signal, comparing San Francisco to the crime-ridden Gotham City.

The story quickly jumped from Twitter to conservative media outlets. Shields talked to anyone who would listen in the days after Lee's death. He told the *Daily Mail* that Lee had fled San Francisco for Miami because of crime: "He did comment on San Francisco deteriorating, which is why he actually had just relocated to Miami." On NewsNation, he said: "The city — it's had problems for a while. But it's very clear to anyone that's been there for a long time that it keeps getting worse. People talk and say they're going to do things, but no one does anything."

Shields knew that he and Lee made a strange pair. He was MAGA. Bob was woke. Shields was a fighter. Bob was chill. But when they met at Coachella, they bonded and then frequently shared long, late-night dinners.

They may have been close, but to me the bond seemed a little superficial. When I spoke with Shields, he wasn't sure what Bob did and said he only realized how wealthy his friend really was from the news. When I asked him to introduce me to more of Lee's friends, he came up with someone saved in his phone as "Mike Party Scene." (Mike never returned my calls.)

But regardless of how close they were, Shields was the first to tweet about Bob, and he and Musk established a narrative that would dominate for the coming weeks.

A perennial Republican candidate in San Francisco wondered if Lee had been killed by someone living at a recently opened homeless shelter, writing on Twitter, "Isn't the location 2 blocks from a Navigation Center?" A conspiracy theorist suggested that Lee had been killed because he worked in the cryptocurrency industry: "CashApp founder Bob Lee was found randomly stabbed to death in San Francisco. The app was a way to send and store currency to get around corrupt big banks and PayPal which politically discriminates. So totally not fishy at all . . ." The blind gossip site Crazy Days and Nights, which mixed well-sourced Hollywood gossip with QAnon delusions, claimed that

Lee's death was connected to his work on a coronavirus tracking app. "Apparently this global health organization didn't like what this A list tech guy was going to say at a conference about his time working with them early on in the pandemic. Now, he is dead. I am sure it is a coincidence."

Most of the rumors were hard for me to believe — I was pretty sure, for instance, that the World Health Organization didn't have a hit squad. But there was one that caught my attention that seemed more detailed and plausible. On the r/conspiracy subreddit on April 6, someone anonymously posted that Lee had been killed as part of an investigation into money laundering at Square:

> I have a few good sources that have confirmed to me the leading theory both at the local and Federal level is that Bob Lee was murdered in a targeted hit over money laundering happening over a long period on CashApp including during his tenure at Square, related to the ongoing SEC investigation if not other investigations. Bob would have provided valuable witness testimony and was killed so he could not. There are little hints. He still had his phone and watch (which was expensive) after the stabbing (a robbery/mugging would have at least taken the watch and phones are stolen all the time in SF). It's unclear if his wallet was still with him or at least my sources don't know. It was also made to look like it could be a random street crime but that is a very safe part of SF where such a thing is pretty much unheard of. Everything points to this being a hit and while there have been many odd deaths in crypto elite, my

sources again tell me this is directly related to long-standing money laundering on CashApp. I do know more specifics about who/why and am 100% sure, but unfortunately I cannot say any more than this or provide sources. Apologies.

Soon after the post went up, it was deleted. I wondered why. Had it been too close to the truth?

4

The Doom Loop

San Francisco is an arrogant place, a strange city that thinks the rules of the world don't apply. And that makes it dangerous. One moment you can be walking down the street and the next get clubbed on the head and wake up on a boat bound for Shanghai. You can walk past the Zodiac killer and not even know it — they never caught him. The city has seen Jonestown, the Zebra murders, Dan White, the Trailside Killer, the Tong Wars, and bombs at the mayor's house. They tried to ban Happy Meals, and they cared more about freeing Tibet than they do about helping their own people. Hell, you couldn't even trust the earth to stay still under your feet there.

At least that's the story that conservatives tell. "San Francisco is like a rogue nation," said Fox News host Jesse Watters in June 2023, a few months after Lee's death. By then it had become a well-worn line. Tucker Carlson — himself born and raised here — told his viewers the same thing a few years before: "It's even worse than you have heard," he said. "Civilization itself is coming apart in San Francisco."

It's not surprising that we play such a role in the imaginations of conservatives. San Francisco has always been a fascinating city, right from the beginning, when the lure of gold caused young men from around the globe to pour in. It was a lawless place, lamented 1855's *Annals of San Francisco*, the very first history book ever written about the city. "Here was a large maritime city, with a population of about twenty thousand persons, and embracing a strange medley of dangerous and desperate characters — without a solitary officer, or a single law to govern or control them. All these rebellious elements had to be subdued, and good citizens made of daring bravados." It was not for nothing we had not one but two Committees of Vigilance — popular uprisings that took the law into their own hands. San Francisco seemed ever poised between law and disorder. As one young immigrant wrote in a letter to his wife during the Gold Rush: "Cards, dice, painted women, obscene prints, gin cock-tails, and brandy-smashers are in large demand and full supply. But then to meet and oppose them there are churches, sabbath schools, active temperance societies, libraries, reading rooms, many good families, and a large number of well-principled and consistent men."

We've never quite shaken the reputation. We are a city of instant riches, not sober industry. We are filled with Catholics and Jews. We are tolerant. We are multicultural. (For the last thirty years, the majority of our population has been non-white.) We are queer. We meditate. We eat vegetables. We sip espressos and thumb our noses at the fly-over states. Some of the right's fantasies are lurid: In 2013, Christian broadcaster Pat Robertson claimed that "some in the gay community" in San Francisco were deliberately infecting others with HIV by wearing hidden rings that cut fingers to exchange blood. Others are more intellectual, like the 2015 essay in the *Claremont Review of Books* that argued San Francisco's well-known self-regard was nothing more than an attempt to "to justify, obfuscate, glamorize, exalt, and deflect attention from House of Bourbon levels of wealth concentration and inequality."

It didn't take long for conservatives to hold up Bob Lee's death as yet another example of lawless San Francisco, ruined by the

Democrats who ran it — the first paragraph of the first story the *New York Post* ran about Lee's death called out the city as "Nancy Pelosi's district," trusting its readers to draw a connection between the two. "West Coast residents have condemned the killing, as a disturbing crime wave grips the region," wrote the *Daily Mail*. (Its only source for that was an actress in Los Angeles who posted on Instagram that "SF is a complete shithole.") Even the religious press joined in, with a correspondent for *The Philadelphia Trumpet* — a Christian magazine out of Edmond, Oklahoma — reporting that the city's "cultural depravity [of] perversion, homosexuality and even transgenderism" had contributed to Lee's death.

But you didn't need to be a tabloid writer, an actress, or a zealot to see that the city was in trouble in the cold spring of 2023. Leaving aside the conservative criticisms from the outside, within the city there was also a sense that something was wrong. We called it the doom loop — an economic forecast about the deterioration of our business district — but it started long before that phrase was coined.

There are as many versions about what happened to San Francisco as there are San Franciscans. There is the leftist critique, that the city sold its soul to the technology industry, importing a horde of well-paid, soulless techies who raised housing prices, gentrified our neighborhoods, and drove out the avant-garde. There was the moderate point of view that the city's problems stemmed from its NIMBYism — homeowners and landlords had enacted an impenetrable thicket of regulations that kept the supply of housing low and prices high.

The problem was corruption. The problem was crime. The problem was the cops. The problem was the buses. The problem was the private shuttles. The problem was tax breaks. No, the problem was too many taxes. The problem was homelessness, drugs, Ronald Reagan, Nancy Pelosi, Scott Wiener, Aaron Peskin, skyscrapers, zoning reform, wealth distribution, disinformation, the school board, too many meetings, not enough community input, not enough affordable housing, not enough market-rate housing, the mayor, the press, too many cars, or too many bicycles.

The only thing we could agree on was that the city's problems were someone else's fault.

The meeting of the San Francisco Police Commission began at 5:30 P.M. on Wednesday, April 5, under the ornate dome at city hall. The committee handled policy and discipline for the police department and rarely generated headlines. The first item on its agenda was a commendation for an officer who had returned a stolen stuffed animal to a little girl. The presentation was jovial, but the mood turned somber as a Black woman named Paulette Brown approached the microphone. Her son, Aubrey Abrakasa Jr., had been killed in 2006, and ever since she had haunted these meetings. Today would have been his birthday, Brown said, holding up a poster bearing her son's face: "Now I've got to go to the gravesite and stick a birthday candle on the dirt."

A chime sounded. Her time was up.

Chief of Police Bill Scott made his regular report. "We have a lot going on with the homicide unit," he said. There had been two killings in the past week. One of those had occurred on April 1. A victim was found with two gunshot wounds at 1:04 P.M. in the Tenderloin, the roughest part of the city. There were as yet no suspects or arrests. The chief was careful not to make the case seem routine, but that's what it felt like. *Expected.*

"Yesterday, there was a homicide that has gotten a lot of attention," said Scott, moving on to Lee's death. He had to hold back some information, but what he could say was this: After 2:00 A.M. on April 4, 911 received a call from a man saying he had been stabbed. He had been taken to the hospital, where he died.

"This is an ongoing investigation that has included officers canvassing the scene, locating evidence. There has been around-the-clock —" Here the chief caught himself, adjusting his words to encompass both the Tenderloin killing and Abrakasa's death. "— *investigations* on both of these homicides, and there is a lot of work to be done. I want to say this: We have a grieving mother of a homicide victim who is here every Wednesday. These types of cases that get a lot of attention, we just need the public to know that our investigators investigate these just as we do any other loss of life.

"We will do everything we can on every case in the city where somebody loses their lives," he concluded, and then asked the commissioners for their questions.

The newest member of the commission, Kevin Benedicto, took a nervous breath. "I know it's very early to have — there's not that much information on the 400 block of Main Street homicide. We don't know yet, or have anything to share, about whether the assault was random or if it was targeted?" he asked.

"Nothing to share yet," said Chief Scott. "Of course, we have discussions about every homicide, but nothing to share, because we don't want to be premature and definitely we don't want to speculate. We are going to be thoughtful about following the evidence and will put out what we can put out when we can. I know it's of interest, as is every homicide. People tend to get a lot more anxiety on random homicides rather than personal disputes. As soon as we have enough information to put out, we will."

Benedicto nodded. "Thank you, Chief," he said. "I just want to say — for the homicide on the 400 block of Main Street — to extend my condolences to the family of the victim — and my condolences to the families of victims who don't make it to the front pages of newspapers, as well. I know the chief said the investigation is ongoing. Any violence, particularly homicides in our community, is always terrible and unacceptable. I know that SFPD is working on this case, as it does in all its cases."

Benedicto's voice sped up as he came to his point.

"I do feel like some people out there on the media and social media are exploiting this horrific crime for political gain. This was a tragedy and a crime. It's under investigation — you heard it from the chief. Yet so much of the coverage in this short amount of time has misrepresented facts, [has been] fear-mongering, and trying to exploit this tragedy. We don't know all the facts. I know the chief will update us when we do. But I find this premature and distasteful to try to fit this horrifying act of violence into a preconceived narrative and use it to advance a political agenda. I'd direct people to read the very moving tribute about the victim that was written by his father." He was referring to a post that Rick Lee, Bob's father, had recently made on Facebook.

"There were some very moving tributes that were covered in the *Chronicle* written by friends and family," added Benedicto. "I would discourage people from reading the fearmongering and the politicization and the things on Twitter, including things by the CEO of Twitter. So, um, thank you."

The *San Francisco Chronicle* had been the Bay Area's leading newspaper for decades. One of its newest competitors was the *San Francisco Standard*, recently founded by the venture capitalist Michael Moritz. Neither of the two news outlets had strict political agendas, but the newer one tended to be tougher on crime than the *Chronicle*, which had shifted to the left recently. That evening the *Standard* tweeted out a clip of Benedicto's remarks in which it made two edits — one to remove Benedicto's mention of its competitor and another to clip out the first part of his remarks, where he expressed his condolences.

"Did this guy just blame @elonmusk instead of offering his condolences and reassuring the public [that] the perpetrator will be found and prosecuted?" tweeted one outraged techie. Benedicto wrote back that, in fact, he had expressed condolences, and the person apologized to him.

But not everyone was so conciliatory. Among those were Garry Tan, the head of Y Combinator, the start-up incubator that had helped birth Airbnb, Reddit, and DoorDash. Tan had become more involved in local politics over the past few years, driven by frustration at the city's progressive faction. "The police commission decided it wasn't about helping protect the public but to virtue signal for the SF political machine," he tweeted. "It must be reformed and Benedicto and his cronies must resign or be removed." That tweet drew the attention of many of his compatriots in the industry, including investor Jason Calacanis, who the next morning wrote on Twitter: "THESE ARE THE LUNATICS RUNNING SAN FRANCISCO[.] EVIL INCOMPETENT FOOLS & GRIFTERS WHO ACCOMPLISH NOTHING EXCEPT ENABLING RAMPANT VIOLENCE[.] VOTE THEM OUT[.]"

5

How Much Tech Can One City Take?

If you were inclined to agree with Calacanis, the case you would make against the city would go something like this:

San Francisco made its first attempt to survey the number of its unhoused residents in 1999. The method was simple. People fanned out across the city and counted. That year, they estimated that 3,610 people were living either on the street or in shelters. The next year, the survey found 5,376 unhoused people, a number that stayed roughly the same for the next decade, before rising in the beginning of the 2020s to 7,000 or 8,000 unhoused people per year. "It's worse than the Third World," local political columnist Phil Matier told CNN in 2023. "Because it's right under the shadow of the rich and the powerful, and it is not only tolerated, until recently it was almost ignored in San Francisco."

A walk through the Tenderloin would make you believe Matier was understating it. Drugs are sold openly. People in the throes of mental illness wander the streets. It's a frightening, filthy place, a sad fate for those people who spend their days there, and a sad fate for the neighborhood.

What Matier was saying was that the problem was not that the rest of the city had to put up with the crime, disorder, and decay. The problem was that for all our wealth, the city's government and nonprofits could not seem to help those who were suffering. In fact, all that wealth we had generated had, in its own way, made it harder to help them. People experience addiction, poverty, and mental illness in every part of the world. But San Francisco had an uncommonly high cost of living, which meant the margin for error was small. It was easier to fall onto the streets here than almost anywhere else in the world.

And that problem, like many of ours, was self-inflicted.

San Francisco's commitment to environmentalism, neighborhood preservation, and community participation meant that the pace of our construction of new housing — market-rate, subsidized, and temporary shelters alike — had for decades fallen woefully short of our need. As a result, the cost of housing had skyrocketed. From 1987 to 2023, the inflation-adjusted price of a home in San Francisco had tripled, and in the year that Lee died, a home sold in San Francisco could expect to fetch prices three to six times the national average for a similar one. The housing crunch hurt renters — about two-thirds of the city's residents — in worse ways. Despite a rent control law passed in 1979, inflation-adjusted rents increased more than fivefold between 1980 and 2023.

Unless you were lucky enough to have bought a home or landed a rent-controlled apartment back then, San Francisco was a punishing place to live. For poor people, people living in gentrifying neighborhoods, young people, or those who had just moved here, it was bad. For those on the cusp of having a place to sleep indoors or not, it was worse than that.

As the tech industry boomed, it was easier to point to an influx of the newly rich as the source of the problems.

Opponents of the tech industry coined a new word for it — hypergentrification — and proclaimed a battle for the soul of San Francisco. For years, progressives had faulted what they called the Growth Machine — an interlocking network of elected officials, business owners, lobbyists, journalists, and others who supported new office buildings and high-end residences as a way to bolster the economy of the city at the cost of degrading neighborhood character, pushing out communities of color, and turning over the city's politics to its richest people. Once their targets had been real estate developers and banks. Now they were companies like Google and Apple.

And as housing prices soared, it was easy for older members of the counterculture to blame techies, rather than zoning, for rising housing prices. In 2012, the journalist David Talbot wrote a widely discussed article that posed the question: "How Much Tech Can One City Take?" "Nowadays, you see Lexus SUVs parked in the driveways on Precita Avenue," he wrote. "Young masters of the universe in Ivy League sweatshirts buy yogurt and organic peaches at the corner stores where Cuervo flasks and cans of Colt 45 were once the most popular items." (In another essay a few years later, Talbot was more blunt, blaming the city's problems on "Stanford assholes.") Soon after, the writer Rebecca Solnit — who sold her condo to a Google engineer in 2011 — joined the chorus, taking aim at the private shuttles that ferried workers from the city to offices on the Peninsula. "Most of them are gleaming white, with dark-tinted windows, like limousines, and some days I think of them as the spaceships on which our alien overlords have landed to rule over us," she wrote in the *London Review of Books*.

The conflict peaked in 2013 and 2014, when protestors blocked the tech buses as they were picking up passengers in neighborhoods like the Mission. (In Oakland, one protester even climbed on the roof of a shuttle and vomited on its windshield.) More than one techie wearing Google glasses got physically accosted. Scooters were thrown into the water. The cabbies protested Uber, the preservationists protested Airbnb, and the drag queens protested Facebook. It seemed like the host was rejecting the graft.

For many techies, though, it was a confusing time. Many of them were *from* the Bay Area, or at least had gone to college here or moved here because they liked the region's vibe. They assumed they had just as much a right to live in the city as anyone else did. They voted for Obama and rode buses and volunteered on the weekends. They experimented with polyamory, dropped acid, and didn't want the police to shoot unarmed Black and brown people. Their heroes were hippie technologists like Grateful Dead lyricist John Perry Barlow, Apple founder Steve Jobs, and Whole Earth founder Stewart Brand — members of the same counterculture that Talbot and Solnit claimed for themselves. So why were they supposedly the problem?

It was now the morning of Friday, April 7, days after Bob Lee died. It was time for Jason Calacanis to record his podcast. Wearing a black T-shirt and posing in front of some kind of alpine scene, he read a bulletin. "Cash App creator Bob Lee, a.k.a. crazybob on Twitter, that was his Twitter handle, was stabbed to death — tragically — in San Francisco earlier this week.

"Any thoughts about that?" he asked his cohosts on the *All-In* podcast. "Have we come to some sort of crossroads?"

All-In may be one of the most popular podcasts about technology, finance, and politics in the world. It is certainly the one whose hosts have the highest combined net worth. Collectively, Calacanis and his cohosts David Friedberg, Chamath Palihapitiya, and David Sacks were worth roughly $3 billion.

Since 2020, the Besties, as they bill themselves, have talked poker, debated investments, and kibitzed about international affairs. They put on a good show — they are rich, smart, accomplished, and funny men. It feels, as *Slate* once described it, like a "safe space for Silicon Valley's money men."

"I used to live two blocks from where the event happened," said Friedberg, speaking in front of an image of Biff Tannen's Pleasure Paradise Casino & Hotel from *Back to the Future: Part II.* (For what it's worth, the character had been based partially on Donald Trump.)

"Where is it?" asked the self-proclaimed "king of SPACs," Palihapitiya, sitting in front of a heart-shaped mirror and wearing an open-necked white shirt. "Is it a bad place?"

"It's in SoMa, in Rincon Center," said Friedberg.

"Is it part of that drug craziness?" asked a confused Palihapitiya.

"No, it's not in the heart of the camping district. It's just a nice area in SoMa — a quiet area," said Friedberg.

But Palihapitiya didn't look convinced, because *all* of San Francisco was crazy, at least on some level.

Friedberg and Lee had started at Google around the same time, before Friedberg left to found a digital agriculture company that sold to the chemical giant Monsanto in 2013 for $1.1 billion. Lee's death reflected his own frustrations with the city. "I went to San Francisco a few weeks ago," he said. "As I pulled up to a restaurant, I joked with my buddy in my car, 'Oh, my car is going to get broken into while we are at dinner because I'm parked on the street.'" Ninety minutes later, they returned from dinner to find a thief had pried open his trunk. As he recounted the indignity, Friedberg got amped up.

"Look, here's the thing. If you park at a parking meter in San Francisco for eight minutes too long, you get a $60 to $100 parking ticket. San Francisco has become an Upside Down town," he said, referring to the shadowy underworld on Netflix's *Stranger Things*. Its leaders had given "those who are lacking in the power structure everything, and [try to] take everything away from those who are at the top of the power structure.

"And by the way, I think this applies in a lot of other ways," he continued, including affirmative action in colleges and diversity, equity, and inclusion efforts by airlines and hospitals. "Did we just flip the power dynamic upside down and give them the end point?" he asked.

Friedberg, like all the hosts of the show, did not return my requests for comment. I couldn't exactly follow the connection he drew between Lee's death, auto break-ins, parking tickets, college admission, and the racial demography of commercial airline pilots, but I think what he was trying to say was this: Human beings are unequal. That's just the way it is. If a government, like the one in San Francisco, attempts to change it, at best it won't do anything, and at worst it will cause harm. Leave the best of us, like Friedberg and Bob Lee, alone.

"It has come to a breaking point in San Francisco," said Friedberg, finally catching his breath. "That's my rant."

"I can't disagree with you," said Calacanis, who turned the conversation over to Sacks.

One of the members of the PayPal mafia — the early members of the payment services company whose ranks include Peter Thiel and Musk — Sacks was interested in politics at a very young age. In 1995, the year after graduating from Stanford, he wrote a book with Thiel criticizing their alma mater for abandoning Western civilization for postmodernity and political correctness. (Sacks has subsequently apologized for several things he wrote there, as well as things he wrote in the *Stanford Review*, the right-wing student newspaper that Thiel founded.)

Wearing a black baseball cap and sitting against a gray wall, he began by saying, "We don't know exactly what happened." But, he went on, "I think we suspect, and I would bet dollars to dimes, that this story is very similar to a case we had in LA recently, the Brianna Kupfer case."

Kupfer's murder was horrific. A twenty-four-year-old UCLA graduate student, she was working at a furniture store on January 13, 2022, when a mentally ill transient with a long criminal record stabbed her to death in an unprovoked attack. Sacks claimed that Lee had likely been killed in similar circumstances — and that the solution was to support the efforts of techies like Y Combinator's Tan to tame San Francisco. "They are setting loose on us a predatory or psychotic element that jeopardizes our safety," he said. "Just vote for whoever the fuck Garry Tan tells you to vote for."

"It's a tragic situation all around," interrupted Calacanis, furrowing his eyebrows to announce that he was no longer hosting conferences in San Francisco. "I do my events in Napa," he declared.

"It takes regime change," said Palihapitiya, an early Facebook employee and now a minority owner of the Golden State Warriors basketball team. Palihapitiya compared San Francisco to New York City during the bad old days: "I grew up in a pretty crappy neighborhood, and you knew who the gangs were," he said. "You knew who the tough guys were. It didn't come at random. It didn't come and stab you to death, right? So you become street-smart in a culture like that, because you know how to avoid it and you know how to be alert. This doesn't feel like that."

"No," said Calacanis.

"This is just like a bad roll of the dice and you could get stabbed to death just walking down the street," said Palihapitiya. "Where are the politicians to stop this?"

"They don't care," said Calacanis.

～

Were you rolling dice with your life in San Francisco? For some people, the answer was yes.

On March 21, 2014, a twenty-eight-year old Latino man named Alex Nieto was sitting on a bench in a park in Bernal Heights eating a burrito before going to his job as a security guard. As Nieto sat on the bench, a white man was nearby walking his dog, which ran up to Nieto for a bite of food. A frightened Nieto pulled out the Taser he carried for work. The dog's owner yelled at him. Nieto yelled back. The man grabbed his dog, shouted a slur, and stormed off.

As Nieto struggled to calm down, a separate white couple came upon him still holding his Taser. They didn't know about the incident with the dog and called the police to report an angry man with a weapon in the park. The police arrived within minutes. Later, they said that Nieto pointed his Taser at them and in response they unleashed fifty-nine shots, more than a dozen of which struck his body, killing him. The district attorney declined to press charges, and protests convulsed San Francisco. Students walked out of classes. Posters went up bearing Nieto's face. Five demonstrators carried out a seventeen-day-long hunger strike in front of the police station on Mission Street.

That was just the first in a series of deaths that shocked the city over the past decade.

On the first day of July 2015, a little more than a year after Nieto's death, an undocumented immigrant from Mexico named José Inez García Zárate was wandering along the waterfront. Over the course of his life, he had been convicted in American courts seven times of felonies and deported from the United States five times. In 2015, he was serving time in San Francisco County Jail on two-decade-old marijuana charges. While he was being held, US Immigration and Customs Enforcement issued a detainer for him, asking to be notified when he was released so that the agency could take custody of him. But San Francisco has a sanctuary city policy, and so instead of turning him over to the feds, San Francisco officials released García Zárate to the streets.

As he wandered, García Zárate scoured dumpsters. He would later say he found sleeping pills in one of them, which he took. Woozily, he picked up a bundle of fabric from the ground. There was a gun wrapped inside — and as he held it, it went off. There would later be conflicting accounts of whether he had pulled the trigger: García Zárate first said he was shooting at sea lions, but at his trial he claimed the gun had gone off accidentally. What was indisputable was that the .40-caliber SIG Sauer fired a single bullet, which traveled through the air, hit the concrete, and ricocheted into a thirty-two-year-old white woman named Kathryn Steinle, killing her.

The gun, it turned out, belonged to a ranger employed by the Bureau of Land Management. Five days before, he had gone to dinner with his family and left it in a backpack under the front seat of his car. Thieves had smashed the window, stolen the backpack, and discarded the loaded weapon. It was like something out of a *Dirty Harry* film. As a result of the city's sanctuary laws, a young white woman had been killed at random by an illegal Mexican felon. As a candidate, Trump made Steinle a regular topic in his campaign speeches, and although her family distanced itself from him, he even mentioned her in his acceptance speech for the Republican nomination. (García Zárate was acquitted of murder and manslaughter, although a jury did find him guilty of illegal gun possession. He was deported to Mexico, and his present location is unknown.)

About six months after Steinle's death, San Francisco police killed a Black man named Mario Woods in Bayview. Woods was boarding a bus when police stopped him because he matched the description of a suspect in a knife attack that had happened nearby. Woods was holding a knife, which he refused to drop. Police opened fire, first with bean-bag guns and then with lethal weapons. Woods died, as did a Guatemalan man named Amilcar Perez-Lopez, who also had a knife, both shot by the police on February 26, 2015. The next year, police killed a Mexican man named Luis Góngora Pat, who at the time was living in a tent on the streets. That was in April. In May, police killed a Black woman named Jessica Williams during a car chase in Bayview. The chief of police handed in his resignation (Chief Scott was his replacement), and in 2019 the city elected a new district attorney, Chesa Boudin, who promised a new approach to public safety.

With the onset of the coronavirus pandemic, life went from uncomfortable to bleak. According to the city government, 1,285 people died of coronavirus. Unemployment shot back up, reaching 13.2 percent in May 2020. In the earliest moments of the virus, there were those arguing that the city had to be shut down to prevent its spread, while others, looking at the history of anti-Chinese xenophobia during previous plagues, cautioned against overreaction. Ultimately, San Francisco weathered the virus better than many other places, in part because our public health officials had been tempered in the fires of the HIV/AIDS epidemic.

But as the lockdown wore on, the number of hate crimes reported against Asian Americans and Pacific Islanders jumped from nine in 2020 to sixty in 2021. The crimes were brutal and random. There was the case in Chinatown of a man attacked in broad daylight by a teenager carrying a plastic baseball bat. There was the time police arrested a man for breaking the windows of at least twenty businesses that he believed were owned by Chinese

Americans. And there was the case of an eighty-four-year-old immigrant from Thailand who was out for a morning walk when, out of nowhere, a man charged at him at a sprint, knocking him to the ground and killing him. Following that death, District Attorney Boudin spoke cavalierly in an interview with the *New York Times*, saying that the alleged attacker was having a "temper tantrum."

To his supporters, Boudin's empathy seemed humane. To his critics, it seemed misplaced. Boudin had been elected on promises to end cash bail, to prosecute police officers, and to divert those convicted of crimes into rehabilitation and restorative justice programs rather than seeking to put them in prison. But while his policies may have been popular, he was not. San Francisco voters organized a recall effort and voted Boudin out of office in 2022. His replacement was a Black woman named Brooke Jenkins who had grown up in the Bay Area.

Boudin was not the only target of the electorate's ire during the pandemic. A few months before voters tossed Boudin out of office, they also recalled three members of the San Francisco school board. The list of complaints against them was long. In 2019, the board voted to destroy a mural at George Washington High School that included depictions of enslaved people and a murdered Indigenous man. The debate split the city, but the mural ultimately stayed in place after a court ruled that the school board had failed to carry out an environmental assessment of the action. (The California Environmental Quality Act is an *astoundingly* capacious law.) During the pandemic, San Francisco schools were kept closed for a much longer period of time than schools in many other districts, fueling discontent among parents and students, especially when the board prioritized its effort to rename many of the districts' schools, including one named for

Abraham Lincoln, whom the board judged insufficiently aboli-
tionist.

The school board might have survived those controversies
unscathed. It might also have survived the disastrous rollout of an
expensive new payroll system that failed to pay many teachers on
time and the abandonment of merit-based enrollment at Lowell
High School, the district's flagship campus. But the school board
and some of its members could not survive a tweet by the board's
vice president in which she used the n-word in reference to Asian
Americans. Or its aftermath, in which she ignored calls for her to
resign and instead sued the district for $87 million. The case was
thrown out of court, but not before parents had begun organiz-
ing a recall, which voters approved in February 2022.

And so, as 2022 dragged into 2023, the city was in bad shape.
The mayor's approval ratings were abysmal. The streets seemed
deserted. The tech companies were laying off tens of thousands
of workers, and their leaders were leaving for places like Miami,
Austin, and Denver.

And then Bob Lee was killed.

— 6 —

Not Random at All

"A stabbing? Every law enforcement person will tell you — your mother who watches *Law & Order* will tell you — that it's extraordinarily rare for people to be randomly stabbed to death," said Joe Eskenazi, the managing editor of the neighborhood news site *Mission Local*. Wearing a 49ers sweatshirt, he was sitting in his cluttered office under a giant poster of a cover of a Tintin comic, recounting the week after Lee was killed.

For more than two decades, Eskenazi has been a local columnist and editor. He's the epitome of an alt-weekly journalist — wiry, intense, and full of obscure pop-culture references. He's righteous, maybe a little self-righteous, but almost always right. When I was in college, I read his work religiously. Later we worked together, and I discovered that he was not only a talented reporter and writer but also a kind and generous colleague.

All of this is to say that when Eskenazi calls bullshit, I listen.

As Joe first examined the case, he noticed a lot of things that didn't add up. There were no bars around where Lee had been found. No strip clubs or late-night restaurants, either. It didn't seem to be a robbery, and he knew that random killings, where the victim and the assailant did not know each other, were exceedingly rare. Eskenazi had been working his phone relentlessly, calling his sources and hearing things he couldn't yet publish. But he knew when he wrote his first column that not everything with regard to Lee's death was as it seemed.

He wrote:

> The public facts in the case remain vague. At present
> we simply have no idea what Lee was doing walking
> alone through a bereft section of downtown at 2:30
> in the morning. We have no idea who stabbed him,
> or why. The fact he still had a phone in his hand to
> vainly call 911 in his dying moments points toward
> this being an entirely irrational, random attack — or
> one that was *not random at all.*
>
> The decent thing to do is acknowledge a tragedy,
> express sorrow for those who have lost a treasured
> individual, and let the police do their work with all
> due haste — and then we can begin politicizing this
> poor man's death to buttress our preexisting world-
> view.

(Had I been Joe's editor, I might have taken that last line out.
It was funny, and a good point, but it was the kind of thing that
would make his critics jump all over him. But then again, it *was*
funny.)

The column continued, referring to the *All-In* podcast, which
had been posted online hours prior:

> Among Lee's fellow VCs and tech executives, this was
> presented as the latest and most egregious example
> of a wave of violent crime inundating San Francisco.
> Less-than-responsible news coverage quoted these
> allegations at face value, the way Ari Fleischer used
> to be quoted at face value talking about weapons of
> mass destruction. That's a problem because the mere

existence of crime, or even a specific crime deemed
extra tragic by outside operators for rhetorical effect,
does not create a crime wave.

Steinle's death was on Eskenazi's mind as he worked. He was
especially frustrated with Tan and the *All-In* hosts. ("You couldn't
pay me to listen to them," he told me.) Bob Lee, he wrote,

> deserved better than to have died, and he deserved
> better than to have been turned into a symbol of all
> that was supposedly wrong with San Francisco by
> rich loudmouths who couldn't find police headquar-
> ters with a flashlight and a million dollars in venture
> capital funding.

It was obvious to him that race played a role: Steinle and Lee
were both white. But many of the others who died — people like
Abrakasa and Nieto — were not. The frenzy that accompanied
Lee's death would not have arisen were he not a photogenic, and
wealthy, white man. If he were someone else, would his death
have been treated as if it were expected?

Joe hit PUBLISH and braced to get jumped on.

"How dare we dishonor this man's death by . . . *checks notes*
. . . trying to make sure other people don't die in similar ways,"
tweeted the blogger Noah Smith. Less than fifteen minutes later,
Tan replied: "Some of us are actually doing something about
it, not just talking." Obviously, what Joe had written had trig-
gered the head of the Y Combinator, because he continued to
tweet about it throughout the evening. "*Mission Local* seems to
serve their local bureaucratic masters over the basic public safety
needs of the people. Journalism should speak truth to power, not

power to truth." Then a few hours later he added, "That article is gaslighting trash."

Joe didn't know it at the time, but two weeks later, his point about which deaths were treated as expected and which weren't would be made for him in the worst possible way: On April 27, a security guard at a Walgreens drugstore on Market Street shot and killed Banko Brown, a twenty-four-year-old transgender man who was unhoused. The guard thought Brown had stolen $15 of candy. Both of them were Black.

"If you're going to point to depressing dystopian conditions in San Francisco," Eskenazi later told me in his office, "it would be these two people who were pitted against each other. That to me is dystopian — a transgender homeless Black person who is just stealing to get by being confronted by an underpaid Black security guard."

7

We Don't Normally
Work Next to Killers

When the police arrived early at the apartment building in Emeryville in the predawn hours of Thursday, April 13, nine days after Bob Lee was killed, Ilya Druzhnikov was meditating. Red and blue flashing lights pulled him out of his trance, and Druzhnikov looked out his window to the parking lot, where he could see a fleet of police cars. Officers were unloading guns and gear from them. Druzhnikov grabbed his cell phone and recorded the scene.

Most people would not expect to see so many police this early in the morning. But truth be told, Druzhnikov was expecting them. Later, someone from the TV news would ask him if he suspected his neighbor was a killer. "Yes," said Druzhnikov. "Of course I did."

"That's the first time I've ever heard somebody say that," said the reporter.

Emeryville sits across the water from San Francisco, splintered by the freeways and tucked between Oakland and Berkeley. California governor Earl Warren once called it "the rottenest city on the Pacific Coast." A small city, it has historically been home to establishments its neighbors didn't want. A hundred years ago, those were speakeasies, racetracks, and bordellos. Today they are Ikeas, Targets, and California Pizza Kitchens.

As an internet entrepreneur, Druzhnikov had founded and sold two companies. And while it could seem like the history of technology in the Bay Area began with people like him, the history of the building he lived in showed that wasn't the case.

The Besler Building had been converted into condos in the 1970s, but before that, it was a factory. Constructed in 1923, the building was used as a manufacturing plant for making cars by Doble Steam Motors, the start-up of a San Francisco engineer named Abner Doble, an MIT dropout. His vehicles ran on steam, not gas, and even by today's standards were impressive contraptions. The Maharaja of Bharatpur bought one, as did the tycoon Howard Hughes, who raced it on the streets of Houston. But in 1931, the company went bankrupt, and the Besler brothers bought it, renamed it for themselves, and converted it to building airplanes until their company, too, folded.

Druzhnikov liked his building. And he liked his neighbors. Among them was the man who rented a unit across the hall and ran his business from it, an IT consultant named Nima Momeni. Druzhnikov and Momeni shared a blunt sense of humor. "You fucking Jew," Momeni would tease him when they saw each other. "You dirty Arab," a laughing Druzhnikov would shoot back, even though he knew that Momeni was born in Iran. Momeni could be salty, but he had an Old World sense of etiquette. Once, when Momeni borrowed a bowl from Druzhnikov, he returned it filled with fresh fruit. (He wasn't the only neighbor who would experience Momeni's generous side.) Another time, Momeni heard Druzhnikov's dog barking inside the apartment, alone, and so Nima let himself in with the spare key and took care of the dog until Druzhnikov returned home.

"It was beautiful," said Druzhnikov. "He was thoughtful, helpful, and friendly."

But Momeni had another side, too. He often threw loud parties that went on all night. He often seemed drunk or high. And he liked his toys; he owned a BMW and a Jeep and a cigarette boat docked in a nearby harbor. He had knives and swords in his apartment.

When he was intoxicated, Momeni would speak nonsensically in a low growl of things Druzhnikov didn't want to know about. Once, he claimed that he had paid someone in cocaine to drive him to Burning Man. He would often talk about prostitutes. (*Mission Local* later found Momeni's phone number on an app that sex workers used to warn each other about potential clients: "Dangerous — uses a lot of coke, erratic in behavior, possessive, heavily armed," wrote one of them. "Definitely a boundary pusher a rough ⊘ snatched me by the hair after I said not to," wrote another.)

He was noisy, too. He liked to DJ — he bought himself an expensive set of speakers — and the sound of the techno music he played would often fill the building. Druzhnikov was resigned to it, but the other neighbors often complained. "Your bass travels through the whole place," Druzhnikov explained to Momeni once. "Dude," he offered, "can I buy you headphones?"

Early in the spring of 2023, Druzhnikov fell into a conversation with one of his neighbors.

"Nima's been acting even weirder than normal," said Druzhnikov.

In March, Momeni's car had been broken into. A few days later, Druzhnikov's car was hit. Nima was convinced that the thieves would be returning, and so he came up with a plan. Instead of reporting the crimes to police, they should rig up video cameras. When the thieves came back, as Momeni was sure they would, they would have video evidence. With that, they could figure out who the thieves were and convince them to return their stuff. Druzhnikov told him that he wasn't interested, and Momeni's scheme petered out.

But soon after, Momeni was caught up in another conflict. Another neighbor who used his unit as an office was a PR consultant named Sam Singer. When he moved in, he hired a crew to do some renovation work. Their noise bothered Momeni, who didn't seem to realize the irony.

"These fuckers doing all this construction noise when I'm trying to work," Momeni told Druzhnikov. "I'm going to get back at them."

Really, you are not aware? thought Druzhnikov. But he let it go, just as he had with the video camera idea. Then a few days later, Druzhnikov's Wi-Fi went out. That was weird. He knew he had paid the bill. He checked the router, and there wasn't anything wrong with it. He rebooted it. Still nothing. And so Druzhnikov had a hunch. Could Nima be up to something?

He texted Momeni about it. Nima wrote back apologetically. Yes, the Wi-Fi was out because of him. It was his fault. He was blocking the signal to get back at Singer. Embarrassed that he had accidentally blocked Druzhnikov's Wi-Fi as well, Nima apologized. The Wi-Fi came back to life.

But a few days later, it went out again. "What the fuck?" Druzhnikov texted, feeling less neighborly this time. "I'm trying to work."

Momeni apologized again, and the Wi-Fi came back again.

Sam Singer was one of the most well-connected men in the Bay Area. His clients included Chevron, the 49ers, Levi Strauss, real estate developers, transportation projects, and even Garry Tan.

When I called him for an interview, the solicitous and conciliatory Singer remembered his dispute with Momeni differently
from how Druzhnikov did. The first time they met, he said, he
told Nima, "I hope we haven't caused too many problems with
the noise." He said, "No, no, no," and added that he hoped his
stereo hadn't bothered Singer. As the two men chatted Momeni
said something about having grown up in Berkeley, and that he
had gone to college at Cal. Singer said he had gone to UC Berkeley as well, and as they said good-bye, Momeni handed him a
small stack of business cards.

"I do IT work," said Momeni. "If you need, just knock on my
door or give me a call."

On the night of April 3, Druzhnikov and the other residents of the
building were jolted awake by a woman pounding on the doors of
their apartments, shouting Nima's name. The next morning, one
of the residents wrote about it on the building's Facebook page:

> Hi neighbors, This morning at 2:30am a woman
> knocked our door loudly and tried to open it. We
> didn't open the door but she wouldn't stop knocking
> so I asked her to leave. She was looking for someone.
> The second time she knocked our door I told her I
> was going to call the police, so she stopped but kept
> roaming around the hallways and screaming "Nemas"
> or at least that's what I understood. Did she knock on
> anyone else's door? She looked young, with dark hair
> and was wearing a black coat. I don't understand, how
> can just anyone get in the building and do that 😢.

They misspelled his name, but Druzhnikov knew who they meant. It was a woman he had been hooking up with, Nima explained.

"She was too drunk, so I wasn't going to sleep with her," Momeni said. "I called her an Uber and sent her downstairs. But instead of getting into the Uber, she stayed in the building. She was so drunk she couldn't figure out where my place was, so she was running around knocking on people's doors screaming 'Nima.'"

This guy was getting more and more weird, thought Druzhnikov.

And then, well past midnight on April 4, Momeni texted Druzhnikov to come over, and to bring alcohol. Druzhnikov grabbed a bottle and went across the hall to Nima's unit. Inside, his neighbor seemed high and drunk. He was rambling — way worse than he usually would. The police were looking for him, Nima said. There had been a fight about a woman.

This wasn't just Nima acting weird. Something was really wrong.

Momeni gestured to an expensive Eames chair he had just bought. Did Druzhnikov want it? Would he take it? Druzhnikov declined and tried to focus Nima on what he was saying. What was this about some fight over a woman? He thought Momeni was talking about the dark-haired woman wandering the halls the night before, the one Nima had said he was hooking up with. Druzhnikov couldn't figure out what else it could have been about. Either way, Nima wasn't making a lot of sense.

Finally, Momeni grabbed a cardboard box and handed it to Druzhnikov.

"I want to get all the drugs out of the house," he said.

"Nima, I'm not going to open it, but look me in the eye and tell me it's drugs," Druzhnikov said. "Tell me that there are no weapons in there."

"Just drugs," said Momeni. "Just drugs. Just drugs. Don't worry about it."

Generally, Druzhnikov thought Nima's drugs were mediocre. His cocaine wasn't that good. But Nima did have something he wanted. He held a small vial of LSD, and shook it tantalizingly. "Here's the acid," said Momeni. "I know you like acid. You can use this whenever you want." And so Druzhnikov nodded and took the box back across the hall to his place.

He hid it in a small storage space near his front door. Over the next few days, he watched Momeni's condition worsen. His BMW vanished from its usual parking place, and Druzhnikov saw his neighbor outside talking to a strange man in a big black truck. Later Momeni asked him if he wanted to take a trip to Colombia with him. Druzhnikov begged off.

And then the police interrupted his morning meditation.

Through his keyhole, Druzhnikov saw the squad assembling outside Momeni's apartment. He heard them pounding on the door and shouting his neighbor's name.

Wow, thought Druzhnikov, *Nima must have been involved in something much worse than just a fight over a woman.*

"*Mission Local* is informed that the San Francisco Police Department early this morning made an arrest in the April 4 killing of tech executive Bob Lee, following an operation undertaken outside the city's borders. The alleged killer also works in tech and is a man Lee purportedly knew. We are told that police today were dispatched to Emeryville with a warrant to arrest a man named Nima Momeni."

Eskenazi's story ran at six in the morning, exactly forty-five minutes after police put Momeni in handcuffs. It was a long and well-edited story. It seemed like Joe and his colleagues had been working on it for more than just three-quarters of an hour.

Facts — at least the facts according to the police — were now replacing rumors as the rest of the local press corps descended on the Besler Building. Lee's death wasn't random. It hadn't come at the hands of some homeless addict. It wasn't a robbery. It certainly didn't seem to have anything to do with a coronavirus app or crypto. San Francisco's liberal lawlessness had not killed Bob Lee. Allegedly, Nima Momeni had.

Within a few hours, the story had received a million views — a huge number for the *Mission Local* site, which might typically receive fifteen to twenty thousand views a day. Eskenazi had thought it might, which was why he was careful not only to break the news but also to provide context.

"San Francisco is home to much in the way of visible public misery, unnerving street behavior and overt drug use," he wrote. "Its property crime rate has long been high, and the police clearance rate for property crimes has long been minimal. But the city's violent crime rate is at a near-historic low, and is lower than most mid-to-large-sized cities. Today's arrest would appear to undermine the premise that Lee's violent death was due to street conditions in San Francisco."

Eskenazi later told me, "My interest here was in making things right with regard to false information being put around for cheap, lazy, destructive politics." But for that to happen, Joe had to be right. And with such a high-profile story, if he made even one little mistake in the details, he was sure that Musk, Tan, or the Besties would pounce on him. As the morning drew on, Eskenazi fretted and fretted. Finally, other reporters filed their stories. He read each one carefully. Each time, they confirmed what he had said. Slowly, he began to relax. As he did, the pressure finally affected him.

"The repercussions of making a mistake in this story, even a minor one, would have been life altering," Eskenazi told me. "I spent a couple hours just out of it. It's like walking a tightrope over a chasm — you could make it, but then you think about what would have happened if you didn't."

Singer found out about the arrest when a reporter he knew called him in disbelief to say that they were at Singer's building. Singer found himself in a strange position for a spin doctor — part of the story. Momeni's arrest was a "total shock," he told the local CBS station. "I'm in the public relations business. We don't normally work next to killers."

In his apartment, Druzhnikov continued to wonder what the police wanted with his neighbor. The cops had arrested him, but they'd also stayed in the building for hours. What were they doing? Finally, his girlfriend went downstairs and asked them. *Murder.*

Druzhnikov's thoughts turned to the box in his storage space. Momeni had told him that there were only drugs in it. He even showed him that vial of acid. But could he believe him? What if there was evidence in there? What if there were bloodstained items? What if there was a murder weapon in his house right now?

That would be bad. As in accessory-after-the-fact bad. Druzhnikov called his lawyers and explained the situation. They told him they didn't handle criminal cases, so Druzhnikov called a firm that did. They asked him for a $10,000 retainer and said they would work with the police to give up the box. To Druzhnikov that seemed like a lot of money for not a lot of help, but then he realized that the lawyers were assuming the worst — not only that was there a weapon in there but also that Druzhnikov had already opened the box and touched it, leaving his fingerprints and DNA on it. That wasn't true, but they didn't know that.

Well, what the hell, he thought. *If that's what they think, I might as well just open the box.*

So he pulled it out and set it on the floor. Druzhnikov took a steadying breath and then opened it.

Momeni had told him the truth. Inside there were only drugs — Nima's lousy coke and the LSD.

8

A Planned and Deliberate Attack

At 9:19 A.M. on Thursday, April 13, 2023, Nima Momeni was booked at San Francisco's Hall of Justice on charges of murder in the first degree, including a sentencing enhancement of allegedly having used a knife to commit a felony. He faced twenty-six years to life in prison.

"This was a planned and deliberate attack," prosecutors wrote in a document in which they laid out the rudiments of their case.

According to the document, San Francisco police had found the dying Lee unconscious on Main Street. As the ambulance took Lee to the hospital, police began canvassing the area for clues. They didn't need to look far. Not only did they find blood on the pavement, but as they shined their flashlights through the fence of a nearby parking lot, they also saw a knife lying on the ground.

After identifying Lee, police began to put together his actions in the days leading up to his death. They interviewed a close friend, who said he was with Bob on the afternoon and evening of April 3. He said that around 3:30 P.M. that day, Lee had invited him to an apartment on Mission and 11th Streets, a few blocks from city hall. When he arrived there, he found Lee along with the apartment's tenant and a woman. The witness said he had never met the man who lived in the apartment, but he knew the woman — they had met through Lee three or four years before. After some time at the apartment, he and Lee left, going to the One Hotel, where Lee was staying.

While they were in the hotel room, the witness said he saw Lee receive a call from the brother of the woman in the apartment. He explained that since Lee had left the apartment, something bad might have happened to her. He wanted to know if his sister had been "doing drugs or anything inappropriate." Bob told him no, nothing like that had happened.

The woman's name was Khazar Momeni, who sometimes went by Tina. Her brother was Nima Momeni.

Bob and his friend parted around 12:30 A.M. on Tuesday, April 4. His friend went to bed. Bob went to Khazar's condo in the Millennium Tower, where she was with her brother. The next morning, the friend called Tina, who told him that Bob had come over "for a second." But she went to bed and didn't know what happened after that.

Police retrieved surveillance footage from the Millennium Tower that helped them discover what did happen. The brother and sister arrived in Nima's white BMW Z4 at 8:31 P.M. They went upstairs. At 12:39 A.M., Bob Lee arrived at the same building. He was inside for about an hour and a half. At 2:03 A.M., Nima and Bob rode the elevator down and got into Nima's BMW. They sat for a while and then drove away. Bob was dressed in black. Nima's clothes were light-colored.

From an apartment building high above Main Street, a Nest Cam captured what happened next. Nima pulled over and parked under the Bay Bridge. The street was dark, although a nearby parking lot filled with construction equipment was illuminated. Two figures exited the car, one in dark clothes and the other in light.

They stood on the sidewalk for five minutes. The video was grainy. It was impossible to see their faces. You could not see who was holding what, if anything, in their hands. What could be seen was that the figure in the black was closer to the fence and the lighter one was closer to the sidewalk.

Then something happened. "The subject wearing the light-colored top appears to suddenly move toward the other subject," said the charging document. Then they separated.

The dark figure moved north. The lighter one moved south before doubling back, crouching on the ground, and appearing to throw something over the fence. The figure then went to the car.

"Shortly after that, the white BMW leaves at a high rate of speed," said the charging document.

Using passcodes given by Lee's family, police unlocked the two cell phones that they recovered from Bob Lee. Reading the logs, they saw the victim had a large volume of ingoing and outgoing calls in the days before his death. One of them caught their attention: a FaceTime call between Lee and someone he had saved in his contact book as "Nima Via Khazar." They also found texts from Khazar to Lee, sent after the incident, in which she appeared to reference a dispute in which her brother was the aggressor.

"Just wanted to make sure your doing ok"

"Cause I know nima came wayyyyy down hard on you"

"And thank you for being such a classy man handling it with class"

"Love you"

"Selfish pricks"

The prosecution asked for him to be held without bail. The judge agreed.

The day after the arrest, the Besties reassembled in front of their podcast microphones.

Sacks began the show by talking about some fans who had begun meeting in person to listen together. He was delighted, saying it reminded him of the Rush Limbaugh fandom. Palihapitiya suggested that Sacks was so happy because he was having sex with men in public restrooms.

They all laughed, and moved on to artificial intelligence, which they talked about for an hour or so. Finally, Friedberg brought up a new topic.

"We saw that someone was arrested for the murder of Bob Lee —" he said.

"I was about to —" Calacanis interrupted.

"It turns out the report of the SFPD's arrest is that it's somebody he knew who also worked in the tech industry," Friedberg finished.

Calacanis interrupted again. "Possibly. Still breaking news."

"Possibly," said Friedberg, who said that although Lee's death was "quite different than what we all assumed it to be," they weren't wrong to have jumped to their conclusion. It wasn't as if San Francisco was a safe city. "I think both things can be true — that we are biased and fill our own narrative by latching on to what something tells us, but it also tells us quite a lot about what is going on in SF," he said.

To the other three men, even that limited mea culpa was a weakness. How could Friedberg give in to twerps like Eskenazi?

"Well, in fairness, in fairness," shouted Calacanis, stabbing his finger in the air and flapping his arms. "I think it's fine for you to make that point. I am extremely vigilant on this show when it's breaking news to say we should withhold judgment, whether it's the Trump case or Jussie Smollett or anything in between, January 6. In fact, quote from Sacks, we don't know exactly what happened yet. Literally, Sacks started with that."

"Yes, correct," said Sacks.

"We do that every fucking time on this program. We know when there's breaking news to withhold judgment. But you can also know two things can be true. A tolerance for ambiguity is necessary," said Calacanis.

"But I'm saying I didn't even do that," Friedberg said.

"But David, that is a fine assumption to make," said Calacanis, pain in his eyes.

"That is a logical assumption," Sacks agreed from in front of a roaring fireplace. "We got all these reporters, who are basically propagandists, claiming that crime is down in San Francisco. They are all seeking comment from me this morning, sending emails and trying to dunk on us."

By now Sacks was warming to the topic of how unfairly he was being treated. "Listen, we said that we didn't know what happened. But if we were to bet, at least what I said, I would bet this is a case that looks a lot like the Brianna Kupfer case. That's not bias; that's logic."

Sacks pointed to three other examples of recent crimes in San Francisco to make his point about "Gotham City." On the evening of April 5, a former member of the city's fire commission reported having been beaten with a metal pipe by a young homeless man in the Marina, one of the city's wealthier neighborhoods. The next week, Whole Foods announced it would be closing its store on Market Street because it could not keep its employees there safe. The same day, the board of supervisors was forced to cancel its meeting because vandals had stolen the copper wiring that connected it to the internet.

"I think there is a pyramid of crime and antisocial behavior in San Francisco that we can all see," said Sacks. "The base level is chaos on the streets, open-air drug markets, people doing drugs.

Sometimes you will see a person doing something disgusting, like defecating on the street or worse. Then you have a level up where you have people chasing after you or harassing you. People have experienced that. I have experienced that. Then there's a level up where there's petty crime. Your car gets broken into. Then you get mugged. Then the top of the pyramid [is] murder. What they are trying to do now is say that because Bob Lee wasn't the case we thought it was, that the whole pyramid doesn't exist. We can all experience it."

"With the disclaimer. With the disclaimer. We always do a disclaimer," said Calacanis, his eyes bulging and his finger again stabbing the air.

"I want to connect one dot, please," said Friedberg. "We filled in our own narrative about San Francisco with the Bob Lee murder."

"No," Calacanis shouted. "We put a disclaimer on it."

"We said what we know and didn't know," said Sacks, shaking his head angrily. "And furthermore, we are taking great pains this week to correct the record and explain what we now know."

Friedberg rolled his eyes.

Calacanis saw him do it. "Is it so hard to be intellectually honest? This is just intellectual honesty," he said.

"Honestly, you are getting soft here, Friedberg. You are getting gaslit by all these people," said Sacks.

"I'm not getting gaslit by anyone," Friedberg replied quietly, more to himself than to the rest of the group. With that, he relented, and in the closing moments of their podcast, the Besties finished by talking about which endangered animals they would like to eat and how much they liked Michael Mann's 1995 action film *Heat*.

"It's up there with *The Joker* and *Reservoir Dogs*," said Calacanis, signing off.

Just what *was* going on with crime in San Francisco? Was it up? Was it down? The Besties weren't the only ones who felt like the city was out of control. What was the real answer? I asked two criminologists exactly that question.

In 2018, Richard Felson and Patrick Cundiff, professors at Pennsylvania State and Western Michigan University, published a peer-reviewed research paper titled "The Gold Rush and Afterwards: Homicide in San Francisco, 1849–2003."

Their discovery: San Francisco was safer in the twenty-first century than it had ever been.

Here is their reasoning: Criminologists assume that many crimes go unreported. But there is one category for which social scientists assume that nearly every time it happens, the police get involved. That's homicide, and the reason is simple — bodies. As a result, homicides are a good proxy for the overall rate of crime. When they go up or down, it's likely that all other crimes — reported and not — have gone up or down as well.

What was even better is that the two professors had in their possession a data set of every reported homicide in the city from the Gold Rush until the turn of the twenty-first century, thanks to the work of retired San Francisco deputy chief of police Kevin J. Mullen, who in 1985 published a book in which he cataloged every homicide he could find in the early days of the city. They pulled the data from Mullen's book and matched it with local and federal records.

In the beginning, the city of San Francisco was in fact quite dangerous — the yearly murder rate was as high as 35 deaths per

100,000 people. Many of those were at the hands of "armed and intoxicated" young men, they said, who argued about "duels and disputes over land, mining claims, and gambling." If it had continued, that rate would rank San Francisco among the most dangerous cities in the country today. But in reality, as the city matured — quite literally its young men grew older — the murder rate fell below 10 deaths per 100,000 people per year, a rate very similar to that of the rest of the country.

As national homicide rates rose in the second half of the twentieth century, the rates in San Francisco rose as well, peaking in the late 1970s and early 1980s at a yearly rate of 15 homicides per 100,000 people. Since then, our murder rate has dropped. According to SFPD data (which goes further in time than Felson and Cundiff's work), in 2023 the murder rate had fallen to 6.7 homicides per 100,000 people, right around the rate for the country as a whole. In other words, homicides had been much more common during the Gold Rush, when San Francisco was an outlier among American cities. After that, however, the rate tended to mirror national trends, spiking in the second half of the twentieth century before declining until today.

So that was one piece of evidence that San Francisco's critics were wrong. Lee's death was not an example of a city that was out of control. It was horrific, but it was not an indicator of a larger trend.

Felson and Cundiff had looked at one city across time. To check their work, I also looked across cities at the same time.

What I found, in data collected by researchers at the Rochester Institute of Technology, was that in 2023, San Francisco was far from the most dangerous city in America. The murder rate in New Orleans, which led all major American cities that year, was 53.8. Just behind it was St. Louis, at 53.7. And not only that:

San Francisco wasn't even the most dangerous major city in California. Oakland had a homicide rate of 30.2 and Compton, 19.4. Many rural areas of the state were even more dangerous than the cities. According to the state department of justice, California's most dangerous county was Merced, where the homicide rate was twice San Francisco's.

Moreover, while being killed by a stranger is a frightening prospect, it is also unlikely.

According to the FBI's National Incident-Based Reporting System's 2021 report, the most recent year for which data was available, 56 percent of male victims of homicide knew their alleged assailant. (Women were much more likely than that to be killed by someone they knew.) In 22 percent of cases, a male victim died at the hand of a stranger. In the other 22 percent, authorities were unable to determine what relationship existed. That means that at best — if every unknown case actually involved a stranger — 56 percent of male-victim homicides came at the hands of a person already known to the victim. Following a more reasonable assumption — that the distribution of the unknown cases matched the distribution of the known cases — around three-quarters of male-victim homicides came from suspects known to the victim. Other studies confirmed my estimate. One put the rate of stranger homicides at 18 percent of all homicides. Another put it in the range of 18 to 25. A third put it precisely at 21.9 percent of homicide cases.

Based on those odds, if you were to bet dollars to dimes that Lee had been killed by a stranger, you would have been a *sucker*. But if you can believe it, that's still doing Sacks a favor. Because he added that he thought it was likely to be not only a stranger homicide but also, in particular, one caused by a person having a mental breakdown. And the odds of that? They are roughly zero.

A study in 2011 estimated the annual rate of stranger homicides in which the killer had a psychosis at 1 per 14.3 million people per year. Extrapolating from that, there are maybe 23 such cases each year in the entire United States. In California, there would be 2 or 3 each year out of our roughly 2,000 homicides per year. Those are not dollars-to-dimes odds, or even dollars-to-pennies odds. Those are Bitcoin-to-cocoa-bean odds. If Sacks were in the habit of making those bets in his professional life as a venture capitalist, he wouldn't be a billionaire. He'd be as broke as I am.

9

There's So Much More to This

Defense attorney Paula Canny was no stranger to high-profile cases. Over her long career, she had defended Barry Bonds's personal trainer during his steroid scandal (he went to jail rather than testify against the star outfielder), had represented the wife of the San Francisco sheriff after he was charged with domestic violence, and had won a $3.6 million settlement for the family of an inmate beaten to death by guards inside the Santa Clara County jail. So she thought she knew what she was in for when she took the case.

On April 14, the day that Momeni was arrested, Canny appeared via Zoom on the local NBC station, her long gray hair framing her face. She spoke quickly. "There's so much more to this, a much greater backstory than is disclosed in the government's pleadings," she said, taking time from her vacation to talk.

"The timing of this is awful," she explained. "Because I'm out of the country, I'm in Paris, the most beautiful place in the world —" Canny paused, mindful of how San Franciscans feel about their own city's beauty. "— *one* of the most beautiful places in the world," she finished.

She explained that in the days since Momeni had retained her, she had gotten to know Nima, along with his family — his mother, his sister, and his brother-in-law. They were still helping her figure out what had happened, but "based on the information that I have, it's not a murder. It's just not a murder charge."

~

On May 2, some of the backstory came to light when the result of Lee's autopsy became public. The medical examiner had worked fast — faster than most people expected, even on a high-profile case.

The results, which the ME's office emailed to the press before it gave them to the prosecution and the defense, showed that Lee had died from a vertical wound to his torso, which had penetrated his heart. There was another slash wound above it, and a third wound to his right hip. The report also showed that at the time of his death, Lee was not sober. There was evidence of cocaine, ketamine, and alcohol in his system (as well as an antihistamine medication).

Canny pounced.

"Didn't I say last week that I thought there were going to be a lot of drugs?" she asked sardonically in a press conference after she returned. "I mean, Bob Lee's system is like the Walgreens of recreational drugs."

"But his cause of death was not drugs," a reporter said. "His cause of death was multiple stab wounds."

"Oh my God!" Canny said, throwing up her hands in annoyance. "I'm not saying that! Let's get it right. You all are educated people. You've all been to college. You all understand that there's a *process* here. My job is to represent him, not give you a story."

"Every recreational drug that a person could take was in his system," she continued. "Put on your thinking cap. What happens when people take drugs? Generally they act like drug people. What do drug people act like? Not themselves. Not happy-go-lucky. Just kind of loser-y. [They] make bad decisions and do bad things."

After hearing Canny's comments, which seemed to be blaming Lee for his own death, District Attorney Jenkins sternly shot back: "Whatever that toxicology test may show, Mr. Momeni is guilty of murder."

Two days later, Canny, who has long been public about having been sober since the 1980s, apologized: "I regret that I characterized the autopsy toxicology screen in such an insensitive and cavalier way. I was out of line and wrong. I am sorry."

On May 18, Canny formally entered Momeni's plea of not guilty. This "was never a case of whodunnit. It was always a case about what happened," she told the press. The fatal stabbing had been "a combination of accident and self-defense."

Two weeks later, Canny was no longer defending Momeni. It was "both with great disappointment and relief" that she was leaving the case, she said. "Shit happens in representing people. It's just like that, you know?" On her way out of court, she added that she was looking forward to a regularly scheduled trip to Nepal, which she hoped would be more "spiritually fulfilling."

PART TWO

10

Work Like You Were Living in the Early Days of a Better Nation

San Francisco is a long way from St. Louis.

Bob Lee's mother was a journalist, covering the courts for a suburban newspaper. Later in her life, she bought and sold antiques, using her research skills to identify old lace at estate sales. Nan was a yellow-dog Democrat who idolized the political columnist Molly Ivins and kept a JIMMY CARTER FOR PRESIDENT button on a corkboard in their home. She clipped coupons for Godiva chocolate and filled the house with books. She watched PBS, smoked cigarettes, listened to Aaron Neville and Leonard Cohen, drank Maker's Mark bourbon neat, and suffered from clinical depression, which she fitfully managed with medication. "If I see one more depression curing drug commercial, I'll shoot myself," she once tweeted.

Bob was born on December 20, 1979, six years after his parents married. He had a brother named Tim, who went by Oliver. Their father, Rick, worked as an engineer for Anheuser-Busch, solving problems in their warehouses and with their shipping. He had grown up in Missouri, moving around the state as his own father, a strict Christian, worked building the highways. It was hard work, but it had some perks — Rick learned to ride a bicycle on an unopened section of I-70. Rick would often use new technology at work, and he introduced Bob to computers when he was young. Bob liked playing games, but what really got him going was designing his own. He started programming in the 1990s, when he was still in middle school, learning how to use DOS to write his own image editors and widgets.

At Lindbergh High School, Lee continued to work on computers. Ironically, given that he would become an expert in Java, he first taught himself JavaScript in 1995 to build websites. (The two programming languages, often confused by laypeople, have nothing in common except part of their names.) Bob loved to tinker, hacking his graphing calculator to program games in assembly languages. He also loved to play water polo, which is where the nickname that followed him throughout the rest of his life came from — Crazy Bob, for his ferocious style of play.

When he was sixteen, Bob found a job building websites for a local advertising agency called Red Rock Communications. One of their employees was friends with Jay Goff, a twenty-six-year-old who had just taken a job as the dean of admissions for Southeast Missouri State University. Goff was trying to beef up the institution's online presence, and on a visit to his friend's office, he asked, "Are you doing anything in terms of the internet? You know, homepage development?" The friend said, "Well, actually we are," and flipped on a computer and noisily used a dial-up modem to go online.

"He showed me these pages that were just unbelievable," Goff told me. "Everything else at the time was blocky and very flat, just replicating printed publications. But these pages were interactive, and they had designs and graphics. I was like, 'What? How did you do this?'"

His friend replied, "I'm going to show you something and you're not going to believe it." He took Goff into a closet in the back of the offices that had once been used as a photo darkroom.

He opened the door, and there, sitting in the darkness, was a scrawny high schooler reading a book on HTML coding and typing on a computer at the same time.

"This is Bob," said his friend.

"Oh hey, great to meet you, great to meet you," said Lee, who hadn't stopped reading the book or typing.

"What are you doing?" asked Goff.

"I'm reading this," said Bob, referring to the book, "and thinking about the different ways I could do this code."

Goff took Lee under his wing. He met Bob's parents and promised them that if their son enrolled at Southeast Missouri, not only would it be tuition-free, but Goff would also look after him. They agreed, and Goff hired Bob as a webmaster. Lee hadn't turned eighteen yet when he started, but he made the most of it, playing water polo, pledging Sigma Chi, contributing to a textbook on Java programming, and working on projects for Goff.

Goff's ward could be wily. When there was something major due, he would have to go hunt Lee down — this was before cell phones had become widespread. "I would drag him into the office, and I'd say, remember, we gotta get this done?" said Goff. Bob would say, "Oh yeah, yeah, yeah — can you find me some Mountain Dew?" and then he would sit in the administration building coding until four in the morning. When he finished, he might sleep a few hours — throughout his life Bob never slept well — and then go to class.

"His work was amazing," said Goff. "Some of those pages he built were still up ten or twelve years later. The IT department didn't know what to do with them, because they didn't understand the background of what he was doing."

The summer before his senior year, Lee took an internship with an advertising agency in Washington, DC. He was there when he called Goff and said he wouldn't be coming back in the fall. "When he left, the only thing he felt any guilt about was disappointing his mother," said Goff. "He loved her. They just had a really special relationship." Neither of his parents had graduated from college, and Bob wished that he had. In the intervening years, Lee would sometimes tell Goff that he was thinking of formally completing his degree, but there wasn't anything he thought he could learn. After all, he had already written a textbook.

"What would I do," Bob would say, "go take classes about the book I wrote?"

In 2001, Bob was living in St. Louis and working as a programmer. He had an okay job, but he knew he could do more. One day that summer, he was driving with a college friend, and he couldn't stop talking about the Code Red worm.

The self-replicating virus was all over the news. It got its name not because it was an emergency, but because the two security consultants who discovered it had been drinking Mountain Dew Code Red when they found it. It worked by exploiting a bug in Microsoft's web server program, IIS. Each time the Code Red worm infected a new computer, it would change the text of any web pages the computer might be hosting to read WELCOME TO HTTP://WWW.WORM.COM ! HACKED BY CHINESE! in red letters. (The worm's creators were never identified.) The worm would then spread to more computers through the worldwide web. Within days of its discovery, hundreds of thousands of computers were infected. The worm was easy to defeat — a reboot would clear it. But many people did not realize it had infected their computers, because it was only symptomatic on computers that were hosting websites. It might have been a funny prank, except that the worm was also programmed to use the computers it infected to carry out a denial-of-service attack on the White House's public website, pinging it with so many requests for data that it would crash. (The White House dodged the attack by moving to a new server.) Later that summer, a new version of the worm was released, infecting hundreds of thousands more computers — and there was nothing stopping a third or a fourth version.

Even though he was just a college dropout in St. Louis, Bob was convinced he knew how to beat the worm. His friend disagreed. "There are people way smarter than you — hundreds, thousands of people working on this across the globe," he said. But Bob was unconvinced.

And so he went out and did it.

After he released the fix, Lee was invited to appear on *The Screen Savers*, a tech news show on the cable channel TechTV. The footage of his interview is still up on YouTube, and it's a time capsule of the turn of the millennium. Bob looked impossibly young, wearing a pale-blue polo shirt and with his blond hair gelled and closely cropped. The endearingly ramshackle set was filled with the digital detritus of Gen X — bulky monitors, unplugged joysticks, and random crap — a joyful aesthetic that Google's and Apple's cold minimalism would soon sweep away.

As a mop teetered precariously behind his head, the host asked Lee where the Crazy Bob nickname came from.

"That's kind of a carryover from when I was pledging Sigma Chi," said Lee, who seemed like he could barely sit still.

The host made a clumsy joke about a secret handshake, and then Lee turned to explaining what he had done to neutralize the Red Code worm. He set up his own server and waited for the worm to attack it. When it did, Lee had written a program that automatically notified the computer the virus came from that it was also infected, telling its owner how to fix it.

"I've gotten a few hundred thank-you emails," Lee bragged.

"So how do people get the software from your site? What's the URL?" asked the host.

Lee stumbled and stammered out the address for his website in a way that made it clear how unfamiliar the internet still was, even to people like him. "It's double-u, double-u, double-u, dot, dee, why, en, double-u, e, be, dot, com, forward slash, code red."

"That's a long URL," said the host.

A few years after Code Red, Bob met his wife the old-fashioned way, at a bar. Krista had just broken up with someone and was out on the town with her sister when Bob struck up a conversation with them.

"He was the sweetest guy. Our conversations, even till the day he passed, never, never fell south. They never lagged. There was always something to talk about," Krista told me.

But their relationship almost never happened.

"When I met him at the bar, I shot him down. I wasn't interested," she said.

Undeterred, Lee struck up a conversation with Krista's sister, who had just moved back home from San Francisco and was looking for work. Bob offered to connect her with his father, who might be able to find something at Anheuser-Busch. He gave Krista's sister his number. A few days later, she gave him Krista's number — and told him to take another shot. "She's not really that much of a bitch," her sister told Bob. "She was just kind of drunk that night."

Krista was annoyed when she found out, and called Bob to tell him she wasn't interested. "Hey man, I'm so, so sorry," she said.

"So," said Bob, "I've got you on the phone. How about we go out?"

Krista laughed. *Why not?*

Lee picked her up in a new Land Rover, which he had proudly bought with his own money. As they were driving, he showed off a brand-new iPod. Krista had never seen one before, and he was explaining it when he took his eyes off the road and crashed. It wasn't an auspicious start to a first date — Oliver and his roommate had to come pick them up from the side of the highway.

"But," said Krista, "we decided, let's just keep going."

By the third date they were in love, and Bob's mother was already teasing them about crashing the Land Rover. "Yeah right," she would say, "you were playing with his *iPod.*"

In the spring of 2004, about forty miles south of San Francisco, Sergey Brin was playing volleyball at the Googleplex, his company's new headquarters, while his company's co-founder Larry Page showed a visitor around the sprawling campus. Google was just about to make its initial public offering, which would make both men billionaires.

Page didn't want to talk about money, though. He wanted to show off a gadget.

He had with him the latest T-Mobile Sidekick, an early smartphone, a handheld device almost like the tricorder, the handheld sensor from the *Star Trek* universe. The Sidekick could make phone calls, send and receive emails, play games, keep a calendar, and more. It looked a little like a Game Boy, but it felt like it had been beamed in from the starship *Enterprise*. Page's visitor, a contributing editor from *Playboy*, struggled to understand it. It was like a "digital communicator that employs voice-recognition technology to place phone calls," he wrote.

After his volleyball game wrapped up, a shoeless and sweaty Brin joined Page and the writer for salads. They talked about the usual subjects: Gmail, "don't be evil," and the ad business. But Brin and Page had larger ambitions for their company.

"We serve the world — all countries, at least a hundred different languages," said Brin. "It's a powerful service that most people probably couldn't have dreamed of twenty years ago. It's available to the rich, the poor, street children in Cambodia, stock traders on Wall Street — basically everybody. It's very democratic."

"The increasing volume of information is just more opportunity to build better answers to questions. The more information you have, the better," said Page.

Less than a decade before, they had been graduate students at Stanford, working on a search engine. Today they were remaking the world. What could come next? What *couldn't* come next? "Ultimately, you want to have the entire world's knowledge connected directly to your mind," said Brin. "Where will it lead? Who knows? But it's credible to imagine a leap as great as that from hunting through library stacks to a Google session, when we leap from today's search engines to having the entirety of the world's information as just one of our thoughts."

That ambition was intoxicating. And it was a hell of a sales pitch. Certainly it was good enough to lure Bob Lee from St. Louis.

Joshua Bloch was a software engineer and one of the foremost experts on the Java programming language. In 2004, he joined Google as its chief Java architect. Before that, he had worked at Sun Microsystems, the company where Java was invented in the 1990s. At the time, Java was the most popular programming language in the world, a feat made possible in part because Sun open-sourced the language, meaning it did not charge fees for its use in general, although it did charge for the use of a few parts.

In his spare time, Bloch and a friend would create "Java Puzzlers," programming games that tested the knowledge of the coding language's many intricacies. As a language, Java has many quirks, and so, as Bloch told me, "We turned them into an educational game."

Here's a sample of one of his puzzles:

> The following program adds two hexadecimal, or "hex," literals and prints the result in hex. What does the program print?

```
public class JoyOfHex {
public static void main(String[] args) {
System.out.println(
Long.toHexString(0x100000000L + 0xcafebabe));
}
}
```

Solution: "It seems obvious that the program should print 1cafebabe, [but] if you ran the program, you found that it prints cafebabe, with no leading 1 digit."

Among those who submitted answers, Bloch recognized many of his friends and colleagues. But among the coders playing his game, one name kept recurring — one that Bloch didn't recognize. *Who is this guy?* Bloch thought.

"There was a good reason we had never heard of him," Bloch told me. "He was working as a consultant at I-don't-know-where."

And so, among the tens of thousands of people who descended on the JavaOne conference in San Francisco in 2004, Bloch sought out one person — Bob Lee, the mystery coder from who-knows-where. The first time they met in person, he was struck by how young Bob was (only twenty-five), how friendly he was, and how limitless his energy was. "He went nonstop," said Bloch.

Bloch would later cohost Java Puzzler games at conferences with Lee, but he'd wanted to meet the young man for a more important reason. One of Bloch's assignments was to seek out the world's most talented programmers — and convince them to work for Google. Bob said he was interested, but wouldn't it be a problem that he hadn't graduated from college?

The answer was yes and no. Silicon Valley may think of itself as a meritocracy that disdains credentials, but this has never really been true. Although it was possible to excel without a degree — neither Steve Jobs, Mark Zuckerberg, nor Bill Gates had one — it helped to have dropped out of the most prestigious schools in the world, Jobs from Reed and the other two from Harvard. By contrast, Lee had dropped out of Southeast Missouri State.

But for someone of Lee's skill, the answer was that it didn't matter. "His undergraduate career was checkered, but that's what made him so amazing," Bloch said. "He was proof there is some meritocracy. He had no credentials, but boatloads of talent." Bob was hired, and he moved to the Bay Area.

In his first two years at Google, Lee worked on ads. That wasn't the most glamorous position, but it was among the most important. Google made many products, but it made its *money* from advertising.

When Lee joined, Google had a problem. It was making too much money too quickly, and too sporadically. It might go from not receiving any revenue from a country like Brazil to receiving a million dollars a day. "The architecture was barely staying alive. It was costing money," said Jesse Wilson, another Google programmer.

Lee could be an intimidating presence. He was quick and confident. He was handsome and athletic. He knew how to talk to people and to charm them. And he was a top-tier coder — rumor had it that Crazy Bob had written a textbook and beaten the Code Red worm.

Before he joined Google, Wilson was used to being the best coder in the company. Now he wasn't even the best coder in the *room*. "He was one of the best programmers I ever worked with," said Wilson. "It was like he could see through the Matrix."

Wilson got to know Lee in meetings, and one day he realized that he had a technical problem that he couldn't solve on his own. As Lee and Wilson started to work on it, Wilson couldn't help being nervous, and Bob could sense it, too. "Jesse, calm down," he said. "Let's focus on the code."

And from then on, the two men were friends.

Lee and Krista had been dating for a while when he took the job at Google. They might have been in love, but they also knew how young they were. The couple decided to break up. "Good luck with your life," Krista told him. Bob went off to the Bay Area while she stayed in St. Louis.

But a few weeks after Lee left, he was back home in St. Louis for Thanksgiving. They spent the holidays with their families — and hooking up with each other. A few weeks later, Krista flew out to go with Bob to one of Google's holiday parties. "We were still together," said Krista. "Obviously."

Krista took a job at a dental laboratory in Santa Maria, on California's central coast, 250 miles from where Bob lived. They were still trying to figure out their relationship when Krista discovered that she was pregnant. And whatever their relationship was, *that* wasn't part of the plan.

"I was just terrified," she said. "I'm twenty-four years old. And this is not the way I imagined my life would go." She called Lee to tell him. He picked up his phone in Las Vegas, where he was out partying with friends.

"I'm going to be a dad!" Lee shouted in excitement.

"I wasn't planning on that," Krista told me. They were both pro-choice, and "I was planning the other direction. I wasn't ready for this." Bob was, however, and upon returning from Vegas he drove to Santa Maria to talk to Krista in person.

"This was meant to be," Bob told her. "Let's have this baby."

Krista looked at him. *Oh God, you're out of your fucking mind.* She quit her job and moved in with Bob. Soon after, they were registered domestic partners.

The family lived in a shoebox-sized apartment on the corner of 24th Street and Grandview Terrace, nestled between Twin Peaks and Noe Valley. There was no dishwasher and only one bathroom. They were young, in love, and tightly packed. Krista was terrified to become a stay-at-home mother, even though Lee was making enough money to support all three of them. It felt too traditional. Too stifling. She was worried that she wouldn't be good at it.

"You're going to be an amazing mother," Lee told her — and she believed him.

"I'm trying to decide on a name for my daughter (any day now), and I'm reading *Atlas Shrugged*," Lee wrote on his blog in 2005, bringing up a character with a unique name. "Any idea how to pronounce it?" he wrote.

Eight people replied with eight different answers. Lee used the name anyway.

Naming a child after a character in a book by an iconic libertarian writer might seem to be a tell about Lee's politics. But it wasn't so simple — the couple named their second child after the protagonist of *To Kill a Mockingbird*, and those who knew him said that Bob's point of view shifted as he matured.

"People from our background, white midwestern lower-middle-class people who are of an engineering mind-set, you read Ayn Rand and you think, *Oh the world is so simple*," said Matthew O'Connor, an engineer who worked with Lee at Square and became a close friend. "Objectivism was a younger part of himself that he never talked about much. It's not an uncommon arc."

In fact, just three years after naming his child after a character in an Ayn Rand novel, Lee was tweeting things like: "It will be awesome if Obama wins this whole thing," and "Holy crap. According to the quiz, I'm most compatible with Cynthia McKinney and should be voting for Ralph Nader!"

One day about a year after Krista gave birth, Lee stayed home from work. Krista thought he was being weird. Shouldn't he be at the office? "Why are you here?" she asked. He mumbled something. She shrugged and went on with her day. Who knew why Bob did any of the things that he did? She took the baby out for a walk and came back to change a diaper. Lee walked into the room.

"I have something for you," he said and pulled out the engagement ring that had just been delivered to the apartment in a brown cardboard box.

"We've got a kid. Can we get married?" he asked.

"Like, I don't know," said Krista. "Not really. But okay. Like, maybe. Like, I love you, but, you know, marriage?"

In January 2005, Larry Page had a meeting with computer programmer Andy Rubin, who had founded a small company called Android.

Android was trying to build a tricorder, and it was far from the only company with that goal. As the power of semiconductor chips steadily improved and the cost of transmitting data wirelessly plummeted, early prototypes for today's smartphones were looking less like science fiction and more like the next major consumer device. Somebody was going to build one, that was certain. It just wasn't certain which company would be selling it.

At the meeting, Sergey Brin raved about his T-Mobile Sidekick. Then the Android team showed off its work. Brin was encouraging. They had another meeting, and then a third.

At that meeting, the Android team launched into a prepared presentation when the Google cofounder stopped them. "Let us interrupt you there. We just want to buy you," said Brin. And so in the summer of 2005, Google did.

By the end of its first year at Google, the Android team made two key decisions: They would use Java to run the phones, and they would scale up. Several hundred people soon joined. Among them was Lee, who moved from advertising to Android. He told a podcast in 2022 that "I was really passionate about mobile, ever since my cousin had an Apple Newton back in the mid-'90s. It was like a touch device you could handwrite on. It was pre-internet, so it was a little before its time."

Lee's job was to build the Android operating system's core library. Those were the most basic parts of the operating system, like the code that parses a URL or tells the phone to download a file. Initially, Google hoped to pay for a license for the Java SE library from Sun. (That was one of the parts that wasn't open-source.) At one point, Google offered between $30 million and $50 million. But the agreement fell apart, as neither side ever felt it could fully trust the other. So that meant that Lee had a lot of work to do.

"It was like a company in a company," Lee told Google engineer Chet Haase for Haase's book *Androids*, a history of the project. "Some people were kind of resentful of being acquired and wanted to keep the scrappiness. In the beginning, we didn't have code reviews, it was a different interview process, people didn't write tests . . . It was a bit of a culture shock for me."

Lee didn't get along with everyone on the Android team, but he loved working with his friends Wilson and Bloch, who joined Bob in an office in Building 44 at the Googleplex.

"The people who made up the original Android team before he joined were very clubby," Bloch told me. "He didn't deeply respect every member of the original Android team. They kind of felt like they knew the way and anybody who joined the team later basically was serving at their pleasure, including Bob. But most of the time, it didn't matter. We had headphones on and we were down in the bits.

"Some people called it a sweatshop," he continued. "I don't think that's fair, but there's a song by the British folk band Oyster-band that has this lyric: 'Work like you were living in the early days of a better nation.' I like that, that's a good phrase." He played the song as they worked because that line, which the band had quoted from a Scottish nationalist writer, captured their mood. They worked like they were living in the early days of a better nation.

That's what it felt like to work at Google. That's what it felt like to live in San Francisco.

The world was going to be connected. It would be different. More innovative. Less hierarchical. More free. And they were building one part of it. They wanted to get it right. And little by little, they did. On the lawn outside their building, whimsical statues of the Android mascot, a little green robot called Bugdroid, began to go up, one for each major release.

"We understood that we were in this position where the stuff we were doing was going to get used by everyone and his sister," said Bloch. "And we might as well do everything we could to make it as good as we could. The group felt like we had one shot at this."

As he worked, Lee had a lot of choices to make. Should the programs be as simple as possible? That would make them take up less memory. But it might mean leaving out options that developers would want to use. Add too many of those, though, and the system would be too complex to be easily used. "Everything Bob was doing was to balance between complexity and affordance to solve problems," said Wilson.

To build the core library, Lee had to use preexisting bits of code, explained Wilson. "A big part of the core libraries is, rather than inventing a bunch of new ways to solve these problems, to take advantage of Java already having APIs," he said, referring to application programming interfaces, software intermediaries that allow multiple systems to interact with one another. "But Android did not borrow code from Java. It took the Java API definitions and did something similar." This difference, though subtle, would become very important later on.

The three men were an odd trio. Wilson was an introverted board game nerd with a wacky sense of humor. One hot summer day he showed up at the office with half a watermelon on his head. He didn't smoke, but he kept a pack of Lucky Strikes displayed on his desk so he could feel like Don Draper, the lead character in *Mad Men*. Bloch was older, a professorial type who would go on to teach computer science at Carnegie Mellon. His idea of a good time was to splurge on the high-end cheese at the Trader Joe's near his house.

And then there was Crazy Bob, the man born without an off switch. Bloch wasn't a fan of social media, but little by little, Wilson and Lee wore him down. Finally, he joined Twitter. By the time he signed up, Lee had nine thousand followers. He was a popular guy. "It was almost like he never got tired," said Wilson. "There was never a Saturday where he wanted to be bored."

On those Saturday nights, Wilson would go home and watch DVDs mailed from Netflix. Lee would call, trying to lure him to join him at Molly Magees, an Irish pub in Mountain View that he frequented. Wilson mostly turned him down. He wanted to rest. By contrast, Bob always wanted to be out in the world doing something.

Most of the time, Lee came back to work on Monday morning with incredible stories of his adventures. But not everything was perfect. One Saturday in 2005, a thief in San Francisco stole the hubcaps right off his parked car. "Someone stole the center wheel caps off of my SUV (I love San Francisco). I think I know where they went," he wrote on his blog, adding a link to eBay. "The damned things are $18 each new. Maybe I'm in the wrong business. ;)"

"He was a young ambitious guy in his twenties," said Marc Fleury, the creator of JBoss. He never worked with Lee, and although they met a few times at industry conferences, he mostly admired Lee from afar. At the time, the community of cutting-edge Java developers was no more than one to two hundred people. "He was a very young programmer back then. Ambitious. Knew how to make a name for himself," said Fleury, who sold his company to Red Hat and retired in 2007.

Part of that reputation came from Guice, a set of Java development tools that was "pronounced *juice*," Lee would often joke, "even though the G is for 'Google.'" (It's programming humor — it doesn't have to be funny.)

Guice allowed programmers to work modularly, meaning that they could test how their code was working without running an entire program at once, which could be time consuming. The fancy term for it was a dependency injection framework, but what's important about it is that Lee was already starting to think not just about how he himself was programming, but how an organization of programmers could work together. In other words, he was thinking like an executive.

"The code was serious wizardry," said Kevin Bourrillion, who worked on it with Lee while they were at Google together. Guice grew like "one cell dividing into two, and two into four." In 2007, Lee and Bourrillion released it as an open-source project. They didn't expect much from it, but it caught on, so much so that the following year Lee and Bourrillion received an industry award for it.

"We went to an event in an auditorium and they announced our names and we went up on stage and got an award. We did not expect anything like that," Bourrillion told me. "Maybe we were supposed to wear tuxes, but I never did."

"I still can't believe it. That was so awesome!" Lee emailed Wilson.

Speaking of tuxes: The wedding was supposed to be in Wine Country, but Krista hated the idea. She was thrilled to be getting married, but the dress, the big party, the fancy venue, the whole thing just wasn't her vibe. She felt like she was doing it for their mothers, not for her and Bob. She didn't know what to do. Could she find a way to get married without having the wedding?

One night, she was out with Bob and their friends. Several bottles of wine had already been drunk when the conversation turned to an upcoming trip they were taking to Las Vegas. As they were talking about Star Trek: The Experience, a live-action attraction at the Hilton that let guests live out their science-fiction dreams, their friend had a brainstorm. "You know, they do weddings there, too," he said.

"It was perfect," Krista told me. "I'm like, 'Should we do this? Should we just elope?'"

"Yeah," said Bob. "Let's do it."

And so, instead of walking down the aisle in a vineyard, Krista put on a cute little silver Dolce & Gabbana dress and walked down the aisle to the salutes of actors playing Federation officers. They showed off the pictures for the rest of Bob's life.

One day at work in the spring of 2009, Lee strolled up to Jesse Wilson and announced that he was raising money.

"Nominally, it was a fundraiser for the American Liver Foundation," Wilson told me. "But Bob just really wanted to swim." Bob was determined to make it from Alcatraz, the island famous for its federal prison, back to the shore of San Francisco. Depending on how you aimed, it was one to two miles of open-water swimming. And the way that Lee drank, his family would joke, the ALF fundraiser was an appropriate excuse to do it.

Lee was being his typical self — excited. As he waxed enthusiastic, the excitement passed from Lee to Wilson. Lee needed a training partner, and to his own surprise, Wilson found himself agreeing to swim with him. It seemed like a fun challenge, and anyway, "It would let me spend more time with Bob."

Over the next three months, Lee and Wilson went to the YMCA each night after work to swim two kilometers — roughly the distance from Alcatraz back to the mainland. A few times, they swam in open water to get used to it.

Mark Twain didn't actually say that the coldest winter he ever spent was a summer in San Francisco, but even though he didn't, he wasn't wrong. The air was hovering around fifty degrees Fahrenheit when Wilson picked up Lee from his condo at six in the morning. They drove an hour to the city, where the two men were supposed to meet the boat that would take them and the other swimmers out to the Rock.

As they exited the car, Lee's face was as pale as the fog.

"I forgot my wet suit," he said.

There weren't very many options. Lee certainly couldn't go back and get it and return in time for the swim. There wasn't enough time for Krista, who planned to meet them at the end of the race, to bring it. There were no wet suits available to borrow. He could watch Wilson from the shore. Or Lee could swim without it.

Out of the hundred or so people swimming that morning, maybe six of them were going without wet suits. And they were not amateurs like Crazy Bob, but instead highly experienced open-water swimmers. The temperature of the Bay would likely be around fifty or sixty degrees Fahrenheit — certainly uncomfortable, and maybe even unsafe. The cold water temperature could cause a swimmer to involuntarily gasp, draw seawater into their lungs, and drown. (Deaths are rare, but they have happened, once in 2013 and again in 2022.)

"Bob was in good shape, but he had the lifestyle of a programmer who drank a lot," Wilson said.

Lee sucked in his gut and made his decision. "Yeah, I want to swim without a wet suit," he said, grabbing a fistful of Vaseline from one of the college swimmers to rub on his body.

As Lee hit the water, the muscles he had honed playing water polo during college kicked into motion. The water was shockingly cold, but he pulled himself forward with practiced strokes. Soon, he found a rhythm. Behind him, wearing his wet suit, Wilson marveled.

Lee's mother, Nan, was back home in St. Louis, anxiously waiting for updates from her son or from Krista. She was worried, although she masked it with humor. "If you drown in the Bay, I'll kill you," she tweeted.

Bob emerged from the water on the shore wearing a smile and Speedo. Krista still swoons when she pictures him.

"Crazybob made it," Nan wrote on Twitter. "In a Speedo. I WILL kill him. CB, you owe Krista BIGTIME!!! for this one."

Bob didn't win the race from Alcatraz. Nor did Google win its smartphone race. At least not the first lap. In January 2007, Apple CEO Steve Jobs showed off the first iPhone, which went on sale that June. On November 5, 2007, Google released the first public beta for the Android operating system. The next fall, T-Mobile released the first Android phone. It was clear that the device was hardly as impressive as the iPhone, but it received generally positive reviews. Its biggest selling point was cost. The iPhone retailed for $599; the G1 went for $179.

Within a year, the G1 had about 6 percent of the smartphone market share. That wasn't much, but as more Android phones were developed and released, phones with the Android operating system quickly began outselling iPhones — by a lot. By the year before Lee died, 70 percent of the phones in the world were running Android, a market share that he had to admit came as a surprise.

"Nobody foresaw how big this stuff was going to get," he said in a 2022 podcast. "Our little team, not only did we develop the OS, we developed all the apps. Nobody else at Google cared. We were super secretive to begin with. We developed the first Facebook app, the first Twitter app, and handed it to them. It was like boiling the ocean. It was super fun."

Today a wide variety of devices use Android, including Wi-Fi routers, headphones, car speakers, and remote controls — nearly every kind of wireless gadget. Lee once used Android to rig up an art-and-light installation at a friend's house, using a smartphone to control the lights in the house when notes were played on the piano. Most of the operating system's uses are not so obvious. You've likely used Android today without noticing it, and when you did, you used code that Bob Lee wrote.

Sun's leaders weren't thrilled, but nothing happened until 2010, when the software giant Oracle bought Sun Microsystems. As the rare funny joke in Silicon Valley goes, Oracle is an acronym for "One Rich Asshole Called Larry Ellison." Oracle sued Google for $8.8 billion in damages, accusing it of infringing on the Java copyrights and patents that Oracle had bought from Sun.

To build Android, Google engineers like Lee wrote millions of lines of new code. They also copied about 11,500 lines of code from the Java API. In most cases, the Google team wrote new implementing code to make those APIs work. In thirty-seven instances, however, Google seemed to have copied the implementing code. It also seemed to have copied the names of those programs and the way they were grouped together. Although Oracle's patent claims had been dismissed, that looked like it could be a violation of copyright. And as Wilson said, "The code that was under contest between Oracle and Google was the code that Bob implemented."

On Monday, April 24, 2012, Lee testified in a San Francisco courtroom. By then he had left Google for a new job as the CTO of Square, but he was enthusiastic about having his day in court — so much so that the judge admonished him twice for giving speeches instead of answering questions. During questioning, Lee said that any similarities between his code and Oracle's happened not because of plagiarism but because there weren't that many ways to write the kind of code that he was working on. "Similarities, paraphrasing, these terms are a contract," he said. "They are very specific rules, and there are only so many ways you can phrase them."

During cross-examination, Google's lawyer asked Lee if he had permission to use any of the thirty-seven Java APIs under dispute. "I didn't know if it was allowed to reimplement APIs, so I asked my supervisor," said Lee. "He said, 'Yes, there is lots of precedent for this in the industry.'"

The initial ruling supported that claim, finding in favor of Google. But Oracle appealed, and the case was tied up in the courts for the next decade. Finally, on April 5, 2021 — two years minus a day before Lee's death — the United States Supreme Court issued a ruling that ended the case in favor of Google.

"I spent ten years of my life on and off writing amicus briefs," said Bloch. "Eventually, the good guys pretty much won."

He might have been one of the good guys, but when Lee left Google, he left behind some sore feelings. While working on Android, he reported to an engineer named Dan Bornstein, who recalled that Lee had a habit of disappearing to work on projects that interested him — like Guice — rather than the ones he was supposed to be working on. When I called Bornstein, I started our conversation by mentioning how well regarded Bob seemed to be by his colleagues. I was, to be honest, buttering him up, but I was also reflecting what I had seen. Bob did genuinely seem to be admired by those who worked with him. Bornstein paused, and I could tell he was thinking carefully.

"He worked on the team for two, two to three years," Bornstein finally said. "I appreciated him for about a year, and then I kind of didn't appreciate him for the rest of the time."

Lee increasingly spent his time and energies in other directions — not only Guice but also giving talks at conferences, working on Java Puzzlers, swimming Alcatraz, seemingly anything that wasn't his actual job. "I think it just wasn't interesting to him," said Bornstein. One day, a fed-up Bornstein received an email from Bob that said, "I've moved to St. Louis."

"I'm like, 'I can't give you permission for that,'" said Bornstein. "And it wasn't long after that he left the company."

11

Bob Had the Mojo

It started in the back seat of a Toyota Camry in 2008, while Bob was living in San Francisco, before he moved back to St. Louis.

Kevin Bourrillion was taking Lee and Wilson from the South Bay to San Francisco, where they were going to attend that year's JavaOne conference. (Lee had temporarily lost his license after a DUI.) As Bourrillion drove, Wilson used his phone to show Lee a new social network.

"The use case for Twitter back then was that if you went to a tech conference, Twitter would solve the problem of coordinating where to get lunch. It was the sandwich app," said Bourrillion. Lee was fascinated. He signed up early enough that his Google handle was still available — @crazybob.

Twitter initially lacked many features. Among those was an easy way to find new accounts to follow. For a prolific networker like Lee, an extrovert in an introverted industry, that was a problem. So in his spare time, Lee whipped up a third-party app that would recommend accounts to follow. He called it Twubble, a portmanteau of Twitter and bubble.

In April of that year, Lee recorded an interview about it. Lee's hair was now closely cropped, but other than the buzz cut, he looked the same as when he had appeared on TechTV to talk about Code Red. "Twitter is this mini-social-network where you can make status updates to your profile. It's kind of like micro-blogging," Lee explained. "A couple weeks ago, I was trying to find some new people to follow. I was going through all my friends and all the people that they follow and picking out new people. Then I thought, Hey, wouldn't it be cool if I could automatically find out who most of my friends follow? Because I'll want to follow those people, too. So it's a really stupid simple idea. It's Twubble."

Among the app's fans was another techie from St. Louis — Jack Dorsey, Twitter's CEO and one of its founders. (Dorsey would run the site off and on until he sold it to Musk in 2022.) Dorsey reached out to Lee, and they had lunch.

"Hey, man, I'm working on this thing. Are you available?" Dorsey asked.

"Yeah, no offense, but you can't afford me right now," Lee responded.

The two men had a lot in common. Dorsey had been born three years before Lee, and had gone to high school about seven miles from where Lee did. Dorsey, too, had been fascinated by technology as a child — his father bought him an IBM PCjr in 1984 and a Mac in 1987, which he used to access the internet before the advent of the worldwide web, going online through a network hosted by Washington University.

After dropping out of college, Dorsey worked a series of programming jobs before finding himself in San Francisco in 2005, working for a floundering podcasting company, when he pitched the idea that would become Twitter. In 2006, he sent the first official tweet ("just setting up my twttr"). The site took off the following year at the South by Southwest festival, but success brought its own difficulties. Dorsey struggled to manage the company, and in 2008 the board forced him out. Around the time he met Lee, he was struggling to come up with an idea for another company, one that would prove that he hadn't just lucked into Twitter by accident.

The inspiration struck when a friend named Jim McKelvey came to him with a problem. McKelvey was a programmer — also from St. Louis — who had a side business making glass objects. One day, a woman tried to buy something from him, but he couldn't find a way to make the credit card transaction work. There had to be a better way to do this, thought McKelvey. So in the winter of 2009, he and Dorsey built a credit card reader that could attach to a mobile phone using its audio jack. Square was born.

"At the time, Jack was very pro–St. Louis," said Wilson, whom Lee would later recruit to work with him at the company.

"Jack had the vision," he added. "Bob had the mojo."

Dorsey never returned my requests to talk. In fact, he never even reached out to Lee's family after his death, but Krista told me the story. Bob was getting restless at Google and frustrated at the cost of housing in the Bay Area. A second child had joined their first, as well as Bob's brother Oliver, who moved in with them when he found a job at the Four Seasons Hotel in Palo Alto. "He was kind of our live-in nanny for a while, too," she said. Bob had enough money now that he could afford to make a change, and like many cities at the time, St. Louis was hoping to incubate its own tech industry. So they bought a house in St. Louis for half a million dollars — barely enough for a starter home in the Bay Area, but enough for what Krista called a "mini Playboy mansion" back home.

Bob intended to keep working for Google, but once Dorsey found out he had moved to St. Louis, he made another attempt to hire him. "Okay, Bob," said Dorsey, "I really need your help on this. Can we come out to the house and have a meeting?"

That was how Krista found herself watching Lee, Dorsey, and McKelvey sit in her living room in St. Louis and sketch out what

Square could become. Lee was fascinated and agreed to join. *What's better, to keep dodging Dan's emails or to help Jack and Jim build a new company?* It was an easy choice.

In December 2021, an older Lee was speaking onstage at a conference about the decision. "Back in 2009, I worked on the Android team at Google, in charge of the code that [underlay] the applications layer," he said. "We had just wrapped up development on the third and fourth Android phones, the Nexus One and the Droid, when my friends Jack Dorsey and Jim McKelvey reached out to me about their new start-up, Square."

Lee explained that he was an enthusiastic amateur photographer — his blog is filled with photos he took of his children, trips to Beijing and Paris, and vacations to Disneyland. Because camera phones back then didn't have built-in flashes, he was fooling around with connecting a flash to his Android phone's headset jack using a rectifier circuit. It was a fun project, but it went obsolete when the Nexus One shipped with a built-in flash.

"My side project went into the dustbin," he said with a laugh. But it prepared him for what came next. McKelvey showed Lee the new invention — a credit card reader that plugged into the headset jack of an iPhone. "I was enthralled, and not just from a technical standpoint," said Lee.

The reader was aimed at small-business owners, promising to improve their existing point-of-sale terminals. Lee knew one such person quite well, his mother, Nan, who had opened an antiques store in St. Louis. "I had seen firsthand how the credit card processors preyed on her small business, making it next to impossible for her to turn a profit," said Lee. "Square could make life better for my mom and millions [of people] like her."

So over the course of one intense night, Lee wrote the code that would allow the reader to work on Android phones. "It was quite the résumé and cover letter. Square offered me a job and I accepted," he said. Lee started as the lead Java programmer. But soon, the company promoted him to CTO. "I was gobsmacked when I found out that Bob was the CTO of Square," said Wilson. "But Bob said, 'I can be the CTO.' Jack said, 'Sure, Bob.' So he got the CTO's salary, not the programmer's salary."

It was a rewarding time to be there — and propitious as well. Lee joined the company not just during the mobile phone revolution that he helped build but also the wake of the 2007–08 economic crisis. As Wilson explained it to me, "It was the Big-Tech-is-good era. It was nothing but upside. Today we've all soured on it, but the vision for Square was that what Facebook was to social and Google was search, Square would be to commerce." And pretty soon, it was clear that Bob needed to move back to San Francisco. He sold the house to Goff, his mentor from Southeast Missouri State, and moved back to the city-by-the-bay.

As the world dragged itself through the Great Recession, San Francisco stumbled. The city's unemployment rate, which had been under 5 percent before the recession began, reached 9.8 percent in August 2009. (The economy was worse in the rest of the state.) Of course, the effects of the downturn were not distributed evenly. Many of them could be felt most keenly in the Tenderloin and SoMa, the area south of Market that historically had been working-class but had been gentrifying since the 1970s. The city seemed bereft of economic ideas. In the 2009 local election, voters were asked to lift a citywide ban on new billboards along parts of Market Street, as if turning it into Times Square would be the fix that we needed. (Voters rejected the idea.)

In 2010, San Francisco mayor Gavin Newsom won election as the state's lieutenant governor, which created a vacancy in the mayor's office. The board of supervisors nominated four candidates, including city administrator Ed Lee, but deadlocked when it came time to vote. Then Lee promised not to seek election if appointed, and the supervisors voted ten to one for him. The city's first Chinese American mayor, Lee was an avuncular figure. He had been a radical lawyer as a young man but mellowed after he began working for the city in 1989. He steadily rose up the ranks, and in 2005, Newsom had appointed him to run San Francisco's bureaucracy.

Lee proved to be a popular mayor. He liked the job, too. So much so, in fact, that in August of the following year, Lee broke his promise and declared his candidacy in the following election, which he won. Lee subsequently ran for another term in 2015 unopposed by any serious candidates.

Like most mayors, Lee — who died of a heart attack in 2017 while shopping at a Safeway supermarket near his home — was close to his city's business community. What set him apart, however, was that the business of San Francisco was now technology, not finance, manufacturing, or shipping as it had once been. In a turnabout from the white flight of previous decades, a new generation of young people — young, well educated, and well off — were pouring into cities like San Francisco. His opponents made it seem like Lee had single-handedly opened the city's gates, but in truth, there was nothing a middle-aged bureaucrat could do to make San Francisco seem cool. That had happened on its own. Lee was merely channeling the tide.

The most notable of his policies was the mid-Market tax break, in which the city agreed to exempt companies from paying San Francisco's payroll tax if they had offices located in mid-Market. Twitter was the most prominent beneficiary of the policy. Its first office was in the South Park neighborhood, just a short way away from the Giants stadium. From there, the company moved around the corner to Bryant Street, and then to another office on Folsom, which is where it was when negotiations over the tax break began.

Twitter's leadership offered the city a straightforward choice: If the city were to lower the company's taxes, it would move into a large empty building that had once housed a furniture mart on the corner of 10th and Market. If not, Twitter would move out of San Francisco.

Although the tax break would later become unpopular with the city's voters, initially it was widely supported. Lee worked with two members of the board of supervisors — one a center-left Democrat and the other a former member of the Green Party — to write it, and it was adopted by an 8–3 vote. Twitter was not the only company to take advantage of the tax break: In 2013, eleven companies did so, including Square. Over the eight years the tax break was in effect (the city chose not to renew it in 2019), the cost was an estimated $70 million in forgone tax revenue — a small fraction of a yearly budget that reaches almost $15 billion.

In December 2009, Square relocated its ten employees to an office in the Chronicle building that once housed the newspaper's human resources department. (You might recognize that building from David Fincher's film *Zodiac*, which was filmed inside.) Two years later, Square had a hundred employees and had expanded to thirteen thousand square feet in another wing of the building. But the office space could not keep up with the company's growth. In 2013, it moved to new offices at 1455 Market Street, which had been built in 1978 as a data center for Bank of America. Furniture wholesalers, newspapers, and banks — a history of the American economy could be written just based on the offices in which Dorsey's companies were located. "We had a giant sense of satisfaction that we were replacing paper check processing with something digital," said Wilson. "Building a brand-new bank felt really exciting. We were not a bank, but we were solving the problems that a bank would solve."

For a moment, it was possible to believe that Market Street was changing. Maybe San Francisco was, too. There were some false starts. A former supervisor opened a dive bar that never caught on. ("Apparently the revolution will not be patronized," sniffed one of the alt weeklies.) The city caught criticism for forcing the guys playing chess to move a few blocks away. But slowly, the neighborhood changed. Fewer drug dealers were hanging around the knockoff clothing and stereo stores. The windows opened for the first time in decades in a ground-floor space that had once been a pool room and a strip club. Now it was a food hall serving Moroccan-Peruvian fusion, vegan Indian food, and raw oysters. In fact, there were two food halls within a short walk of each other — a fancy grocery store, coffee shop, and bodega also opened downstairs at the Twitter building. Sometimes I would get coffee there. It was convenient, and I couldn't justify the $5 for a small tea at Chai Bar up the block. New apartment buildings were sprouting up. The best known of these — at least the one that advertised the most heavily — was NEMA, right across from the Twitter headquarters. For a while, you couldn't go to any local website without seeing an ad touting the building's amenities. It got so bad that when I once joked on Twitter that it seemed like the apartment was the home of Patrick Bateman, the lunatic yuppie from *American Psycho*, two people accused me of having stolen their joke.

Bob started at Square on a Monday. The programmer Matthew O'Connor started on a Tuesday. That meant he knew Lee was an earlier employee than he was but couldn't remember the exact numbers that they were, twelve, thirteen, or fourteen. (I checked: Bob was thirteen.)

Before Square, O'Connor had been a consultant at Twitter. Even though he had been there for some of the site's most memorable early days, like Obama's election and the day the plane landed in the Hudson River, it was rare in the tech industry for a contractor to get hired full-time at the same company. So when Dorsey asked him to join Square full-time, he jumped at the chance.

Lee was still in St. Louis, and O'Connor always thought of him as a midwesterner. *Nice. Considerate. Polite.* "He'd carry in your groceries or change your tire," said O'Connor. "Even if you were a stranger, he would help you carry your couch up the stairs. It also comes with naïveté. Bob had a lot of that in him, too."

When Bob and Krista moved back to San Francisco, they found a place in Outer Richmond, a more suburban part of the city near the Pacific Ocean. She can still taste the pastries they would buy from Devil's Teeth Bakery. Krista got a job as an event producer, working for touring acts like the Wu Tang Clan and Dave Chappelle, a job that allowed her and Bob to channel their love for nightlife.

During the day, Lee and O'Connor divided the workload between them — Lee oversaw technical projects while O'Connor managed the workers. Even though he was a Java expert, Lee was no longer restricting himself to the programming language. He worked on hardware, software, and the intricate system by which banks, credit card companies, and a host of other firms moved money around the world. "We were like the early settlers," said O'Connor. They did everything. "If he had to write C code, he would write C code. If he had to write JavaScript, he would write JavaScript. If he had to write assembly, he would write assembly. He was a rare type."

"I guess the most jarring thing for me was I mostly focused on Java prior to Square. Now, being the CTO, I'm technology agnostic. We use a wide variety of technologies," Lee said in a 2011 interview. Once, that even meant hauling out an oscilloscope to figure out why the credit card swipes were sometimes failing to register. Other times it meant working on projects that were a little larger.

In 2010, Facebook founder Mark Zuckerberg announced that he would donate $100 million to public schools in Newark, New Jersey, buying himself a wave of good publicity ahead of his not-so-good portrayal in the film *The Social Network*. Governor Chris Christie and Mayor Cory Booker joined him on Oprah Winfrey's talk show to accept the money. To make the transfer for the TV cameras, Zuckerberg had to actually move the money from his account to the school district's.

Enter Square.

Lee and O'Connor worked a series of late nights to get the transaction ready, and when the big day came, they were on hand on the set to flip the switch remotely from San Francisco. There was just one problem. The live segment took too long, and *Oprah* had to go off the air. And so while "technically, we were on *Oprah*," said O'Connor, their part was only shown to the studio audience.

After their job was complete, the two men, who had been up for more than twenty-four hours, crawled into their respective beds. When they finally reemerged, it was time to party. They started at the Tempest, the dive bar adjacent to the Chronicle building popular with reporters and bicycle messengers. Then they went somewhere else. They might have gone somewhere after that. O'Connor's memory is hazy.

He did know where they ended up — the bar at the Four Seasons Hotel, where Lee's brother, Oliver, was now a manager.

That was often where they ended up. It was an opulent place for the boys from the Midwest to find themselves, certainly a long way from the sketchy bars in East St. Louis that Bob and Krista used to frequent. At the time, Lee often said that for ambitious young businesspeople, going out late was the new hitting the golf course.

One of the biggest figures to straddle politics and technology in that era was Harper Reed, who would become the CTO of President Barack Obama's 2012 reelection campaign.

"I grew up with the same sense of limitlessness that Bob did," Reed told me. "The peak of that techno-optimism might have actually been around the same time as the Obama campaign."

The day before Reed interviewed for the campaign CTO job at Obama headquarters, he had been hanging out with Lee. At the time, Lee would often carry fistfuls of Square readers, which he would use to demonstrate the technology to anyone whose hands he could press one into. Lee gave a bunch of the readers to Reed, who was enthralled. Reed had them with him when he went in for the interview the next day. He explained to the campaign leaders that they could use a new form of technology to process political donations via credit cards. The staffers seemed skeptical, and so Reed pulled the readers out of his bag and showed them off to the assembled politicos.

Not only did he get the job, but the Square readers proved so effective that the Federal Election Commission had to rewrite its regulations to clarify that the readers were legal ways to raise campaign money.

By now, Lee had made himself a home in San Francisco. He knew all the right clubs. He danced to DJs all night. Bob was always ready for a good time. He was a regular at Atelier Crenn, the Michelin three-star restaurant in Cow Hollow, where the menu for the twelve-course tasting menu was written as a poem and dinner cost $450 a person, not counting drinks. "He went there a bunch," said O'Connor. "He took me once. I was a vegetarian at the time, and he arranged it so they accommodated me. It was a phenomenal meal."

O'Connor continued, "He always made the people he was around feel safe, but it was intense." At raves, Bob would often be seen in the VIP section. If he recognized someone, he'd wave them in. He had season tickets to the San Francisco Opera. He'd belt out Johnny Cash's version of "We'll Meet Again" at karaoke, as well as the theme song from *Star Trek: Enterprise*, the latest installment in the franchise. (Most Trekkies didn't warm to it, but O'Connor and Lee did.) Invariably, he referred to people he knew — whether at work or on the town — as his best friend. "We never worked together, but we became friends throughout the nightlife scene," said Michael Schultz, who worked at Google at the same time as Lee. "He never failed to introduce me as 'My friend Mike, one of the most brilliant people I've ever worked with.' We never worked together, but he wanted me to feel good."

Lee was friends with several well-known DJs like Rob Garza, one of two musicians that made up Thievery Corporation. He hung out with Metallica drummer Lars Ulrich. (Supposedly, he and Ulrich would later date the same woman. Through a representative, Ulrich declined to comment.) Once, Lee talked his way backstage at a play in Los Angeles to meet George Takei, the actor famous for playing the helmsman of the USS *Enterprise* on the original *Star Trek* TV series. In fact, Krista proudly said that her former husband had met not only Takei but also other *Star Trek* actors LeVar Burton, Jonathan Frakes, and Gates McFadden, "who he had the biggest crush on." He and John Perry Barlow, the Grateful Dead lyricist and web pioneer, would wander the streets of New York together. They were fond of a burlesque club called the Box. One night while they were in the audience, the actors pretended to murder someone on stage. Barlow leaned over to Lee and said, "Back in old New York, there's a chance that would have been real."

"He had a thing for nightlife. He would throw money around. It didn't matter to him," said Bloch, the programmer who recruited Lee to Google. When Lee left the company, he took Bloch and the others on a celebratory outing to Ridge Vineyards, the home of the Cabernet Sauvignon that put California wine on the map. It was a long way from the Mountain Dew he used to drink, but Lee seemed to Bloch to retain his sense of innocence. "There was a childlike aspect to Bob, and I mean that in the best possible way. He loved to play with toys. He loved to tinker and to build," said Bloch.

"For how hard he partied, he was always there the next day," said O'Connor. "I think he burned the candle at both ends. I often suspected he was self-medicating depression or anxiety."

Whether they were at the Four Seasons, Monarch, Audio, or the Tempest, it seemed like Lee's energy was inexhaustible. They would go to parties, and he would talk about technology the whole night with O'Connor. Little by little, he realized that Lee was doing the same thing with other people who were passionate about completely different things — photography, their homes, their families, whatever. Lee's intensity seemed to have only one setting. *On.*

One person who hated the nonstop carousing was O'Connor's ex-wife, who grew increasingly frustrated about Matthew's late nights with Bob and Krista. Over time, they worried O'Connor, too. One moment in particular stood out.

"We were at some underground club, and I knocked on the bathroom door. It was the most innocent thing in the entire world. I had to pee really bad. This lady opens the door and says, 'What the hell is going on?' There were drugs involved, obviously."

O'Connor protested that he was just trying to use the bathroom. But the woman, who was dating the party's organizer, thought Matthew and Bob were trying to see her naked and started yelling that she was going to kill him.

"Bob stood up for me. He could have gotten super angry, but he acted as the peacemaker," said O'Connor. "After that, we got the fuck out of there."

Looking back, O'Connor still thought that neither he nor Bob did anything wrong. But that wasn't the point. The problem was that they put themselves in a situation where things could have gone very badly very quickly. O'Connor didn't go to many parties like that from that point on, but he knew Bob never stopped.

One Friday afternoon, Bob came home and told Krista he had some work to do. All weekend she heard him clacking away on his keyboard. She slipped him some food but mostly stayed out of the way. She was accustomed to her husband becoming obsessed with work sometimes. When they were first dating, he once bolted out of the bed in the middle of the night because some code had come to him.

Bob had been kicking around an idea for the past two years. Why was it so easy to send a text or a tweet but so hard to move money around? Square prototyped a version of his idea, but the project languished until one day when Square employees were volunteering to clean the streets of mid-Market near their offices as part of the deal for the tax break.

As he cleaned up trash, Lee thought about problems he was having paying the family babysitter. (People who went out as often as Bob and Krista needed one badly.) If he used PayPal, the system would hold on to the money in the transaction for too long — sometimes more than a month. But if he wanted cash, he had to use a barely functioning ATM at a corner store near the office, which charged a $6 fee for every transaction. As they worked to sweep up the streets, Lee was complaining to Dorsey about all of it, Jack interrupted with an idea — could you send money by email? Bob thought about it, and then had a flash of insight. He raced home to get started.

Bob showed up at the office on Monday with the rudiments of a new app. Two weeks later, they had a functioning prototype of Square Pay. Jack renamed it Square Cash before it launched, but as it grew more popular, people began calling it Cash App.

"Bob was the person who thought up the app and made it happen," Wilson told me.

For Cash App to work, two things needed to happen. Transaction fees needed to come down, and Square needed to find a way to move the money around. The first hurdle was overcome in 2011, when Illinois senator Dick Durbin added an amendment to the Dodd-Frank financial bill that limited the fees that retailers could charge for debit card processing.

That took care of the cost, but Lee still couldn't figure out how to actually move the money around. That was when he hit on the solution — the unlinked refund.

Most refunds that credit cards process are linked. That means that the source of the transaction is the same as the recipient of the refund. (In other words, the card you use to pay is the card to which the refund goes.) But the network also allows for unlinked refunds, in which the account that gets the money back is not the one that paid in the first place. Most people never used it, but it was a function that had been built in to the system and never exploited. *What if I used unlinked refunds to send money?* thought Lee. Then all people would need to do to send money was punch in their card numbers.

Cash App took off slowly at first. It almost didn't make it. There was plenty of competition, including Venmo, another app that let people move money around. But Cash App had one advantage over Venmo — it's not a snitch. Venmo is notorious for its openness, requiring people to indicate what their transactions are for and pushing people to use it as if it were a social network. By contrast, Cash App doesn't broadcast any information.

Cash App first took off in Atlanta, where it was a particular hit within the Black community, spreading from there through the rest of the South. Hundreds of rap songs have mentioned Cash App in the lyrics, most notably Roddy Ricch's 2020 hit "The Box." Square didn't anticipate rap fans to be its audience, but it embraced the development, with Dorsey hobnobbing with Jay-Z and Beyoncé and buying a majority interest in Jay-Z's streaming platform, Tidal. Once, the company enlisted rapper Megan Thee Stallion in an advertising campaign called "Investing for Hotties." Rapper Kendrick Lamar appeared in another ad.

"It's funny to think it was all born of a simple hack born of impatience," Lee said at a conference.

One night in 2015, Bob and Krista were lying in bed. They had just gotten back from Vessel, a nightclub they loved. They had just found out that a couple they were friends with was breaking up, and it made them reconsider their own relationship, which had had its own challenges. Krista recalled the conversation for me.

"I never want you to hate me," Bob told Krista.

"Honey, I could never hate you," Krista told Bob.

"You've given up so much for me. I know that you were never meant to be this doting housewife."

"No, honey, it's okay," she said. "I love you, and I'm glad to be the one behind the man."

"I don't want that for you," he said.

She thought about it, and found herself agreeing with him. "You're right," she said. "You know, I don't really want that, either."

And so they decided to separate.

"And it was fantastic," Krista later told me. "We would often joke that it's because I love you that I don't want to be with you anymore. We'd seen so many couples fall apart, and we didn't want to be those people."

A few weeks later, Bob went off to Burning Man for the first time. He stayed for two weeks. "It was fantastic," said Krista. "I got a whole place to myself. I loved it. I absolutely loved it. He got back, and he was this whole new enlightened person."

12

We Shape Our Buildings

Bob Lee's friends weren't exactly sure what to think about Tina, but they knew they didn't like her very much. She wasn't included in their group texts. She wasn't invited to parties, although she and her brother would sometimes finagle their way into them anyway. She seemed messy — she was always starting drama. They heard she liked to play the victim. She exaggerated. She was erratic. She couldn't be trusted. They heard a rumor that she had once attacked a former boyfriend with a knife. And yet Bob seemed to like her.

"Bob and Khazar have known each other since 2020," said Krista. "There was a possibility that they were lovers, but they were never dating. Any girl that Bob actually liked and was dating, I would get to meet her. He didn't even know her last name. She was just a party girl. Just a bimbo."

Before the 1906 earthquake, Jackson Square had been the most notorious red-light district on the Pacific — the Barbary Coast, where cocaine and morphine flowed, sailors bought sex, and the police were afraid to go. It had long since been cleaned up. Today it's home to advertising agencies, boutique stores selling Aesop soap, Allbirds shoes, and a bookstore that only sells architecture titles.

It was here in 2013 that a club called The Battery opened its doors, started by a San Francisco couple who sold Bebo, a social network they had founded, to AOL for $850 million. The BBC deemed the purchase "one of the worst deals ever made in the dotcom era," and the AOL CEO who negotiated it was forced out of his job.

According to one puff piece in a luxury magazine, The Battery was envisioned as "a private social club for the likes of fringe artists and tech moguls to commingle á la Gertrude Stein's Parisian salons or the Algonquin Round Table." A membership cost $2,800 a year, with an additional initiation fee of $1,000. As of 2023, the paid membership was around five thousand people.

It's a strange hybrid of a place, a little too sexy for business and a little too buttoned-up for vice. But that was the chimeric scene that Lee was now firmly a part of — and that was where he met Tina. The lines between business and pleasure were thin. Every art show was a chance to size up a new investment opportunity, and a new potential investment contact could easily find themselves hanging out with Lee well into the night.

The club's five stories hold a restaurant and several bars. There are event spaces, a gym, and a sauna. Downstairs, koi fish swim in a pond. Upstairs there's a small hotel. An unconfirmed rumor that I've heard from several different people is that Beyoncé stays there when in town. (I don't know if that's true, or just something The Battery wants people to think is true.) The club hosts karaoke dance parties, magic shows, and conversations about "Emerging National Security & Defense Challenges Around the World."

On the front door there is a sign that reads, WE SHAPE OUR BUILDINGS. THEREAFTER, THEY SHAPE US. I used to work around the corner and would pass it on my lunch breaks on my way to Safeway to buy a sandwich. Every day I would look at the sign, and every day it would confuse me. I still don't understand it.

"I love the interior designer," Krista said. "But they should have been a little more selective on who they let in."

She threw a party there in 2018, after the Golden State Warriors won the NBA championship. Another time, she and Bob rented the whole bottom level, the first-level bar, and the penthouse upstairs for a private party. "It was supposed to be invite-only," she said, "but the next thing you know, it's full of escorts. I'm not knocking the profession. It's wonderful, it's great, whatever. But when you're doing an event like that, it's the last thing you want. Yet The Battery just lets them in."

Krista wasn't clear exactly how Bob and Tina met, but she knew that once they met, she slid into his DMs: *Come to my place. Come over, come over.*

"No, I'm good. I have a girlfriend," Bob wrote back, according to Krista.

"Your girlfriend doesn't mean shit compared to me," she reportedly wrote.

Krista made a sour face as she told the story. "So high and mighty, you dirty skank," she said, adding that she didn't think Khazar was even a member. "I think she's just a ho that hangs out there."

A few months after Lee's death, I had lunch there.

The Asia-Pacific Economic Cooperation summit was in town, and while the presidents of the United States and China were meeting discreetly in a mansion in the suburbs on the Peninsula, the city's streets were packed with foreign leaders, factotums, and security agents. Several blocks downtown were fenced off temporarily. I parked my Honda Civic on the street near my old office as protesters marched in the distance.

The place was busy. It felt a little like the members lounge at an airport — transient, tony, and transactional. I sat down to lunch — a lab-grown fake-meat cheeseburger and french fries. As I bit into it, a big glob of mustard fell and plopped onto my dress shirt.

Krista was right to remark on the interior design. It is something, that's for sure. The club is covered in fabrics of every color, texture, and pattern. Garish contemporary art fills the walls. A photorealist painting of Chinese tanks rolling into Tiananmen Square is on display inside the front door. (I wasn't sure if we were meant to root for the tanks or not.) The vibe was neoliberal-colonial hell. Diving helmets and fencing masks. One wall had dozens of small prows of ships nailed to it, each of which had a different figurehead. There were patterns on patterns on patterns covering every available surface, sort of like those Magic Eye posters that had been popular in the 1990s. Taxidermied heads of all kinds of animals filled the walls. The interior designer, Ken Fulk, the trendiest aesthete in San Francisco, loves taxidermy.

I went to the unisex bathroom to clean off the mustard from my shirt. Inside, each of the stalls had placards bearing the name of one of the seven deadly sins. The one marked LUST was twice the size of the others. The bathroom's wallpaper was printed with drawings of aristocrats fucking each other on couches in pairs, trios, and more.

By some alchemy I could never unravel, Fulk was the most sought-after interior designer in the city. Taxidermied heads hang in restaurants, offices, and private residences, a sharp rejection of the organic, post-hippie style that had dominated the Bay Area when I was growing up, which I suppose explains why his style was so widely embraced. I will give Fulk this: His taste is so awful that it must be authentic. But why it is so popular with other people, I can't determine, except that once you start working for famous people, you tend to keep working for other famous people. In 2014, Fulk designed the wedding of Napster founder Sean Parker. It cost $10 million to turn a grove of coastal redwoods into a fake *Lord of the Rings* cosplay set that netted a $2.5 million fine from the state government. When Kamala Harris was the state's attorney general, she faced an official investigation for having accepted Fulk's free help redecorating her loft. She ended up paying him over $10,000.

After returning to my table, I gazed at the people eating lunch. The women were dressed sensibly, mostly in muted jewel tones. The men wore vests from which you could read their place in the status hierarchy as easily as if they were badges of rank on military uniforms — North Face for the junior partners and Arc'teryx for the senior ones.

I had come to try to capture a glimpse of how Lee and Khazar might have moved through this space, to better understand the world they inhabited.

Bob must have been charismatic; she must have been hot. He must have seemed rich; she must have seemed fun. Maybe they only had a superficial connection. It was here that the chain of events that would lead to Lee's death began. And yet I couldn't seem to extract any meaning from my time inside the club. It just seemed like an ugly, overdecorated dining room filled with people not so distinguishable from Lee.

As I finished my cheeseburger, I felt like I had failed. Any of these men could have been Lee. Were it not for his death, Lee would have been just another face in The Battery, and I would never have come here trying to better understand him. That's when I thought again about something that Harper Reed had told me. *Bob was interesting, but he wasn't that interesting.* Lee was a talented programmer and manager, but not more than that. He had been at the right place and at the right time at least twice, and might have done so a third time. But he was not a household name, not a mover and shaker. He was no Peter Thiel or Mark Zuckerberg.

The truth is this: The tech industry is lousy with men like Bob Lee. Any of these men could have been him. And maybe that was the point.

Bob left Square in 2014. Krista remembered being at a Fourth of July party at the house of venture capitalist Ron Conway, a confidant of Mayor Lee's. Conway and Jack Dorsey cornered her. They wanted to know where Lee was going next.

"Bob's not going anywhere next," she said. "He just wants some time off."

Lee spent the rest of the summer traveling up and down the East Coast, including Miami, where he was living at the time of his death. He did some investing and worked for a while at Present, a social network start-up aimed at women that failed to catch on. (It was a new experience for Lee, to be part of something that failed.)

Now that his work life wasn't so stressful, Lee could spend more time enjoying himself. One morning in 2016, Krista awoke to several missed calls from him that had been placed at five in the morning. She called him back.

"Do you have the breakfast of champions at home?" he asked.

"Yeah," she said. "I have a few things here."

It was a Tuesday morning around 6:00 A.M. The kids were away at camp. Krista was headed to the gym, but first she gathered up some drugs, bottles of Champagne, orange juice, and vodka and took them to Lee's new apartment. The smell of men who had been up all night partying hit her as she opened the door.

"I walked in, and Bob was with John Mayer, Dave Chappelle, and our friends. I dropped off the supplies and was laughing my ass off. It was quite the motley crew."

～

At Google, Lee had known a professor at the University of Maryland named Bill Pugh, an influential figure in the Java community. In fact, Google cofounder Sergey Brin had taken a class from him as an undergraduate, and he brought Pugh to the Bay Area to work for Google during the summers and while he was on sabbatical. Lee and Pugh had a lot in common. They both went to Burning Man regularly, and when Pugh was in town, they would hike through the mountains or hang out around the pool at Josh Bloch's house talking about their plans for next year's gathering.

By the end of March 2020, people like Pugh were talking about how they might use their technical skills to help the fight against the virus. "There was a lot of discussion about using Bluetooth and cell phones to find out if you were near somebody who had COVID," Pugh told me. Pugh grew fascinated with the idea, blogging about it, writing white papers, and sending out an endless stream of tweets and updates on LinkedIn. Eventually, Google and Apple announced they were jointly working on a framework for contact-tracing apps.

As it turned out, Lee was thinking along similar lines. He reached out to Pugh. "Bill," he said, "I'm working with a group that's trying to build an app for the World Health Organization on top of this framework. Would you like to come on and talk?"

Pugh said yes.

The idea was to build a single contact-tracing app that could be customized for each country it would be used in. The group received permission from Apple to start work shortly before Pugh joined the ad hoc group.

Lee's role on the project relied less on his technical skills and more on his professional network, finding the right people, making introductions, and acting as a rainmaker. Eventually, it ran into too many hurdles to succeed, and so Lee ended his involvement, and

Pugh joined Apple, where he worked on another contact-tracing app that, according to a study published in *Nature*, prevented an estimated one million infections.

During the pandemic, Lee's lifestyle changed in several ways, not least of which was that his divorce became official. He and Krista had been separated for some time by then, but they hadn't realized the paperwork hadn't gone through. Then one day, Krista was at the car dealership buying a new car, a Porsche 911. She placed a call to move the money, and her accountant asked whether she wanted to use her individual account or the joint one. *The joint one*, wondered a confused Krista.

"You guys still have a joint account," said the accountant.

She called Bob. "Sweetheart, I hope that you don't mind, but I'm taking a hundred grand out of the account," she said.

"Whoa, what are you doing?" he asked.

"Well, apparently you're buying me a Porsche 911."

"Okay, that's your divorce present from me."

Krista called the car her Divorce-sche. Bob took it out one time from her house and ripped the bottom while parking. After that, she didn't let him drive it.

After Krista moved to the North Bay, Bob decided to leave the city, too. He found a house in Mill Valley, on the top of a hill and surrounded by redwoods. Krista called it the vortex, because once you were up there, there was no daylight. It was a bachelor pad that he shared with his father, Rick. (Nan died of cancer in April 2019, not long before the beginning of the pandemic.) But Bob did not stay in the tree house for very long. At her nephew's graduation party in 2022, Bob told Krista that he might be selling it.

She laughed. He had barely moved in and furnished the place. What did he mean he was selling it?

It turned out that someone who recognized the house and was

a fan of the architect made an unsolicited request to tour it. Lee agreed, and to his surprise, that person ended up making an offer to buy the place. Lee didn't know who the buyer was, and he and Krista were laughing as they speculated whether it was the pop star Lady Gaga, whose relationship with a techie was rumored to be getting pretty serious.

It wasn't her, but Lee counteroffered, the buyer accepted his price, and within a week, Lee needed a new place to live. "It was so fast," said Krista.

Lee wanted her and the kids to move with him, but Krista demurred. The kids were now old enough that it would be hard to uproot them, and she had a life of her own — a new boyfriend whom she loved and her own business growing cannabis. Lee didn't even know where he was headed.

"Maybe I'll move to Mexico City," he told her. "Maybe I'll move to Austin. Maybe I'll move to Miami."

"Okay, how about you do this, honey? Why don't you visit all these places?" she said.

Lee sold his Mill Valley house for $4.43 million — almost double what he had paid for it four years earlier in 2018 — and spent a few months on the road. Eventually he decided to buy a condo in Miami, where he and Rick lived in a fifty-three-story building on the waterfront just north of downtown, with a room-mate, a DJ named Dangerous Rose. Rick marveled at the life he was now living. He took his grandchildren to the carnival, drank mimosas for lunch, had oysters for dinner, and gazed at the fat green lizards clinging to the sides of the trees in the sun. Things had shifted so fast.

13

Miami Has This Energy

"I met him pretty soon after he lost his mom," said Sara Drakeley, who at the time was the CTO of MobileCoin, which is now called Sentz, the company where Lee was working as the chief product officer when he died.

"I think it changed him. I wonder if it was different before that, or if something about his mom passing really made him embrace humanity in a way," she said.

When Drakeley became the CTO of MobileCoin in March 2021, she started looking for someone to bounce ideas off. The company had just closed its Series B funding round, and she thought it would be helpful to find an adviser who had faced similar challenges. "I asked our investors if they had anyone in their Rolodex who could provide guidance," she said. They knew just the guy. In fact, he was one of their investors.

"During our first calls, it was the peak of the pandemic. I didn't have my daughter in daycare, so she was just in the background while Bob and I were chatting about technology and how to build an engineering organization."

Lee's advice was that MobileCoin was now sitting on a lot of cash thanks to its Series B funding round. It was a lot of fuel that should be put to use. As they talked, Lee developed a deeper understanding of the company's potential. He thought that it could be a global version of Cash App, which was still only available within the United States. The prospects were exciting, and the more they talked, the more wound up Lee became. Drakeley said, "He got so enthusiastic that ultimately he was like, 'Actually, I would like to join.'"

The new sense of purpose was good for him. As his friends often noted, when Lee wasn't working hard, his boundless energy went in other, more destructive directions. A bored Bob was a dangerous Bob.

At MobileCoin, Lee took a roving role, working across every part of the business, something like a mini CEO. Sometimes he would advise Drakeley on how to manage engineers. Sometimes he would recruit designers and programmers. Sometimes he would get down into the bits and program something. "He did that two or three times where it would be like some problem seemed impossible," said Drakeley. "And he'd come back the next day and be like, 'I think I got it.'"

On December 16, 2021, Lee had his coming-out party as an executive for MobileCoin, giving a speech at its first corporate conference in San Francisco.

Lee's speech was bookended by several other presentations. In the first one of the day, MobileCoin CEO Josh Goldbard spoke loftily about privacy, freedom, and the future of the human species while wearing a strange-looking hat, sort of a baseball cap with spikes through it. Drakeley went last. Her topic was "constraints." (To understand gender roles in the tech industry, just read that again.) Lee was somewhere in the middle. I watched a video recording of Lee's talk to prepare for my interview with Drakeley, who took over as CEO in May 2023, just after Lee's death.

I told Drakeley that Lee looked tired in the video. He didn't have that energy that I was used to people describing him as having. "He was so nervous before that talk," said Drakeley. "He really wanted to make a good impression. He was coming in at this really high level of leadership, and although he had earned my trust, obviously, that was one-on-one."

He opened with a joke, or at least an attempt at one. "I'm Bob Lee," he said by way of introduction, "and I'm MobileCoin's freshly minted — not mined, that would be Bitcoin — chief product officer."

The joke bombed. Programmer humor hadn't improved in the two decades Bob had been in the industry.

"Now that I'm at MobileCoin, we'll continue the mission I started at Cash App — making payments better for everyone by finding efficiencies, exploring underused functionalities, and legitimizing new methods of payments with the world at large," he said.

But for that to happen, MobileCoin would have to survive.

In April, the price of a MobileCoin, which had been around $2 to $6, rose suddenly, climbing to almost $70, before crashing a few weeks later. (At the end of 2023, MobileCoin was trading around 50 cents.) It looked as if the currency had been caught up by a pump-and-dump scheme, with investors driving up the price to unsustainable highs before cashing out near the peak. Worse, rumors were circulating online that it was an inside job. Rumors were also spreading of some kind of inside deal between Mobile-Coin and messaging app Signal, which Goldbard denied.

It took the financial journalist Michael Lewis and reporters at the *Financial Times* to unravel what had happened: In March and April, a trader with an account on the now-bankrupt FTX cryptocurrency exchange cornered the market on MobileCoin, along with another rarely traded cryptocurrency, BitMax. The trader realized that there was a flaw in FTX's software that would allow them to borrow bitcoins against the value of their holdings in MobileCoin and BitMax. By inflating the value of their holdings, this trader, who was never publicly identified, was able to convert their position into $600 million worth of Bitcoins before disappearing and sticking FTX with a rapidly depreciating pile of MobileCoin and BitMax. The loss was bad enough, but making things worse, Alameda Research, the hedge fund run by Sam Bankman-Fried, secretly compensated FTX for its losses, which totaled more than $1 billion. Bankman-Fried would later be convicted in the United States of seven counts of fraud, money laundering, and conspiracy.

When speaking to me, Drakeley chose her words carefully when talking about the confusing situation. "We had got to get it right given the resource constraints that we had. That can be difficult in any organization, because there are so many competing priorities," she said.

Drakeley and Lee grew close professionally as they worked together, even though she was in Lake Tahoe and he had since moved to Miami. Drakeley remembered being surprised the first time that Lee referred to her as his best friend. "I was like, *What?*" she said. "We don't know each other." But then, she realized, that was just the way that Lee was. "It was like he got you. He saw who you are. I met the Dalai Lama once, and it felt like that — to be instantly seen by this human somehow. Bob had that quality."

They bonded over their jobs, to be sure, but also over their shared love of *Star Trek*, their families, and the books that Lee shared with her, many of them technical textbooks on programming, sorting and searching, and fundamental algorithms. Drakeley had been a computer animator earlier in her career, and when Lee found that out, he excitedly showed her a four-hundred-line graphics renderer that he had written years before. "He was so proud of it," she said.

But more than that, Lee shared with Drakeley his sense that even as challenging as MobileCoin could seem, things would work out in the long run. Just look at Lee. He had his share of successes, but also plenty of failures, like Present, the women's social network that went nowhere. For somebody like Lee, a failure was never the end.

"It was really important to him that he had failed multiple times as a founder," Drakeley told me. "That was important. It made him a better executive. He very much impressed that upon me. If you want to get philosophical, you can think about San Francisco in the same way. Can it maintain that resilience and optimism?"

If there was ever an exact opposite of the cute little statues that Google commissioned to celebrate each launch of a new Android phone model, the Miami Bull — a symbol of Miami's growing status as a center of the cryptocurrency world — was it. The Android statues looked like Baby Yoda. The crypto bull looked like an American mercenary would ride it through the streets of Baghdad during the Iraq war.

Standing eleven feet tall and weighing a ton and a half, the bull debuted at a cryptocurrency conference there in 2022. It had pistons for legs. It had glowing blue eyes. (Everything in crypto has glowing eyes for some godforsaken reason.) It cost a quarter million dollars — about five Bitcoins at their value at the time. It looked like a rejected sketch for a Transformer. It *was* a rejected sketch for a Transformer — its creator had been a concept artist on one of those incomprehensible action films and had dusted off an unused design.

During the pandemic, Miami was one of several mid-tier American cities vying to attract techies giving up on San Francisco. The city-by-the-beach sold itself as a fun-house-mirror version of the city-by-the-bay: warm, cheap, business-friendly, and always down to party. For a moment, Miami looked like the next great American city

"Miami has this energy just like what it used to be in Silicon Valley," Lee told Drakeley once. "There's a lot of hope about the future."

Techie cantons have littered American cities for a decade or more, including one that Lee and Dorsey tried to nurture in St. Louis. Many of these attempts failed, or at least fell far short of their ambitions. It was hard, nearly impossible, to defeat the network effects that kept cities like San Francisco in place.

But the path dependency of regional economies had never seen a crisis like the pandemic. As workers fled in search of cheaper housing costs, new and exciting places to live, or proximity to the families they left behind, cities like Miami marketed themselves to techies as places to ride out the end of civilization. As one coder who left San Francisco explained to me, working in the Bay Area began to be seen as a tour of duty in a foreign country.

In a way that San Francisco never really was, Miami was the center of crypto. It happened almost at random. The inventors of Ethereum, the second-most-traded cryptocurrency, had rented a house in Miami while they were working on it and debuted their work at a conference held in Miami in 2015. The NFT fad had also hit Miami hard after a pair of literary-minded thirty-something men met at a Miami bar and created the Bored Ape Yacht Club, whose non-fungible tokens ran on Ethereum and were shilled for by celebrities like Paris Hilton. The boom was in full swing when FTX signed a $135 million, nineteen-year deal for the naming rights to the stadium where the Miami Heat played basketball. If you were a conservative in tech, the question was not whether you would stay in San Francisco. The question was whether you should move to Austin or Miami.

Lee stood out among the techies who moved to Miami because, unlike many of them, he was a liberal Democrat. Far more common were conservatives like the venture capitalist Keith Rabois, who bought a mansion in Miami for $28.9 million in 2020. After having made San Francisco his home for two decades, he told *Fortune* it was "impossible to stay" in a city that he thought was "just so massively improperly run."

From Miami, Rabois continued to snipe at the city he used to call home, saying things like, "If you are under 30, you are sacrificing your career ambitions by remaining in the Bay Area," and "San Francisco is Detroit and Miami is the future." But it wasn't just liberalism that pushed him out — it was also the NIMBYism. In 2017, Rabois bought another house on the same street as his home in San Francisco's Glen Park neighborhood. He planned to remodel it, but his neighbors were so opposed to his plan that they created a website to detail everything that was wrong with the proposal. (In 2023, a defeated Rabois sold the first house to former Obama campaign manager Jim Messina for $8.7 million.)

Rabois wasn't the only conservative tech baron who packed up and left San Francisco. The same year he bought his mansion in Miami, his friend Peter Thiel spent $18 million on the Miami waterfront property that had been the set of MTV's *The Real World* in 1996, at which he hosted the city's mayor soon after he moved in. Among the other notables and semi-notables who decamped from San Francisco to Miami were Reddit cofounder Alexis Ohanian, venture capitalists Shervin Pishevar and David Blumberg, Shutterstock founder Jonathan Oringer, and Zao Yang, the creator of FarmVille, who complained to the local press that San Francisco hadn't appreciated his genius enough.

In a way, none of this was new. Florida has for many decades been a state for rich conservatives to flee to after they have made their money in other parts of the country. Florida is warm, it has no income tax, and its politics are conservative. But if people were motivated by crime to leave California, as many claimed, they may have been acting more from their feelings than the numbers. In 2022, Miami had 47 homicides, which is a homicide rate of 10.7 per 100,000 people — significantly higher than San Francisco's homicide rate. As Kevin Bourrillion pointed out to me, "The idea that Bob moved to Miami because of crime is bizarre. Miami of all places. What are you talking about?"

The morning that she found out that Lee had died, Drakeley knew what to do. Someone else who worked at the company had died the year before, and she had done the same thing that time. She picked up her phone and called every person who worked at MobileCoin. There were fifty of them. It was a long day. "I hope I never go through anything like that again," she said.

On Hacker News, the bulletin board popular with the industry, Goldbard praised Lee: "I had the distinct pleasure of working with Bob daily for the last few years. Bob was an incredible human being who I will miss every day. He was my friend and someone who drank deeply from the cup of life. He had a way of seeing the world that was enchanting. He was a visionary in so many ways."

And then the company went silent.

There wasn't much else to say, and the circumstances in which he had died were not yet known. Maybe his death had something to do with the app. Maybe it had something to do with crypto. Maybe it was something else entirely. Things were tense enough inside MobileCoin as it was — Goldbard would soon leave — and Lee's death only exacerbated the feeling of chaos that had enveloped the entire crypto industry in the wake of FTX's collapse and the bust of the NFT fad. "It's kind of like, you know, someone turned on the light and the cockroaches started scattering. It's probably good for the industry that the bad actors are being rooted out," said Drakeley.

"For it to turn into such a public thing, the whole company, we just, we went completely silent. We were like, 'We're not going to engage.' We're just not going to engage with the world right now. We're going to succeed with what we're building and then emerge once it feels safe again to do so," said Drakeley.

In the end, she's not sure how well she really knew Lee. He only showed her what he wanted to show her.

"He was so open and authentic," she said. "That didn't necessarily mean that he was open and authentic about every part of himself and every relationship he'd had. It was like, *Oh yeah. Of course there's more to this person.*"

14

The Lifestyle

The month after he died, the *Wall Street Journal* made an attempt at finding out more about Bob Lee's life away from work.

"In certain wealthy tech circles it is known as 'The Lifestyle,' an underground party scene featuring recreational drug use and casual sex," the newspaper wrote.

"To some, 'The Lifestyle' is narrowly focused to describe people who might engage in various sexual activities with different partners," it went on. "In San Francisco, it is used more loosely to describe an underground party scene that has evolved since the city's early days as an incubator of the countercultural movement."

Many details in the article had already been reported elsewhere — Lee was a well-off executive who liked to stay out late, Nima Momeni was a hanger-on, and his sister was glamorous but listless. But this part about The Lifestyle — capital T, capital L — was new.

Could there be some kind of secret society right under our noses? One that was made up of the city's richest and most powerful? Had Bob Lee been a part of a scene out of *Eyes Wide Shut*? I imagined masks, occult rituals, and secrecy. Maybe Khazar was a part of it, too? Maybe that's why Bob had died? It was as if all the rumors and conspiracy theories about the Bohemian Grove, a club in the redwoods that includes some of the world's most powerful men, had been updated for the digital world.

But Krista wasn't having any of it. "She disputed that Mr. Lee was a 'party boy,'" reported the *Journal*, "and said she had never heard the term 'The Lifestyle.'" Was she covering for him? Or had the East Coast paper simply dressed up Bob's life in scare quotes to give its audience of investment bankers and Republican staffers a thrill? There was a lot that seemed to hinge on the capital T and the capital L.

Mike Bailey, a good friend of Bob's, denied that there was any such thing as The Lifestyle. The two men had been especially close when Bob was living in Miami, and Mike was sure that if Bob was up to something like that, he would have told him, or maybe even invited him to join.

When I talked to Harper Reed, who was quoted in the *Journal* article, he agreed that the paper was probably playing up something that was real, but not as salacious as it made it seem. Of course there was *a* lifestyle in the Bay Area, he told me, but people were doing drugs, having sex, and going to parties in the rest of the country, too.

When I asked her, Krista chalked it up to a misunderstanding. The lifestyle was what people in the polyamory world, who dated multiple people simultaneously, sometimes called what they were involved in. Krista had embraced polyamory after they separated, but Bob never did. "He was extremely faithful," she said.

"San Francisco social life was fantastic," she added. "The media turned it into something about drugs, sex, and 'The Lifestyle.' There was no lifestyle. Like, yes we did like to attend parties and clubs. I don't think that's anything that's unheard of. He wasn't in some weird sex cult, like that article tried to make it seem."

All of them could have been trying to deflect me from the truth, of course. Maybe the first rule of The Lifestyle is not to talk about The Lifestyle. So for a few months, I followed the lead, talking to anyone who might have run in the same circles in San Francisco to see if they had heard of it. A few people said they had, but each time I pressed them for details, it turned out that they had only heard of it after the *Wall Street Journal* story. (The reporters who worked on the article did not return my requests to talk.)

What Krista and Bob's friends told me squared with my own sense of what dating in the Bay Area was like. It also checked out with what other people said after the *Journal's* story came out. There were multiple threads on Reddit calling foul on the story. "Probably a case of a few people using a phrase and the media pretending it's a distinct organization," wrote one person.

"My married partner and I identify with being part of what would be considered 'The Lifestyle' here in SF, although I would stress it's a vibe rather than a specific singular group of people," another person wrote. "Realistically it's house parties, play parties, some of the dating apps but also you'll see large numbers of the community attend certain public events like DJ nights etc which attract a similar crowd. [It includes a] big overlap with burning man, Tulum vacationers, ayahuasca rituals etc."

As I was investigating the rumors, chasing down each scrap that I could find, I also happened to be reading *The Damned*, a novel by the French writer J.-K. Huysmans. Published in 1891, its main character is a thinly veiled stand-in for the author drawn into the clutches of a satanic cult that haunts Paris. It's good stuff. The novel is filled with church bells, alchemy, languid dinners, intellectual debates, evil women, and desperate chases through gaslit streets. Throughout it, the narrator moves closer and closer to a cult — The Lifestyle, if you will — made up of the rich and powerful. At the end, he finds them, observes a Black Mass (which the real-life Huysmans supposedly based on one that he attended), and is seduced by one of the satanists, who "initiated him into obscenities whose existence he never suspected," in the back room of a wine shop.

It's tawdry and exciting, but it ends up being nothing. A middle-aged man having sex. Was this really the damning secret? I guess I shouldn't have been surprised when *Law & Order* ran an episode with a story that was just distinct enough from Bob Lee's actual death to avoid legal repercussions, filled with intimations of dangerous sex. (In the end, the killer is convicted, despite concerns that a surveillance video of the killing may have been faked with artificial intelligence.)

What I knew for certain about Lee's last days in town was this: Lee was in the Bay Area to attend a school play — *High School Musical*. He attended with Krista and Krista's partner. Afterward, they went out to dinner with Mike Bailey, who had known the Lees for almost twenty years.

At dinner, Lee seemed distracted, engrossed with something on his phone. Bailey thought he was texting with someone. But after fifteen minutes, Lee showed them what he had been doing. He had been using the AI software ChatGPT to plot how Krista might run for president. "It was just the funniest thing," said Bailey.

After the play, Bob and Krista's partner went to the Regency Ballroom in San Francisco, where they attended a dance party held by a Burning Man–affiliated group called Opulent Temple. It was billed as a White Party — guests were asked to wear only white. But as a way to stand out, Lee was dressed from head to toe in black. DJs played well past two in the morning. There were belly-dancing and aerial performances, and at midnight, Sufi dervishes performed an ecstatic whirling dance. Bob and Krista's partner partied all night and then went to an afterparty at a plastic surgeon's office. Early on the morning of April 1, Bob went to Khazar's apartment. He was there for a little while, and then left.

Early on the morning of April 3, Bob returned to Khazar's apartment, this time in the company of a friend named Jeremy Boivin. They hung out for a while and then split up. Khazar and Jeremy went to the beach, and then back to Jeremy's apartment. Bob went to work, and then met up with them at Jeremy's in the afternoon. From then until Lee was stabbed, the events were under dispute.

15

A Really Good Heart

Before she left the case, Paula Canny filed a thicket of support letters for Nima, asking for the court to release him pending the trial. They painted a sympathetic picture of Momeni.

"I have known Nima his entire life," wrote his mother, Mahnaz Tayarani. "As a mother, I believe I know my son. Hence, I would like to tell the court about Nima."

Tayarani married young, and gave birth to Nima, her first child, when she was twenty-three years old. A year later came his sister, Khazar. The young family lived in Tehran, but as Tayarani explained, when Nima was fourteen, she decided, "I had no choice but to take my children from Iran."

"I had endured years of abuse and violence at the hands of my husband. I left Iran to start a new life in America," she said. The three of them settled in the Bay Area, where Tayarani had friends, and Nima took care of his mother as he grew older. When Nima was twenty, Tayarani applied for a dental hygiene program at a local college. She was accepted but worried that she would not be able to afford the tuition. When she told Nima, he said, "Mom, go for it! I will help as much as I can." She burst into tears.

Nima also looked after his sister. When Khazar broke up with a boyfriend, Nima invited her to live with him. "Nima took care of her," Tayarani wrote — and others as well. "He frequently buys groceries for elderly people in need," she said, and he "bought a computer for the office manager at my office when he heard that her laptop had been stolen."

"We are all very sorry about Bob Lee," wrote Tayarani. "I know with all my heart that my son would never intentionally kill another person, much less hurt another person. That is not in his nature."

"My brother means the world to me," Khazar said in her letter, "and I believe he feels the same way about me. He is protective of me, but never controlling. He watches out for me as I do for him. We are close friends, and as close as a brother and sister can be."

The letter from Khazar's husband, Dino Elyassnia, was shorter, but it was written on the official stationery of his plastic surgery practice. "Nima has always acted appropriately, respectfully, and cordially," in the ten years that he had known him, said Dr. Elyassnia, who offered to use his residence in the Millennium Tower as bail surety for Nima.

A longer story came from a friend of Nima's mother, who only gave her first name — Soheila — and wrote that she first met Nima in 1999, when he was a teenager. He and his sister were standing on both sides of their mother as they came off the plane on their first day in San Francisco. Soheila, who had left Iran years before, thought that Nima and Khazar shared a sense of shock and confusion, "both clinging to their mother, and the innocent plea in their eyes made them look alike."

Soheila and Mahnaz had been high school classmates in Mashhad. Shortly after they graduated, Mahnaz married a "handsome dentist with an artistic streak" and moved to the country's capital. Her friend was jealous, but what she did not know was that Tayarani was being abused. "As it is with women in Iran, they tend to hide their domestic violence issues as private, shameful matters," wrote Soheila. "Perhaps that was why I did not hear from her much after the wedding."

More than a decade later, Mahnaz reached out to Soheila. This time, the full story poured out. "When I heard of her husband beating the children, having affairs, and abusing her, I vowed to help her escape." After first arriving in San Francisco, Mahnaz and her children slept in Soheila's son's bedroom. Slowly, the family adjusted. The children enrolled in high school and learned English. Mahnaz found a job in a flower shop and rented an apartment. The transition had been difficult, but as the years passed, to Soheila it seemed successful.

"I watched Nima and Khazar go through culture shock as well as the economic shock of adjusting to a new standard of life," she wrote. "Nima always stayed in touch and I watched him as he grew into a man; kind and generous and ready to help whenever he was needed."

The last time Soheila saw Nima was March 20, 2023 — Persian New Year. It was a happy holiday. Just a few weeks before, Nima and Khazar bought Tayarani a new BMW. "It was symbolic of how far they had come in this country, to finally achieving economic freedom and stability. Mahnaz was so content that her children had grown up and that she no longer had to worry about taking care of them," wrote Soheila.

"When I read in [the] papers that he was a suspect in Bob Lee's murder, I was shocked. It would have been less surprising to hear that he had been hit by a meteor than to hear this news," she wrote. "I hope that Nima will have a fair and impartial trial, and I hope that his family (namely Mahnaz and Khazar) do not have to suffer any further."

Two of Nima's friends wrote letters in which they attested to his kindness. One wrote that he had been to parties with him, "and only once seen too much drinking as a cause of a guest getting unruly. In this case, a girl was too drunk to drive." Nima took her keys away, and in reaction she raised a "loud ruckus outside his apartment and cracked his car windshield."

Two of Nima's neighbors wrote letters, too. One of them said that they had met Tayarani outside the building. "I stopped and told her to please tell Nima I am thinking of him. I told her Nima has always been sweet, kind, and generous toward me, and to please let him know I am thinking of him. She said I could help him by writing to you and telling you how I feel about Nima."

"I would by no means ever want my name in the media," they continued, "but I am willing to say that Nima is always kind toward me."

The other letter was from Nima's downstairs neighbor, who wrote that they had met three years before, shortly after Nima moved in. Nima's Jeep had been broken into, and he asked if the neighbor's security cameras had any footage of it. "Unfortunately, he had to reach out to me several times over the last few years regarding vehicle break-ins and vandalism," he wrote.

Nima was a considerate neighbor, often leaving bottles of wine at his door as a token of apology when his parties went a little long and were a little loud. Nima's neighbor would sometimes go upstairs for lunch at Nima's apartment. Every time he left, Nima would ply him with gifts — "a bowl of whatever produce he had recently purchased: pomegranates, berries, figs, oranges, etc. I was almost embarrassed to receive this level of generosity."

Nima's generosity extended to his unhoused neighbors, too. Once, his downstairs neighbor saw Nima talking to a man who had been camped out on the street near the building for months. One day, the man had returned to his corner to find his belongings gone. He was sobbing on the sidewalk when Nima "walked over to him, put his [hand] on his shoulder, exchanged a few words with him, and passed him money to help him out.

"This is the Nima that I've gotten to know," concluded the neighbor. "I write this to counter the unfairly negative portrayal of him I've seen in the media from people who've never met him, seemingly based solely on selected, salacious bits of information. The Nima I know has a really good heart."

After reading the letters, I sought to discover what I could find out for myself about Nima, since the family was not talking to the press.

When the Momenis first arrived in the United States, they lived in Albany, a pleasant city in the East Bay just north of Berkeley. Nima and his sister graduated from high school there, and so one day I traveled to the Albany public library to find their yearbooks. I wanted to find out who their friends might have been and what their younger lives had been like.

But the yearbooks made them seem like ghosts. Neither was recorded as being in any clubs or on any teams, although I did end up later finding one person who remembered Nima taking lifeguarding lessons with him. They were represented only by their portraits. Khazar looked poised and self-possessed, her hair neatly tied back and a faint, closed-lipped smile on her face. Nima looked a little rough. He wasn't scowling, but wasn't smiling, either. He looked on edge. The image reminded me of what one of his friends had written in a support letter, that Nima qualified for free school lunches but was too proud to take them.

Another piece of information I found about Nima came from the Albany Police Department.

On the evening of January 18, 2005, it received a call saying there had been a street fight outside the Momenis' apartment. It was between Nima and two other young men. Nima had stabbed one of them with a knife and sent both of them to the hospital.

In Nima's bedroom, police found 15.7 grams of marijuana divided into four baggies, as well as an earnings stub from a part-time job, a leather jacket, a pack of Wrigley's chewing gum, a pack of Swisher Sweet cigars, some speakers, a receipt from traffic school, a black knit cap with the Metallica logo on it, two folding knives, a butterfly knife, and a box cutter.

"It was possible this was a dispute over drugs," the police wrote in their report. Prosecutors declined to file charges.

That seemed to be the first encounter between Momeni and law enforcement, but it was not the last. In 2011, he was stopped near the Oakland airport for speeding and then arrested when police discovered his license was on hold for a prior DUI. In Momeni's car, they found a knife. Nima pleaded no contest to one charge of speeding and one of carrying a switchblade. Two years later, he pleaded no contest to a charge of selling a switchblade, and that time he served ten days in jail. In the summer of 2022, police cited and released Momeni on allegations of battery after a woman alleged that he had grabbed her arm and pushed her. "She believes that he may be bipolar, because one minute he will be fine and the next he will go off for no reason," the police report read.

Although Momeni claimed to his neighbor Sam Singer, the PR consultant, that he had graduated from UC Berkeley, the school said it could find no record of him enrolling there. On his LinkedIn, Momeni also claimed to have attended Laney community college in Oakland and Vista College, a for-profit school in Texas that shut down during the pandemic.

Whatever the truth was, Momeni's job required no more formal education than Bob Lee's did. Nima was an IT consultant who worked at two small companies in Silicon Valley before founding his own firm.

After his arrest, one of his former coworkers told the press he was "completely taken aback." He and Nima had bonded over a shared interest in Zoroastrianism, the ancient Persian religion. Momeni wasn't a member of the faith, but he was fascinated by it. They lost touch after he changed jobs, but "at least in my interactions with him, I didn't see any signs of anger, any red flags, at that point," said the co-worker.

In 2010, Momeni filed the paperwork to open his own business, Expand IT Services LLC. According to his LinkedIn page, his clients were involved in health care, finance, technology, manufacturing, and the service sector. He wrote: "Our service/solutions portfolio includes: IT solution design and helpdesk support; networking, cybersecurity, VoIP, and monitoring; regulatory/compliance and security audits (ISO, PCI, HIPAA); hosting, virtualization/cloud services; and database, website, and application services (CRM, MRP, etc.)."

For a time, Momeni prospered. He was genuinely good at his job. Although people could sometimes find it difficult to understand him — his English was accented and his voice was gruff — he was good with technology. He knew how to make things work. But at some point, the business fell apart, and the state suspended its license. In 2021, Momeni revived his company, but by then, his friends said he was struggling with drugs, taking cocaine daily, and acting strangely.

Momeni was also a heavy smoker, a habit that annoyed his neighbors. "All the neighbors hated — HATED — this guy," wrote one on Nextdoor after the arrest. "He was rude, stunk up the hallways with his cigs (which was illegal), yelled all the time, completely inconsiderate, refused to pay rent for four [or] five months. Just an awful human being. But even though he was such a lowlife, we were shocked that he's accused of killing someone."

~

By 2023, things had changed for the Momenis. Nima's mother had moved to Mill Valley. His sister had gotten married. Now Khazar lived in the Millennium Tower, the high-end building near the Embarcadero, where she and her plastic surgeon husband, Dino, owned two units.

As it happened, the Millennium Tower was famous, but not for the right reasons. After it opened, the fifty-eight-story building, one of the tallest in San Francisco, began to sink, causing its floors to tilt. You could put a marble in one corner of the room and watch it roll to the other corner. Lawsuits followed, as did metaphors. As the *Chronicle*'s urban design critic John King noted, "In weird yet undeniable ways, [the] Millennium Tower has come to symbolize the hubris and fragility of today's San Francisco — and how buildings only capture the public's imagination when they tap a nerve that goes beyond aesthetics."

Khazar's husband Dino Elyassnia's family had fled Iran during the revolution, settling in the Bay Area. He studied at UC San Diego and earned his medical degree at USC. He followed two of his uncles into plastic surgery and built a thriving practice. In 2018, Elyassnia was featured in *Town & Country*, which touted him as "the Corrector of Billionaire Tech Necks." (There might have been a little hype there — Elyassnia's Instagram page features more nose jobs than anything else, and the identity of his billionaire patients was never revealed.)

On his Instagram, Elyassnia occasionally shared photos of himself and his wife. One of the photos was taken for a profile of the doctor in *Haute Living*, another luxury magazine. "She packs bags for the homeless," he said in that article, "and she's taken me shopping for gifts for underprivileged families. She has been my guiding light." In the photo, he wore a black suit and perched on the arm of a cream-colored couch with the couple's Yorkshire terrier Cookie in his arms. Khazar stood next to him in a low-cut scarlet dress, giving the camera a charged look.

"I'm grateful for my wife," Elyassnia wrote in the caption. "Spending three months isolated together, around the clock, gave me a whole new perspective on what an amazing human being she is. Not only is she better than me in every way, but she is truly gifted when it comes to understanding the human condition which translates into an unbelievable level of kindness and generosity to others. Ultimately I'm most thankful for having her as an inspiration in my life and a constant reminder of what matters most on this earth is the impact we have on others."

It so happened that the week I was looking at his Instagram, I also had an appointment with my dentist. His office is in an art deco skyscraper on the edge of Chinatown, a building filled with medical offices. I thought that I was taking a break from work as I chatted with the hygienist, but when I told her about the story I was working on, she was surprised. Not only did she know who Dr. Elyassnia was, but his plastic surgery practice was in the very same building. "We were shocked," she said, when she and her colleagues made the connection from Bob Lee's death to Elyassnia. "We see him at Christmas parties and in the elevator. He's always so friendly."

PART THREE

16

A Sudden Heat-of-Passion Quarrel

When Momeni's new lawyers rolled in from Florida, they weren't licensed yet to practice law in California. So as they got up to speed on the case, Saam Zangeneh and Bradford Cohen also had to get their own paperwork in order.

Although they weren't well known in the Bay Area, back in Florida the two men had high profiles. Zangeneh, whose Instagram bio read "101% Persian," had once represented a hit man who killed a criminal law professor in Florida State University during a child custody dispute. (*Dateline* made an episode about it.) By way of introduction, Zangeneh asked me to refer to him in this book as having "the physique of an Aryan god." (He seemed to be joking, but only slightly, although he later clarified that he meant Aryan as in Iranian, not Nazi.) Cohen had been a contestant on *The Apprentice* in 2009, and his clients included the rapper DMX, basketball player Dennis Rodman, wide receiver Plaxico Burress, and the rapper-turned-reality-TV-mainstay Vanilla Ice. The rapper Kodak Black has his name tattooed on the inside of his wrist. ("He's a good guy," said Cohen. "He's been over to the house for seder a few times.") Two other rappers have Cohen's name tattooed on them, too.

The two men had worked together before, representing rapper Pooh Shiesty on charges related to a 2020 shooting at a hotel in Miami. (He pleaded guilty to lesser charges.) Zangeneh reminded me a little of the actor Joe Pesci, tightly wound and motormouthed, which would make Cohen the Robert De Niro of the duo, a little more reserved and watchful. Zangeneh loved showing off his watches. Cohen told stories about drinking in Las Vegas with Prince Harry. They went bouldering at the gym on the weekends and wandered the city on rental bikes. The first time I saw them getting coffee at the Social Cafe, the coffee shop next door to the courthouse, they were literally throwing money around, tossing cash on the counter, and offering to buy coffee for everyone in the place. God help me, I genuinely liked them, although I shuddered to think what their hourly rate was.

Zangeneh and Cohen were there early on July 31, when sheriff's deputies took Momeni from his jail cell and into a courtroom in San Francisco's Hall of Justice. Backed up against the I-80 freeway, the hall is an imposing building, all granite and concrete. It has the institutional smell of a city hall or a library — old paperwork, creaky ventilation, and sweat. But if Momeni was sweating, he didn't want us to know. He strutted in with his chin up and his shoulders back. He swaggered as if he were Pooh Shiesty. His mother caught his eye and made a heart sign with her hands. Krista glared at him.

That day's hearing was to determine if Momeni would be held without bail pending his trial or if the court would free him until then. Although the proceedings were a mini trial, the standards, and stakes, were lower. The prosecution did not have to show enough to convict Momeni beyond a reasonable doubt to convince a judge to continue to hold him.

Assistant District Attorney Omid Talai, a trim, scholarly man who headed up the office's homicide unit, laid out the evidence against Momeni methodically. Here was security footage of Momeni and Lee together. There was a picture of a knife that police found at the scene. Here was a crime scene investigator's report that found Lee's DNA on the blade and Momeni's on the handle.

Zangeneh and Cohen tried to find holes, raising questions, for example, about why police did not take fingerprints from the knife. They also questioned why police had not interviewed a potential witness, a man named Napoleon who had been sleeping on the street behind some garbage cans.

Joining Cohen and Zangeneh were three other lawyers. Mike McMullen was Zangeneh's partner, more bookish than Zangeneh. Tony Brass was a longtime fixture of the San Francisco courts who had been a prosecutor before becoming a defense attorney, often for police officers. Zoe Aron, the fifth member of Momeni's legal team, had grown up in San Francisco before practicing in Los Angeles. When needed in court, Aron would pile her two dogs into her car, zip up I-5, and crash at her parents' house. During court appearances, Nima would politely pull out her chair for her to sit.

"I think that when you look at the totality of the circumstances, all of what was presented can only result in a sudden heat-of-passion quarrel," Zangeneh said, but while a jury might believe that, for now, the judge did not, ruling that Momeni would stay in jail through his trial.

"It's what we expected," Zangeneh said after the hearing.

Standing outside the courtroom wearing a black leather jacket and a long gold necklace, Krista talked to a group of reporters. "What are you feeling right now?" one of them asked her. "It would involve a lot of bleeping," she said. She laughed and then her face turned sad. "I'm extremely grateful to the team who tried to revive Bob. I think that was one of the most heartwarming yet heartbreaking things to hear."

"This idea that they were friends, that they were bro-ing out?"

asked another reporter, referring to something the defense attorneys had said inside.

"Interesting use of slang on that one," said Krista. "They were acquainted through Tina, but I don't think that they were friends. I had never heard him mention him. We were very close, we talked all the time, and I don't think I ever heard Bob mention the name — either of the names to be honest with you. No, I'm sorry, I don't think they were friends."

She had time for only a few more questions.

"Do you think Nima did it?"

"Yes. Yeah, he's admitted to it, saying it was self-defense. He stabbed him. The fact that he stabbed him multiple times — it is disgusting. If this was supposed to be self-defense, like they seem to claim — you know, Bob was a smaller guy. Nima is substantially larger than him. He could have shoved him, pushed him, punched him. That would have been sufficient. Bob was one of the most non-violent men that you probably would have ever met. Very respectful — more loving. If there was an argument, he would prefer to handle it with words and dignity rather than violence. I've never seen him be violent, in any way, shape, or form."

Krista had to go, but her words were clear: *It wasn't like Bob stabbed himself.*

The case moved slowly. Murder cases almost always do.

A few months later, we reassembled for another hearing. Zangeneh and Cohen stood outside the courtroom with Tayarani, whom they shielded from the press, waiting for Brass to join them. Cohen, who was bald, made a joke that Brass was late because he was fixing his shoulder-length hair.

"Can you tell us what the motions are?" I asked. Cohen demurred.

"Change of venue?" I guessed.

Cohen didn't say anything, but Zangeneh caught my gaze and raised his eyebrows. *Good guess.*

A short woman in a dark suit passed by. As she did, the news reporters suddenly rushed to follow her. She talked to them without breaking her stride.

"Who is that?" the attorneys asked me.

"Christine Pelosi," I said.

Blank looks.

Nancy's older daughter wasn't as well known as her sister, the filmmaker Alexandra Pelosi, but in San Francisco she had a modest profile for having sat in a number of unelected positions as a proxy for her mother — Electoral College member, Democratic Party delegate, and various charities. The Pelosis had been at the center of yet another one of San Francisco's high-profile crimes when an intruder broke into the home of the former Speaker of the House and attacked her husband with a hammer. It's a small city: The attacker was an activist who a decade earlier had protested a bill restricting public nudity that was written by the Castro supervisor, now a state senator, who was presently engaged with Christine in a behind-the-scenes competition for Nancy's seat, should she ever vacate it.

A guard led Momeni into court around 9:41 A.M. He was wearing an orange jumpsuit and had restraints on his arms and legs. He saw his mother as she made a heart sign with her hands. He nodded back to her.

Standing in front of Judge Eric Fleming, a friend of Brass who was supposed to go with him up to Tahoe soon, the attorneys agreed to begin the trial on March 15, 2024. "The Ides of March," said Zangeneh, who must have known how Julius Caesar died — stabbed with knives.

At this point, Zangeneh made two motions, one to get Momeni's BMW out of police impound (Nima needed to sell it to raise money to help pay for his defense) and another to change the venue.

Two days before the hearing, the *San Francisco Standard* had published a story that was ostensibly about how Momeni was preparing for trial while being held in jail. But what was really interesting were the four photos that it ran of Momeni posing inside his cell in his orange jumpsuit. That was unheard of — to photograph a defendant in an ongoing trial inside his cell. What could possibly prejudice a potential juror more than that?

According to the freelancer who took the photos, he had been there working on a different project, recognized Nima, and asked if he would like to be photographed. Nima said yes. Momeni smiled for the camera. He posed with his hands on his balding head. He did not express agony or remorse. He looked like he was preening. Next to him was a pile of books — a biography of Napoleon, a psychology textbook, and a book by the mythologist Joseph Campbell.

But his attorneys said there could be no meaningful consent for a prisoner inside the jail. "I've never in my twenty-seven years seen a photographer go into a jail before the trial. It's hugely prejudicial, and it's next-level stuff," Zangeneh said to the judge, his voice rising in anger that seemed only half theatrical.

The judge promised to consider it and added that the sheriff was looking into what had happened. (The editor of the *Standard* later sent out a statement that read: "A freelance photographer had permission to take photos inside the jail and Nima Momeni gave the photographer permission to have his photo taken. We contacted Momeni's legal team prior to publication and they did not raise objections or concerns about the publication of the images. The Standard believes the images were entirely newsworthy.")

Talking to us outside, Zangeneh stared hard at the reporter from the *Standard*, threatening a civil suit and suggesting criminal penalties. Zangeneh wondered aloud if the website's tech billionaire owner had conspiratorially ordered the story on behalf of Lee's family: "I'm not sure there's a nexus between Bob Lee's family, Big Tech, and the *San Francisco Standard*, if there's some sort of marriage that is going on here to be able to influence the jury," he said. "There may be. But I will tell you what, we are going to look into it."

After the lawyers stalked off, I hunted down a copy of their pretrial motion, hoping to read more about the photos. But in addition to the photos, the motion contained something that the lawyers had not mentioned in court — claims about why Paula Canny, Momeni's first attorney, had left the case.

According to the paperwork, Canny had discussed the case with the former mayor of San Francisco, Willie Brown — and after talking to him, her "perspective of the case shifted dramatically." The inference seemed to be that Brown had leaned on Canny to settle the case on manslaughter charges — against Momeni and his family's wishes. The motion went on to say that Canny had introduced the Momeni family to another lawyer, as a potential attorney for Khazar's husband. That attorney, who also met with Brown, urged the family to strike a plea deal.

The alleged interactions sounded nefarious, but it was hard to judge. Brown worked as an attorney before going into politics and is well known in San Francisco for offering his opinion on all and sundry in a variety of ways and settings, sometimes in a column he once had in the *Chronicle*, other times over long lunches at

John's Grill, a downtown restaurant. But Brown no longer held any office or much influence.

One thing seemed clear: There was no way the trial was going to start on the Ides of March.

When March 15 rolled around, the only hearing the judge was prepared to hold was on the change-of-venue motion.

As usual, an orange-clad Momeni entered in shackles. His mother rose and greeted him by making a heart sign again with her hands. She sat alone. Her son didn't have the same swagger as before. He looked haggard. I could have sworn that the bald spot on the back of his head had grown larger. Krista entered wearing large sunglasses, a leopard-print dress, a leather jacket, and heavy boots. The kids sat on one side of her, Bob's father and brother on the other.

The defense had commissioned a public opinion survey of potential jurors in the Bay Area, trying to bolster its contention that their client could not receive a fair trial here because too many people had already made up their minds about him. It would be like trying the murder of a player on the Lakers in Los Angeles, they said. Of the one hundred respondents, seventy-seven said they had seen information about Bob Lee in the media, thirteen that they had seen the photos of Momeni in his jail cell in the *Standard*, and ninety that Momeni was either certainly or probably guilty.

After the defense finished, the prosecution responded, criticizing the design of the survey. In particular, the survey had only included ten respondents who were Asian Americans. That was dramatically less than the proportion of San Franciscans who were Asian American or Pacific Islander — just short of 40 percent.

"I know how this is going to sound," said Fleming, "but you haven't practiced in this community. There are going to be a lot of potential jurors who are Asian American. Many of them get their information in different ways, like in the Cantonese newspapers." This sort of thing would happen often to Zangeneh and Brass throughout the proceedings. They would make mistakes that only someone who lived here would notice. Often they were subtle — like mangling the name of the Embarcadero, calling the Millennium Tower the Millenial Tower, and dropping the -s at the end of Caltrans, the state's transportation department — but they struck me as the kind of thing that a juror might notice.

Zangeneh and Cohen tried to push back, but the judge ruled that the trial would stay in San Francisco. In the back of the courtroom, reporters celebrated the fact that they would not have to relocate to somewhere like Sacramento or San Diego to cover the story.

After the ruling, the defense attorneys shrugged. They said they had never expected to win that motion.

17

The DNA Is Going to Be
a Problem for Us

A judge was assigned to the trial, and there was some back-and-forth about timing. March turned into April, and July turned to August. The summer passed slowly.

Every morning on my way to court, I walked down 6th Street, one of the most notorious stretches in the city, if not the entire Bay Area, when it came to urban dysfunction. Even before 9:00 A.M., dozens of people were already out, some of them using drugs and others talking to themselves. A few enterprising folks set up blankets and sold groceries on the corner, hawking cherry tomatoes, heads of cabbage, and cans of energy drinks to anyone who passed by. One morning, I watched a man steal an electric scooter parked on the sidewalk while onlookers cheered for him.

Arriving at the courthouse, I would often stop for a coffee at the Cuban place next door to the Hall of Justice and take in the scene. As the self-driving Waymos, the Cybertrucks, and the Rivian SUVs cruised slowly by, they passed an abandoned black limousine across the street, its hood popped open and its side covered in graffiti. A woman smoking a joint cackled as she saw a man fall off the gyroscopic hoverboard he was riding. Standing next to them, a man was inexplicably holding a fishing pole.

I read the news on my phone. Kamala Harris, once San Francisco's district attorney, was now the Democratic nominee for president. Donald Trump's running mate, J. D. Vance, had once worked here as a venture capitalist. David Sacks, the *All-In* podcast cohost, had pushed hard for Vance to be named to the ticket, and he'd been rewarded with a Tuesday-afternoon speaking slot at the Republican convention in Milwaukee. "In my hometown of San Francisco," he said, "Democrat rule has turned the streets of our beautiful city into a cesspool of open encampments and open drug use."

"This guy will be my friend for life," said Zangeneh, standing outside the courtroom and hugging Talai, who beamed back. They showed off photos of their children and talked about their summer vacations. The mood on August 23 was so jovial that you could almost forget what everyone was there for.

Every day that there were pretrial proceedings, Krista and her family and friends arrived wearing necklaces made to honor Bob with pendants on them that said LOVE AND EMPATHY. Krista often accessorized with easter eggs that referenced her former husband in some way, like the chunky boots she had worn to Burning Man. One day she wore a second necklace with the word DISCO on it. "This is in honor of disco nights," she explained in a way that didn't actually explain anything. Another day she wore fishnet stockings, setting off a round of gossip among the journalists and trial-watchers. Krista either didn't notice or didn't care. "Bob loved these," she told me.

Courtroom 28 was a cold place. The air conditioner didn't work correctly, blowing cold air through the vents even when the chamber was already frigid. The room was paneled in blond wood. There were no windows. The seats were uncomfortable.

Wearing a purple face mask, Judge Alexandra Robert Gordon, who had been assigned the case, entered from the back carrying a large Mason jar filled with water and slices of lemon. "I've discovered through the pandemic that when I wear a mask all day I get totally dehydrated," she said as she took her place.

"All right, let's do this," she said, taking a sip.

As the attorneys discussed the schedule, Momeni's mother entered carrying a large bag. Half a dozen of her friends sat around her as she distributed balloons, signs, candy, and a homemade cake. They were celebrating Nima's fortieth birthday.

Zangeneh asked about various formalities. Would it be okay if he brought new clothes to the jail for Nima to wear? Of course, said the judge.

What about a haircut?

"I'd be shocked if they let you bring in a barber with sharp scissors," said Gordon, laughing.

"I like to push the envelope, so to speak," said Zangeneh, laughing as well. "Or the clippers in this situation."

As the guard led Momeni in, Tayarani stood and unfurled her sign. HAPPY BIRTHDAY MY SUN, it read. She had drawn a sun and a heart on it. Nima saw it and smiled, almost embarrassed, as he waved to her and sat down.

For the next hour, the prosecution and the defense wrangled over the witnesses they planned to call. The two sides agreed to finalize their witness lists by the end of the day. There would be a brief hearing for everyone to check in with one another on September 6 — the judge would have to use Zoom, since she would be on the East Coast, dropping one of her kids off at college — and then the proceedings would pick up again on September 16.

As the hearing wrapped up, Zangeneh rose with one more request. "His family has baked him a cake," he said, gesturing toward Nima's mother. Would it be possible for his client to have a slice? His mother rose expectantly and came toward her son, separated from him by a low wooden railing.

"If it were up to me, I would say yes," said Gordon. "But the sheriff's office has rules."

Tayarani looked crestfallen.

"The value of the gift doesn't reside in the object," Gordon said philosophically, addressing Nima. "There are people who love you." With that, the guards led Momeni out again. In the hall outside, Tayarani pressed slices of the cake into the hands of reporters. I took a piece. Why not? It was a small good thing. As I left, she pressed another slice into my hands. I walked out with Brass, chatting with him about the case. There was a lot in the defense's favor, he said, "but the DNA is going to be a problem for us," he added, almost as an afterthought.

Through the early fall, the two sides traded pretrial motions. Some were uncontroversial — they agreed that all the surveillance video collected by the police would be given to the jury to watch if they wanted.

But some of those motions required more debate.

For instance, the defense wanted to be able to use Lee's nickname — Crazy Bob — as a reason to show that Momeni might have been afraid of him. But the prosecution objected. Talai pointed out that in almost all circumstances, nicknames were not used in criminal proceedings. Judge Gordon said that Crazy Bob couldn't be mentioned in opening remarks, but that Momeni was free to talk about it if he wanted to.

On September 26, we were scheduled to start a hearing on qualifying one of the defense's expert witnesses a little later in the morning, but I didn't have anything else to do, so after I bought my coffee from the Cuban place, I settled into the back of the courtroom and watched Judge Gordon schedule a different trial with Dane Reinstedt, the other prosecutor on Momeni's case. There was a lull when they finished. Cohen and Aron were at the copy shop, running off three hundred copies of their jury questionnaire, while Brass and McMullen sat bored at the defense table. Copy duty seemed the more interesting job today. A little later, Zangeneh walked in.

He had just sat down next to them when suddenly he jumped up and strode quickly out of the courtroom. As he passed me, I could see he was on his phone, and I could hear him say, "Six bodies!" with a look of intensity on his face.

The other members of the team shrugged at each other. Saam always had something going on.

A few minutes later, he returned. "Do either of you want to go to the Caribbean with me for the weekend?" he asked his colleagues. They looked confused. "I'm taking the private jet," he said. "I need to be there for thirty-six or forty-eight hours. If you want to come, there's twelve seats on the plane."

They looked even more confused. The prosecutors and the judge were paying attention now.

"I'll tell you what's happening," said Zangeneh. One of his clients was being held in MDC Guaynabo, a federal prison in Puerto Rico. There had been a turf war between rival drug dealers, and another organization had shot his client eleven times, including twice in the head. "His brain was on the floor. Eight percent of it is missing," Zangeneh said. "But he lived, and after he got out of the hospital — I'm not saying this is what he did, this is what they say he did — he killed the family members of the four people who shot him. The allegation is that he killed sixteen people associated with the hit. Family members first." Prosecutors in Puerto Rico had just released a new indictment that claimed he

Bob Lee in 2021 when he became Chief Product Officer of MobileCoin. *MobileCoin*

Khazar Momeni *Instagram*

Nima Momeni's profile picture on LinkedIn *LinkedIn*

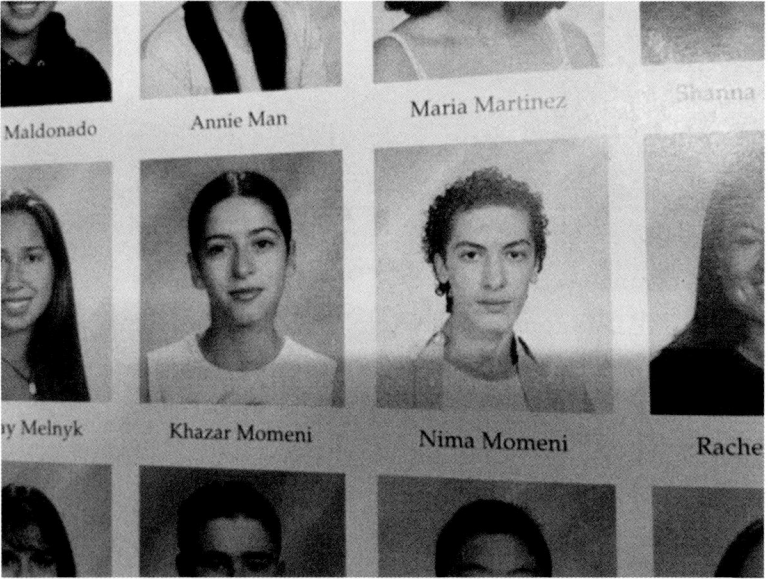

Khazar and Nima Momeni in their high school yearbook.

Bob Lee's headshot on Twitter (now X). *Twitter*

Android sculptures at the Googleplex.

The Millennium Tower.
Wikimedia Commons

The San Francisco-Oakland Bay Bridge seen at night. *Wikimedia Commons*

The Portside Building, in front of which Bob Lee was found unconscious.

The view from Main Street where the stabbing took place. To the left of the photograph is the parking lot where police found the knife.

Khazar Momeni testifying during her brother's trial. *Vicki Behringer*

Momeni and his attorney, Saam Zangeneh, reenacting Momeni's account of Lee's death — that Bob attacked him. *Vicki Behringer*

The prosecution playing surveillance video it said was of Momeni reenacting the stabbing to a private investigator. *Vicki Behringer*

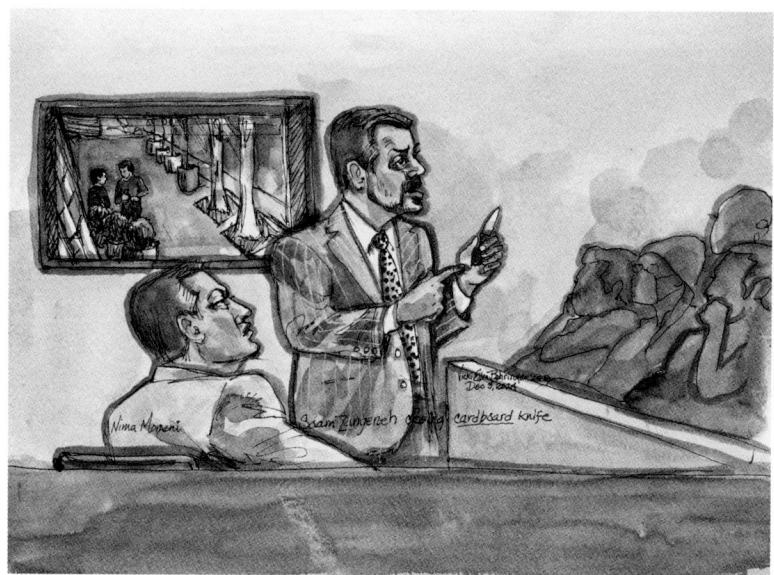

"It's the knife!" said Zangeneh in his closing argument, showing the jury a video he said put the weapon in Lee's hands just hours before his death. *Vicki Behringer*

Momeni reacting to the jury's verdict — guilty of murder in the second degree.
Vicki Behringer

The San Francisco skyline at night. *Pexels*

had ordered another six killings while in custody, said Zangeneh with a weary sigh.

"So I've got to deal with that. Anyway, do you want to fly with me?"

The other lawyers declined. Zangeneh didn't seem put off. Frankly, it didn't seem like he wanted to go, either.

"You know my exit strategy, right?" he said. "In three years, I'm not going to be a lawyer. I'm going to be the ice cream guy. I've got an ice cream place and a gelato place in Puerto Rico, and I'm opening an ice cream place in St. Thomas."

The judge finally interrupted him. As much as she wanted to hear more about his ice cream plans — we all did — it was time to start the hearing.

With his serious demeanor and tight haircut, Steven Pomatto looked like the cop he had been for twenty-three years before his recent retirement. Explaining his background under questioning from Brass, he said that before joining the SFPD, he worked on a bomb squad in the United States Navy. As a police officer, he had started out on patrol before being promoted through the ranks. He had reviewed reports on the use of force, worked in internal affairs, and trained recruits at the police academy in the use of force.

"What about hand-to-hand combat?" asked Brass.

"I was the supervisor of the defense tactics division at the police academy," explained Pomatto. "That includes defending against knife attacks."

The defense wanted the judge to allow Pomatto to testify as an expert in hand-to-hand combat, to tell the jury what he thought could have happened during the fatal encounter between Momeni and Lee. To prepare, they had given him a dossier of material on the case, including the grainy video of the confrontation. Pomatto said he had reviewed what he had been given and, from that, "came up with a reasonable explanation of the incident." And his explanation was very different from the one that his former colleagues in the SFPD had advanced. Nima had not been holding the knife. No, not at all. According to Pomatto, Bob Lee was holding the blade and had attacked Nima, not the other way around. So how did Lee end up stabbed to death? Momeni had redirected the knife back at him in self-defense.

A few months prior, Krista had suggested, though not in so many words, *It's not like Bob had stabbed himself.* And now here was the defense, saying just that.

"Is it your opinion that it is reasonable — beyond reasonable — that Mr. Lee drew the knife and then Mr. Momeni turned it on him?" asked Brass.

"Yes," said Pomatto.

"Explain."

"Given the way the knife projected, the direction of the wounds, the position of the people, and the shortness of the incident, there's a high probability in my opinion the *deceased* had the weapon in his hand," said Pomatto. "If the defendant had the weapon in *his* hand, the physical evidence would be different."

According to Pomatto, when Lee drew the knife from his pocket, Momeni, having been trained in self-defense, would have known not to grab at the blade itself but rather to immobilize the arm that held the weapon by grabbing it at a joint — like the wrist or the elbow — and pinning the arm to something. In this case, that was Lee's body. When the knife was pinned to his hip, "it would be highly reasonable that would be where the first stabbing would occur," said Pomatto. After that, Lee had then gotten his arm free — it would have been an easy pin to break — and then slashed at

Momeni twice. Each time, Momeni would have grabbed Lee's arm and redirected the knife back at Lee. That would account for the two long horizontal slashes across Lee's chest.

"Is that something that you see in the video?" asked Judge Gordon, taking over the questioning from Brass. "Or is something you think is a reasonable scenario?"

"The video doesn't dictate it," said Pomatto. "What I am getting from that is that they were in close proximity to each other. I am using the coroner's report for the location and direction of the wounds."

"Do you see Mr. Momeni using self-defense tactics in the video?" she asked.

"No," said Pomatto. "I'm basing that on my training and experience with weaponless defense."

Talai took off his glasses, put his head in hands, rubbed his brows, and then leaned over and whispered something to Reinstedt. They both smiled ruefully.

Pomatto was now holding a pen in his hand, demonstrating with it what he thought could have occurred. "If you are holding a knife like this," he said, holding it up like he was the slasher in *Psycho*, "you would get vertical wounds." He changed his grip and moved his arm to his waist. "And if you are holding it like this, you would be poking someone and would get erratic wounds. But in this instance, you have wounds that are consistent with the decedent holding the knife and moving it like this." Extending his arm, Pomatto slashed the knife horizontally through the air, and brought it back to his own chest.

Judge Gordon interrupted him, asked him to stand up, and to demonstrate with her. He stood in for Lee as she stood in for Momeni, and he walked her through the same three motions again. They grappled together for several minutes.

"I've never had quite such a graphic display," said the judge, a little out of breath, after Pomatto sat down.

A few minutes after Talai began his cross-examination, Cohen and Aron entered the courtroom, each carrying heavy cardboard boxes with copies of their jury questionnaires. Momeni pulled Aron's chair out for her, as he always did, and she sat down. She produced a legal pad with pink paper and began taking notes while sipping water from a large pink water bottle.

"I was still at the police academy when this happened," Pomatto was telling Talai. "But I didn't know anything about this case." After the defense hired him, he talked about it with another defensive tactics instructor whom he knew. With the aid of a rubber knife, the two of them had worked out what they thought could have happened, within a reasonable degree of certainty, said Pomatto.

"What does *within a reasonable degree of certainty* mean?" asked Talai.

"It's what a reasonable person would determine."

"Is it the same as possible?"

"More than possible. It's a higher standard, in my opinion," said Pomatto.

Talai asked questions for a while, and then came to his point — that Pomatto seemed to be basing his opinion on a hypothetical given to him by the defense, asking him to say if it was possible or not. That Pomatto had not independently come up with a theory.

"Let's assume you never spoke to the defense, but you got all this information. Would it be your opinion that this is the most likely scenario?" said Talai, over Brass's objection.

"With the brief and the physical evidence, this is the most probable," said Pomatto.

"What about without the brief?" asked the judge.

"Without the brief, my opinion could change a little bit," said

Pomatto, saying it might change the sequence of the wounds but not his opinion on how they were caused. Appearing skeptical, Talai thanked Pomatto and he was excused.

With that Pomatto left the room. Judge Gordon asked Talai what he thought.

"I'm concerned for the years he was a peace officer, frankly," he said. "I don't see how this witness should be allowed to testify. Many of his answers made no sense or were non-responsive. Imagine a scenario where a DA would come in and say I want my homicide inspector to say, 'I see something in this video that none of us can see, but that I know from my training that this is what happened.' He literally tells us the exact sequence as if it was a Jason Bourne or *Mission Impossible* movie."

For now, Judge Gordon would leave it there. She said she would rule on whether Pomatto could testify only after Momeni took the stand. Brass and Talai thanked her, by which time Zangeneh was already out the door.

The final major pretrial motion seemed like an exam question from law school, but it was not merely an academic exercise.

Before Momeni's arrest, the police had taken a surveillance video of him standing in the parking lot of Canny's office, talking to a private investigator who worked with her. Neither man knew he was being recorded. As they smoked, they were talking, and at one point, Nima swung his arm three times horizontally through the air and then made a motion as if he were throwing a free throw in basketball.

In the eyes of the prosecution, it looked as if Momeni had been caught on camera reenacting what he had done. But the defense argued that a jury should never be allowed to see the video, asserting attorney-client privilege over it.

"It's like a blue book exam," said Brass. There were many legal questions to work through. Did the privilege apply to people working for attorneys who were not themselves lawyers? Did it apply even though they were standing in a place that was publicly visible? Was the parking lot a public place, or did the fact that it had a PRIVATE PARKING sign posted on it mean that they would have reasonably expected they were speaking in private? Did the law that said attorney-client privilege did not apply to conversations that could be overheard apply here? Did it matter that there was no sound, only video, in the recording?

Although the judge did not allow us to observe the hearing, we could read the motions that were filed.

The prosecution argued that "the video of the Defendant making gestures that correspond to the wounds suffered by Mr. Lee is highly relevant both in identifying the Defendant as Mr. Lee's assailant and as evidence of the specific actions of the Defendant." At the time of the parking lot conversation, "the specific details of Mr. Lee's injuries were not yet publicized," which meant that it was highly unlikely that Nima would have known about them "unless he were the perpetrator of the assault." The video did not show Nima acting in self-defense, any struggle over the knife, or any expression of fear on Momeni's part.

But as important as the recording might have been if it were deemed admissible evidence, the defense was asserting that it was covered by attorney-client privilege, which extended to the private investigator since he was working for Momeni's lawyer and discussing the case with him.

Not so fast, responded the prosecution, which said that the California Supreme Court had held in a 2019 decision that "statements observable by third parties are not confidential communications that qualify for lawyer-client privilege." The gestures that

Momeni was making in the parking lot were plainly visible, which meant that they were not confidential. But, the defense argued in turn, "at the time of the video, Mr. Momeni was under the reasonable expectation that he was not being surveilled or followed [...] His actions were clearly intended to be confidential."

They were thorny questions, and ones that might decide Momeni's fate. When the hearing concluded, the attorneys were silent as they exited. They would not tell us what the judge had ruled. We would have to wait for the trial to find out.

18

I Can't Talk About That

It was now October, and opening arguments were coming soon.

Before that, Judge Gordon ruled on yet another batch of motions, including how many of the texts sent between Nima and Khazar would be included at trial. Printed out, the texts ran to 376 pages. The judge asked the two sides to work together to come up with a manageable amount. They agreed.

"Do we want to address the defense filing from this morning?" asked Reinstedt, bringing up a new topic: The defense had asked for Krista to be barred from attending the trial.

"Your Honor," said Reinstedt, "it's a big ask to have her excluded from the entire trial. The court has discretion over which witnesses can be excluded, but victims also have the right to observe proceedings. It's important for her to be present in the trial regarding the father of her children."

The judge turned her gaze to the defense team. Zangeneh rose, evidently frustrated. "What's going on is Miss Lee is getting information from the SFPD and attempting to intimidate other people and to act as an un-deputized police officer," he said.

According to the defense, in September, when the prosecution added Khazar to its witness list, the district attorney's office was trying to serve her with paperwork summoning her to court. Initially, the office could not find her. Krista had found out, and had been texting mutual friends, trying to track her down. Around the same time, Sergeant Brent Dittmer, the lead inves-

tigator on the case, had finally secured an interview with Jeremy
Boivin, the friend of Bob's at whose apartment he had been in the
hours leading up to his death. Boivin told Dittmer that Krista had
told him to talk to the police.

"It's witness tampering, witness intimidation," said Zangeneh.
"If she is sitting here, she can see how the case is going, and
witnesses can see her. She has shown an affinity for getting
involved in a way she should not."

Outside the courtroom, Cohen handed out copies of the
motion. I read it over lunch. It was fascinating, because not only
did it talk about Krista's texts, but it also provided the actual
transcript of Boivin's phone call with Dittmer. Boivin had so far
declined to talk with me. In fact, other than talking to a writer
for *Rolling Stone*, he hadn't talked to any other media as far as I
knew. I had briefly spoken to Boivin when he was in court, asking
him to talk. His lawyer took down my number and never called.
My follow-up emails went unanswered. Boivin evidently did not
want to talk — when one of the TV reporters recognized him and
tried to get him to speak, he ran away through the wrong door,
setting off the court's fire alarm.

So barring some stroke of luck, this transcript would be the
closest I would ever come to talking to one of the most important witnesses in the case. It also raised a question that the trial
never really answered. Why had Jeremy not been the one who
had gotten stabbed?

"Well," said Boivin at the onset, "Krista told me to talk to you I
guess."

"I appreciate you doing this voluntary call with me," said Dittmer. "You're in control, okay? If there's something that you don't
want to answer, just say 'I don't want to answer that.' All right?"

"Okay," said Boivin.

Dittmer told him he wasn't interested in talking about Boivin's current legal troubles — he was on trial on drug charges — he just wanted to talk about Lee and Momeni. Boivin said he understood.

"How long have you known Bob Lee and his family?" asked Dittmer.

"I think we met in 2019," said Boivin. "We met after a club one night. He came over."

"What was your relationship with Bob?"

"Well, we were just good friends. We went to this one dealer together twice." (The word *dealer* was in brackets in the transcript and had two question marks after it. It's possible Boivin said something else.) "He had been over for Thanksgiving dinner, holidays, because I couldn't go home to see my family for whatever reason," said Boivin.

Some of his previous legal issues were relatively minor: In 2014, a Bay Area couple who had rented a bedroom from Boivin sued him in small claims court for $1,930. "Through alcohol abuse and domestic violence, it was made unlivable," they wrote. The court dismissed that case. Two years later, Boivin faced two new civil claims. One was for $2,827 from a subtenant. The other was brought by Boivin's landlord who said he owed $7,958 in unpaid rent, but Boivin claimed the landlord was retaliating against him for requesting repairs to his apartment. The court found against Boivin in both cases.

But some of his legal troubles were more severe: As Nima's trial was ongoing, Boivin was facing his own charges of drug possession. And in 2020, Boivin was arrested for allegedly raping an unconscious woman — his housekeeper. He was charged with seven counts of sexual assault, along with charges relating to drug possession. (In the *Rolling Stone* article, Boivin's attorney denied a claim that Bob Lee had paid Boivin's bail in that case. His lawyer also told the magazine that he "has not and does not presently sell any drugs to anyone.") The charges were dismissed, and Krista told me, "We later found out that some other drug dealer blackmailed him. Set him up, more or less. It was that guy's girlfriend who said, 'Oh yeah, she was raped and sodomized.'" Krista added that Boivin never took drugs himself.

As part of their investigation in that case, San Francisco police arrived at Boivin's apartment, where they saw Boivin wearing a backpack and placing two duffel bags into his car. They arrested him, finding a large amount of cash in his pockets. Inside the duffel bags they found three empty jugs marked GBL, a drug similar to GHB; as well as marijuana, pills, gummies, MDMA, baggies, two radio jammers, a two-ounce gold bar, a five-ounce silver bar, and a one-kilogram silver bar. Inside the backpack, Boivin had $31,704.08 in cash. Inside the apartment, which had security cameras mounted on the outside that fed video to a wide-screen television, police found more drugs "than could be consumed by any one person within the span of several months," according to court documents. Boivin's apartment had jugs of GBL and bottles of GHB, canisters of nitrous oxide, Modafinil, LSD, "Femalegra" pills, LSD tabs, methamphetamine, Xanax, MDMA, ketamine, cocaine, DMT, Sidalist, Kamagra, quetiapine fumarate, sertraline, tadalafil, and "a number of white and blue pills, orange pills, and red and blue pills," according to court documents. They also discovered accounting records that could only be read under black light, and fake identification documents.

Boivin's legal troubles continued. In 2023, he was arrested again for drug possession, and his landlord sued him for more than $92,000 in unpaid rent. On November 7, Boivin and the landlord settled, with Boivin agreeing to move out and to pay $50,000 and the landlord forgiving the remainder of the debt.

"Did you ever provide drugs to Bob?" Dittmer asked.

"I can't talk about that," said Boivin.

"Did you ever see Bob take drugs?"

"I can't talk about that."

"Did you ever see Bob when he was under the influence of drugs?"

"I can't talk about that."

"Did he have a temper or anything? Did you ever see him get into arguments with people? Fights? Anything like that?"

"Not even a little bit," said Boivin. "I'd trust him with anyone, anything in my life. I'd leave my girlfriend with him. I'd leave my cat with him. He's 100 percent a solid dude. He's guaranteed. He'd take care of whatever you needed."

Dittmer asked if Bob ever carried weapons. Boivin said no. He asked if he knew how Bob met Khazar. The Battery Club, Boivin replied. "They were friends," he went on. "Acquaintances, I'd say, more or less. Out and about in The Battery. I'd known Bob for years, but I'd never heard of Khazar before that day." He had never heard of Nima, either.

Boivin explained that everyone had ended up at his apartment because he and Bob had been at Khazar's the night before, after which Bob left to go to work while Jeremy took Khazar to the beach. After Bob was finished with the interview, he came to Jeremy's apartment.

"What's your relationship with Khazar now?" asked Dittmer. Boivin sputtered.

"Uhm . . . we are . . . uh, uhm . . . I don't know if I should talk about that. I mean . . ."

"Okay . . ."

". . . we're not, we, we see each other on occasion."

"Are you friends? Or is it a romantic or sexual whatever? Describe it however you want."

"Ehm, so . . . I don't think I should speak about that. Yeah, I don't think it's really too relevant to the current issue," said Boivin.

"When did you last see her?" asked Dittmer.

"Her birthday, three days ago," said Boivin.

Boivin grew similarly evasive when Dittmer asked him if they were doing drugs while at Boivin's apartment, but what he did say was that he ordered pizza around 5:30 or 6:00 P.M., around the time that Bob left and a friend of Khazar's arrived.

"We were just chillin', hangin' out. We were gonna go swimming down at the pool," said Boivin. "That, that, that eventually did not occur."

"It's September of '24, right?" said Dittmer. "This is a long time after this happened. We've never talked about it, but Khazar and her friend, did they take any drugs before this pool thing that was going to happen?"

Boivin replied that he couldn't talk about it. "But one thing I have to say is," he added, "if I was a guy that was doing anything rude to anyone, why is it, why do you think Khazar would have me over the same night later, or then spend the next six days with her after? Okay? There's nothing. I didn't do anything wrong to either of those girls. I was cordial, I was trying to be hospitable, of course."

Getting emotional, Boivin continued: "It's getting blown out of proportion. Their lawyers are feeding — making this story that is absolutely ridiculous. They're all playing into it. Or they decided to make a story that everyone needs to think. Outrageous. Really, really. I feel really upset about it. It's taken a toll on my life."

He said Khazar had gotten sick and called her brother to come pick her up. When Nima arrived, along with Khazar's husband, it was the first time Boivin had met either of them. To him, Nima seemed like a bully. He had a "tough guy sort of demeanor." He was angry, Jeremy suggested, because Khazar's friend and Nima had slept together the night before. (I couldn't verify or disprove that the woman was the dark-haired woman heard calling Nima's name in the hallway of the Besler Building.)

Jeremy said the two women left so quickly that Khazar ended up with his glasses and he with her jacket. So, he said, he went to Millennium Tower to exchange the items. When he was there, Nima grilled him.

"What did he question you about?" asked Dittmer.

"Just, like, what had gone down," said Boivin. "Why, why, you know, why, and, it had to have gone down the way it did go down, and, just, like, they were grilling me about this, that, and the other thing.

"Khazar was cool," a nervous Boivin continued. "She was like, 'No, you didn't do anything. We're fine. She's like, 'Nima, leave him alone.' Blah, blah, blah. This, that, and the other thing.

"I'm not going to lie to you, it wasn't a friendly conversation," he said.

"Did he threaten to harm you?"

"There's been some insinuations of harm coming my way, or getting the cops called on me. I can't really recall any exact details to be honest with you."

Boivin said that he left, but then returned to Khazar's place early on the morning of April 4, just after Nima and Bob left, although Boivin didn't know that at the time. Boivin said that he stayed with Khazar in the Millennium Tower for the next four days, and in that time they never talked about Lee's death.

"Have you talked about the case?" asked Dittmer.

"Uh, she doesn't really want to talk about it. We're so wrapped up in our separate ways, with our own lawyers and ramifications, that we don't really talk about it now."

Dittmer asked if Nima seemed like he was under the influence of something. Boivin evaded. "Uh, he seemed like, uh, on the same wavelength as about everyone else that night," he said.

"Do you think Bob would have been upset at Nima for any reason?"

"Absolutely not. This narrative that they are playing is absolutely ridiculous. Absolutely not. A hundred percent. A hundred percent not. On my name."

"There's been public speculation that Bob and Khazar were involved in some way."

"One hundred percent not. Never once, never once have they been involved."

Here, at the end of the interview, Dittmer asked the question that the defense had made so much out of: "Regarding speaking with me, who have you spoken to about us talking?" he said.

"Um, my lawyer and Krista. Well, Krista told me to talk to you, I guess," said Boivin.

"Have you spoken to anybody from Nima's legal counsel?" Dittmer asked.

"No. I was just going to, but I didn't," said Boivin.

"It's your decision. Do you know if Khazar's been in touch with Nima's lawyers?"

"I don't think they are talking to each other right now, to be honest with you."

"Sitting where we are right now, do you have anything to add?" said Dittmer.

"I really don't want to go to court. I don't want to be subpoenaed. I really don't want to go to court about this," said Boivin.

Boivin never appeared at trial, nor did he ever agree to talk to me.

As questioning for jury selection started, it was pretty obvious that some would be dismissed.

When asked to introduce themselves with an interesting fact from their lives, one of them cheerfully admitted that in 1973 they had driven a stolen car across the country.

"You knew it was stolen?" said the judge.

"I was hitchhiking. It was a convertible," he said, as if that explained it. "Sorry."

Other potential jurors indicated that they had read about the case in the news, or had known Bob, or would have a hard time believing the police, given the deaths of people like George Floyd and Alex Nieto. One woman said that as a Buddhist, she was opposed to sitting in judgment of anyone. "Karma is not for me to decide," she said. Another woman was an attorney whose brother-in-law was currently incarcerated after having been convicted of killing his wife with a knife. There were a handful of people who seemed mentally unwell or could at least fake it. An anticipated three-month jury duty commitment was a big ask, and as it looked more and more likely that they might have to serve, a number of potential jurors suddenly discovered financial or family conflicts.

Finally, a jury was assembled: twelve men and women and five alternates. It seemed like a cross section of San Francisco — white, Black, Asian American, and Latino. Some were obviously well off, like one Harvard-educated man who worked at a start-up. Others seemed middle-class. One juror told the judge she was worried about being identified in the press. Another was a young man with dark hair who struggled to keep an odd smile off his face during much of the proceedings. One was an older white man who dressed every day in black jeans, a black jacket, a black baseball cap, and a rotation of black T-shirts, including one that had a picture of the floor of the House of Representatives on it with the caption HYPOCRITES written in capital letters.

19

You Are Sitting in Court
with a Murderer

It was eight thirty on the foggy morning of October 14, 2024 — Indigenous Peoples' Day — when Tony Brass parked in the lot next to the Hall of Justice and entered. In the hallway outside, Nima's mother was waiting for the bailiff to open the courtroom. Department 28 was at the end of a long corridor on the second floor. She sat on a hard wooden bench as a reporter asked her to clarify something she had heard.

"No, we're not Zoroastrian," said Tayarani. "But Nima is very interested in it. Right thought, right speech, right heart." The reporter asked about what she herself believed in. "I believe in God," said Tayarani. Brass walked up and hugged her, and then the doors opened.

One by one, the other attorneys entered the room. Judge Gordon took up her position behind the bench.

Before the bailiff brought in the jury, she explained, there were some final pretrial motions for her to rule on. One of them was the defense's motion to exclude Krista from the courtroom.

"I find there has been no meaningful showing that Miss Lee's presence will provide a substantial risk," said the judge, who added, "I will admonish Miss Lee that as a witness she cannot talk to other witnesses. I cannot keep her from speaking to the press, but anything she says will be fodder. One hopes she exercises care in speaking to the press."

And so, after that ruling, Krista and the family entered. Her face, framed by her blond hair, looked drawn and weary. She had dark bags under her eyes, a colorful scarf around her neck, and dark sunglasses perched on top of her head. With her were the children; Bob's brother, Oliver; his father, Rick; and Krista's partner. ADA Talai hugged them each and spoke to Rick as they sat down.

"Finally," said the judge, "I have been given requests to permit taping, video audio recording, and photos. I have denied those requests, but I have been asked to reconsider." She said that she had, but that her conclusion was the same. Members of the press would be allowed to take notes on our laptops, but not to record the trial. Cell phones would have to stay in our pockets for the duration, too.

It was now 10:00 A.M.

"I think we are ready to start this trial day," said Gordon. She stood, and the jury entered.

"In the case of *The People of the State of California versus Nima Momeni*, said defendant is accused as follows," said the judge reading from a piece of paper. "Count one, said defendant did commit a crime of murder, did murder a human being, Robert Lee. It is further alleged that the defendant did use a deadly weapon, to wit, a knife."

She finished and looked up. "Mr. Talai," she said. "Are you ready?"

"Stabbed through his heart and left to die," Talai said slowly, emphasizing each word.

"Our victim was stabbed repeatedly, once in his chest, once in his hip, and once literally puncturing his heart. Robert Lee, known as Bob, just a forty-three-year-old man, was driven to a dark secluded area after 2:00 A.M. and was stabbed. He immediately began bleeding profusely and taking his last breaths."

Momeni sat impassively, his mother behind him, separated from her son by a low wooden rail. Talai pointed to Nima.

"Ladies and gentlemen, you are sitting in court with a murderer," he said. "Sitting behind me is a coward who stabbed a man three times. Sitting in court with you is a man who drove Bob under the Bay Bridge after 2:00 A.M. and stabbed him three times, once puncturing his heart."

Krista sobbed and pulled her children close.

"So what happened, exactly?" said Talai. According to him, Bob had flown back to San Francisco from Miami, spending the weekend with his friends and family. It was a blur of activity for an outgoing man — a school play, dinners out, parties, and catching up with old friends. One of them was a tech entrepreneur named Borzu Mohazzabi, who went by Bo. He met up with Bob around 4:15 P.M. on April 3 at the apartment of Jeremy Boivin. Bob was finishing up some work, and Bo hung out for a while with Jeremy and a woman named Khazar Momeni. Bo and Khazar knew each other. Talai wouldn't call it dated, but four or five years ago, "they had hung out." Khazar wasn't happy to see Bo again and asked Jeremy to tell the men to leave. He did.

As Bob and Bo entered the elevator at 5:12 P.M., security cameras showed them passing a woman coming up to Boivin's apartment, a friend named Aranza Villegas. They didn't know her, and they passed without interacting with her.

"It was a normal, uneventful Monday," said Talai. They went to the bar on the ground floor of the One Hotel, where Bob had been staying, to have a drink. It wasn't the first substance they had used that day — at Boivin's there had been a bowl of cocaine and a tank of nitrous oxide. But from the security cameras in the bar, it appeared that Bob and Bo were not very intoxicated. After having a drink, they went to Lee's hotel room, where Bo hoped to show Bob an idea for an app he was working on.

Throughout the afternoon and evening, Bob was placing and receiving many calls and texts. Bo thought that was normal — his friend was always doing that. But around 9:00 P.M., he noticed Bob having a phone call that struck Bo as strange.

Bob put it on speakerphone. There was a man on the other side of the line asking questions. "What happened at Jeremy Boivin's apartment?" he said. "What was happening with my sister? Did anything inappropriate happen? What about the girls getting naked?"

Bob explained that the man was Nima Momeni, Khazar's brother, and that he was trying to calm him down. Nima seemed to think that something bad had happened to his sister. If anything did, Bob and Bo weren't there when it occurred. But the questions continued: "Were you there with some other guy? Who was that? What were you doing over there? Who was your friend? What was his name?"

"Get off the phone with this fucking guy," said Mohazzabi. "He's crazy."

Bob did, and he and Bo continued their night. At 10:22 P.M., security cameras recorded them walking in the front door of The Battery, the members-only club less than a mile away from Bob's hotel. An hour later, they returned to Bo's apartment, where Bob said hello to Bo's fiancée, who was preparing to go to bed. Bo decided to call it a night, too, and around 12:30 A.M., Bob left. The two friends agreed to meet at SFO airport the next morning to fly to Miami.

"And when Bob left," said Talai, "he was Bob. Mellow. Happy. That was the last time Bo saw Bob."

Bo thought that Bob was going back to his hotel to sleep. But that's not what happened. Instead, Bob traveled to the Millennium Tower, where Khazar lived, arriving there at 12:40 A.M. on April 3. He went inside and spent about eighty minutes upstairs with her and her brother. At 1:58 A.M., security cameras in the elevator showed Bob and Nima leaving together.

From the Millennium Tower, Nima drove Bob to a spot on Main Street under the Bay Bridge. They sat in the car for about twelve minutes and then exited. A security camera perched high on an apartment building looking down on the street showed the two men standing on the sidewalk together for about five minutes. The video was grainy, but it was possible to know who was who from the color of the clothes they were wearing — Nima in white and Bob in black.

"Then, all of a sudden," said Talai, "you see the defendant immediately and quickly advance toward Bob."

That was the moment at the center of the case, and although neither side would say it to the jury, you couldn't see in the video what happened. Was Nima holding the knife? Was Bob? All you could tell was that the two figures suddenly came together and then broke apart. It was a gap in clarity that both sides were going to try to fill, the one to convict Momeni and the other to show him not guilty of murder.

Talai gave his account of what happened: Nima stabbed Bob and then, as Bob was dying, threw away the knife and "popped into his nice white BMW and drove like a maniac back to the East Bay," said Talai.

"And that, ladies and gentlemen, is our case."

He paused. But, he continued, there was more. Nima smirked as the prosecutor went on.

"We will give you evidence straight from the defendant that gives us not only the obvious motive, and his lies about what happened, but will give you a glimpse into this individual," Talai said. There would be text messages. There would be witnesses. And, he said, revealing how the judge had ruled on the surveillance video taken in Nima's previous attorney's parking lot, there would be a video that showed the defendant reenacting the crime. "No defensive tactics," said Talai. "No attempt to take a knife away from Bob. One, two, three stabbing motions, and then he throws it away."

But wait, there was even more — after police recovered the knife, they tested it for DNA. They found Bob's on the blade of the knife and Nima's on the handle.

It was just like Brass had told me: *The DNA is going to be a problem for us.*

20

The Gold Club

"Six. Six hours," said Saam Zangeneh, buttoning his suit jacket and rising to stand in the cold courtroom at 1:38 P.M.

"The evidence is going to show that from 8:00 A.M. on March 31 until 2:30 in the morning on April 4 — that's ninety-one hours — Bob Lee slept for potentially six hours. It's not because he's an insomniac. This period of time was fueled by substance abuse. Mostly cocaine."

His job as a defense attorney, said Zangeneh, would be to educate the jury on the real facts of the case, not to give them the tunnel-vision version the prosecution would offer.

Zangeneh's account started this way. At ten in the morning on Monday, April 3, a security guard at the Millennium Tower knocked on Khazar's door to respond to a noise complaint. She opened the door, barked at him, and went back inside. Next, a man came outside. Reeking of alcohol, he tried a different tactic to make the problem go away — offering the guard $60 to ignore the complaint. "That man was Bob Lee," said Zangeneh.

That afternoon, Bob arrived at Boivin's apartment, where there were a lot of drugs. Not just the cocaine and whippits that Talai mentioned, but also LSD and GHB. Bo showed up around four and almost immediately made Khazar feel uncomfortable, staring at her as he did drugs.

After Jeremy kicked them out, Bob and Bo kept partying. They had plenty of supplies — in the elevator, Bo showed Bob a baggie full of cocaine.

Back inside the apartment, Boivin served Khazar and Aranza shots of GHB, which he mixed with fruit juice in a shot glass. "If you don't know," said Zangeneh, "it's a date rape drug." Although they took it willingly, they passed out in Jeremy's bedroom. When she woke, Khazar was distraught. Trying to focus, she called her brother, her husband, and her mother for help. Soon, Nima and Dino arrived to take her home. In the car with her brother, Khazar told Nima that Boivin had drugged and sexually assaulted her. Jeremy Boivin, Zangeneh emphasized, not Bob Lee. "There was never a mention of Bob Lee.

"Is there more?" he continued, pointing to the prosecution. "There's more."

"The evidence is going to show that at 11:17 P.M., Bob Lee messaged Nima, 'Gold Club? 😊😊😊' That's a strip club. The evidence is going to suggest that Bob was inviting Nima to go to a strip club. Is that the narrative they suggested? Does that make sense? This motive they are telling you about? It doesn't exist. We have the text messages to prove it," said Zangeneh.

When Bob arrived at Khazar's apartment, said Zangeneh, there had been no argument. In fact, the two men, Bob and Nima, were enjoying themselves so much that finally Khazar had to kick them out so she could go to bed. The men went downstairs to Nima's car and tried to figure out where to go. They drove around for a while, and then stopped and got out at "the one place on the road where it was all lit up," said Zangeneh.

And now it was Zangeneh's turn to fill in the gap in the footage. "We will show you that at two thirty in the morning, after a ninety-hour drug-fueled bender, Bob Lee took a knife out of his pocket to attack Nima," said Zangeneh. "And what did Nima do? He defended himself. In the struggle, Bob cut himself on his hip and then slashed at Nima, but Nima succeeded in redirecting the blade back at him."

This, said Zangeneh, not mentioning how hard the defense had worked to keep the video out, was what the surveillance video taken in the parking lot showed. Nima was showing what *Bob* did.

And why was there DNA on the knife? Well, obviously it had gotten there when Nima picked up the knife to throw it over the fence.

"All we ask is that you pay attention. Bob Lee was sleep-deprived. At two thirty in the morning on April 4, Nima was forced to defend himself, forced to stand his ground," said Zangeneh. "It's terrible. Somebody is dead. Nobody likes that. But in this state, in every state, you have the right to use self-defense."

21

Help

"Help, help, help, help," Bob Lee said in agony.

"Where are you?" asked the dispatcher.

"Help. Help," said Bob.

"Sir," she repeated, "Where are you?"

As he listened to his son's last words, Rick shut his eyes tightly as Bob's brother, Oliver, held their father's body in his arms.

"Help me," he said just before the end of the call. "I'm in the street."

The rules for testimony were these: The first side examined the witness, and then the other side performed a cross-examination. Then the first side went again. After that, there was an indefinite number of rounds of questions, but in each round questions could only be asked about the answers from the previous round. Then the judge asked the jury to write down any questions they might have, which she looked at with the attorneys. They selected which questions to allow, and the judge read them to the witness. Then the attorneys were allowed to ask follow-ups if they had any, and then, finally, the witness was excused. For some witnesses, the whole process lasted no more than an hour. For others, it lasted days and days.

Officer Joseph Rinaldi had been the first officer to arrive on the scene, and the first witness to take the stand on behalf of the prosecution. He told ADA Reinstedt that when he arrived, he observed an adult man on the ground. "He was unconscious," said Rinaldi. "He had blood on his clothing and was not responding to officers attempting to speak with him."

Reinstedt played the footage of that moment captured by Rinaldi's body camera. There were two large monitors in the courtroom, one to the left of the judge and another to her right. The lights in the courtroom dimmed as the jury watched. The scene was dark, illuminated by flashing red and blue lights from the police car. Rinaldi stood over Lee's body. "Hey, my friend," we heard him say. "Hey. Where were you stabbed, man? Where were you stabbed, man?"

It was a terrible thing to watch the recording, to see Lee's body on the ground, knowing that he would never regain consciousness. Bob's eyes were closed. The skin of his face looked clammy. His mouth was slightly open.

"Get the med kit," said Rinaldi in the video, "He's not doing so hot. I'm not feeling a pulse."

After the ambulance crew took Lee to the hospital, Rinaldi and other officers secured the scene and looked for evidence. His flashlight cutting through the night, Rinaldi saw blood on the sidewalk and smeared on the Portside building's call box. Following the trail to the intersection of Main and Bryant, underneath the Bay Bridge, it looked to him that whatever had happened had started there.

As Rinaldi was searching, another officer called out to him. They had found something. Rinaldi went over to the Caltrans parking lot. With their flashlights they could see a knife on the ground just over the fence. It wasn't hard to imagine that it might be important, and so Rinaldi and the other officers set up a vigil over it, watching the knife in the lonely, dark hours until the crime scene techs arrived after daylight to take it.

"Wasn't there another person at the scene?" asked Cohen during his cross-examination, referring to an unhoused man that the police had found sleeping not far from where Lee was found. Yes, said Rinaldi, but he hadn't seen anything. "Didn't you go several times to your police car when you were supposed to be watching the knife?" asked Cohen. Yes, said Rinaldi, but each time, someone else took his place.

The first day of testimony was over. The judge stood as the jury exited. Zangeneh winked at his client, and Nima was taken back to jail, disappearing into the corridor at the back of the courtroom.

The next morning, Sergeant Paul McIntosh testified, explaining that he was the one who first saw the knife in the parking lot and had assigned Rinaldi to watch over it as he called Caltrans to get them to send someone to unlock the gate, which they did after dawn.

Zangeneh cross-examined, and just as Cohen had done the previous day, probed the police officer for weaknesses.

"Officer McIntosh, if Rinaldi went to his car to warm up, did anybody else watch it?" he asked, mispronouncing McIntosh's name as he spoke.

"I don't know," McIntosh said.

Zangeneh played surveillance footage from the Caltrans parking lot. "Would you describe that Caltran lot as dimly lit or illuminated?" he asked, missing the -s at the end of Caltrans. (*He wasn't from around here*, as the previous judge had put it.)

"Inside the parking lot is illuminated," replied McIntosh. The attorney was trying to show that the area had been much better lit than the police claimed it was. If so, that would undercut the prosecution's claim that Momeni had planned to kill Lee.

Zangeneh played another clip of security camera footage from a different camera, which showed several cars driving on the block of Main Street in the minutes leading up to when Momeni parked his car there. He counted them for McIntosh: *One, two, three* — all the way to twelve passing vehicles in the half hour before Nima parked. There were also two people who walked by. *Not so dark, not so deserted. Maybe not so planned.*

Finally, Zangeneh cued up another part of McIntosh's body camera footage, in which the police officer was looking at Bob's driver's license with another officer. They read out his full name to each other — Robert Lee.

"At least he wasn't named Robert E. Lee," we heard McIntosh say in the video.

"That wouldn't go over so well if he went to school in Oakland," said the other officer.

"Was that a racist joke?" asked Zangeneh, looking for evidence of potential bias.

"I don't think it was a racist joke," replied McIntosh. Zangeneh tried to press him on it, but the judge told him to move along, and so he did. (Later, outside the courtroom, Bob's father, Rick, explained in his genteel baritone that in fact the family was related to the Confederate general, but only distantly. On Bob's mother's side, the family had lived in St. Louis for eight generations; on Rick's side only for three. "We're the newcomers," he said.)

Next to take the stand was Rosalyn Check, the crime scene investigator who arrived at the roped-off block of Main Street at little after 8:00 A.M. on April 4 with two of her colleagues. They mapped and took photographs of the potential evidence that had been found, which included not only the spatters of blood and the knife but also two iPhones, a PopSocket, a vape pen, a small plastic baggie, and a wrapper from a chocolate bar. It wasn't clear which of those items, if any, had come from the victim or the assailant. Maybe they were just trash.

Check was then called to the One Hotel, where the police were searching Lee's room. She explained to the jury what she had found there: two small empty bottles of Hangar 1 vodka, one small empty bottle of Don Julio tequila, a few cans of beer, and an open bottle of white wine. She also found a white powder residue on the side table that looked like cocaine, and more drugs in the bathroom. After she was done, she went back to her lab to examine the most important thing the police had found so far — the knife.

In the lab, she realized she had a decision to make. In her experience, it would be possible to test the knife for fingerprints or for DNA, but not for both. If she dusted it for fingerprints she might dilute the DNA too much to get a reading, and if she swabbed it for DNA she would likely smudge off the fingerprints. It was going to be one or the other.

Check went for the DNA.

It was easier to establish identity using DNA, and she doubted she could even get fingerprints from the knife handle if she wanted to. She knew that because she had tried to get prints from similar rubber surfaces many times before, including from other knives, guns, and even a baseball bat. She couldn't. So following her usual procedure, Check examined the knife for DNA evidence. Her decision paid off. She was able to get two samples — one from the blood on the blade and another from the handle. Later, the police would match those samples with the decedent and the defendant.

McMullen had many questions for her about the crime scene in his cross-examination. Did she know if the knife had been guarded the whole time before she arrived? What were the roles of the other two investigators there with her? How far was the knife from the fence? He asked a lot of questions about that — a line of inquiry that didn't seem to go anywhere or mean anything.

Next there was the matter of the wrapper, the piece of trash that came from a Riesen candy. In one police photo taken at night, it was not there, but in another photo of the same spot in the morning, it was. For McMullen, that suggested the scene had not been as well secured as the police were making it seem. For Check, it suggested that the wind had blown some irrelevant trash around.

"What we can agree on is that a chocolate bar ended up next to a pretty substantial piece of evidence?" asked McMullen.

"Yes," said Check.

"That's not acceptable, is it?" asked McMullen.

"Well, no," conceded Check.

"I would imagine that changes your opinion as to just how well secured this crime scene was?" said McMullen.

"No, it doesn't," said Check.

"Let's talk about the knife," said McMullen, changing subjects. "You didn't test the knife handle for fingerprints?"

"I did not," she said. McMullen was asking why, when, from outside the courtroom, I could hear the sounds of people chanting, their words muffled and indistinct.

"I've processed guns with rubber grips, other weapons, and I've never had luck," Check was saying. "It's not that I go out of my way not to do it."

The sound was now so loud that I couldn't focus on her testimony. I went outside to see what was happening. At the other end of the marble hallway, a group of people were clustered in front of another courtroom. They were either on their way in or out, I wasn't sure. As I came a little closer, I could hear their chants. "Free Palestine," they were shouting. "Free, free Palestine."

I figured these had to be the group of protestors who had walked onto the roadway of the Golden Gate Bridge in April there for their own trial. Although the Palestinian cause was certainly not unpopular in the Bay Area, District Attorney Jenkins had decided to charge them with false imprisonment, conspiracy, and trespassing. I watched them chant for a while and then went back down the hall, where Reinstedt was now performing his redirect examination.

"Mr. McMullen asked you about how the rubber was not a particularly suitable surface for fingerprints," he said. "You said you'd tried a number of times?"

"I've tested on a similar surface hundreds of times," said Check. "Anything with a rubber grip surface. If there's an opportunity to take fingerprints, we'll try."

"Have you ever got prints in hundreds of attempts?"

"No," said Check.

"Was anything out of the ordinary in the processing of this knife?" asked the prosecutor.

"The rubber was degraded. It was coming apart. You might have better luck fingerprinting a new knife, but not one where the grip is falling apart," said Check.

Nima's mother, Mahnaz Tayarani, cut a lonely figure in the cold courtroom. Sometimes she sat with friends or with a friend of Nima's, a dark-haired man around the same age as her son. Often, she was alone. She drove each morning across the Golden Gate Bridge in the BMW that her children had bought her, ate her lunch alone inside her car, and drove back as soon as the day was over. Tayarani often wore thick glasses and soft clothes in neutral colors, her white hair cut into a chin-length bob resembling Anna Wintour's. She slept poorly. She tried to go to yoga early in the morning and kept up with her work when she was able.

At first, Tayarani shied away from talking to anyone before or during breaks from the proceedings, sitting alone on the hard benches outside Courtroom 28. She politely declined to talk to the journalists who approached her. Slowly, over time, she began to open up, often chatting with the courtroom sketch artist, a woman around the same age as her. I began arriving early to sit with the women before court began. Sometimes Tayarani did not want to be disturbed. Other times, we played Sudoku or Wordle together.

"Nima was very caring," Tayarani told me one morning. "He loved to feed birds." The pigeons would line up at the window of his apartment, waiting for him to feed them, and after he was arrested, she had to clear out a large bag of birdseed from his Jeep. Her son was gentle with animals and plants — he tended to a large potted tree in his apartment in the Besler Building and had a fishtank where he kept several fish, including a yellow-and-black angelfish. She searched for a picture on her phone. "When he got it, it was as small as your thumb," she said, "But when he was arrested it was as big as your hand."

Mahnaz took care of Nima's apartment for several months after his arrest, before he finally gave up the lease. She gave away some of his other fish, but she cared for the angelfish as much as she could, feeding it and cleaning the tank. But finally, one hot day, she was away, and the water temperature in the tank changed. Another fish, a bottom-feeder, must have sensed an opportunity, because it attacked and killed the angelfish.

"I was mortified," she said, "but Nima consoled me. He said, 'Mom it's not your fault.'"

22

Bob, This Is Fucking Crazy

The next witness to take the stand was Bo Mohazzabi. Bo was a dark-haired man around Bob's age. The two friends had been together for much of April 3 and 4. Mohazzabi, who was wearing a suit jacket with no tie, explained that he had first met Bob through his brother, who met Lee in 2011 at an Android conference.

"Bob was legendary in the open-source community," said Mohazzabi. "He developed the Android operating system."

The morning of April 3, 2023, was normal, Bo said. He woke up around 6:00 or 6:30 A.M. "I hydrated, meditated, and started to work around 8:00 A.M.," he said. Mohazzabi had done a juice cleanse that weekend and had used the time to brainstorm about a start-up idea. He was hoping to see Bob, not just to hang out with a friend he hadn't seen in a while, but also to talk to him about his business plan. The two men texted throughout the day.

Around 3:30 or 4:00 P.M. on April 3, Lee invited Mohazzabi to meet him at Jeremy Boivin's apartment. So Bo ordered a Lyft and arrived at the thirty-eighth floor of Boivin's building at 1550 Mission Street at 4:11 P.M. When he arrived, Lee was in another room on a conference call for work. So while he waited for his friend to finish up, Mohazzabi made small talk with Boivin, whom he had never met, and Khazar Momeni, whom he had.

"I met her through Bob in 2017 or 2018 at Bob's place," he said, his tone of voice indicating he did not want to fill in the exact contours of their previous relationship. "We sort of kept in touch. I once went to her apartment. We hung out a few times."

"When did that end?" asked Talai.

"In 2017 or 2018. I would guess it was a few months," said Mohazzabi.

"Why did you fall out of touch?"

"I just chose not to interact with her. I would say — yeah — I was not interested in having a friendship," said Mohazzabi, measuring his words carefully.

At Boivin's apartment, Mohazzabi said he talked with Jeremy about the companies they had worked for, while Khazar remained quiet.

"Did you see whippits?" asked Talai, referring to nitrous oxide.

"Yes," said Mohazzabi, who said that Khazar was taking hits from a red canister of the gas. Bo said he also took one hit, as well as a shot of tequila. Boivin also had a bowl of a white powder on the coffee table, although Bo was evasive about what was in it.

"It could have been cocaine powder?" asked Talai.

"Sure," Mohazzabi said. (For what it's worth, nitrous oxide is a legal substance; cocaine isn't.)

Done with work, Bob came out of the back room, and the four people hung out for a while. A little after 5:00 P.M., Jeremy pulled Bob aside for a brief conversation. Bob returned and told Bo it was time for them to leave.

"I said, 'Great,'" said Mohazzabi. "I didn't necessarily care to be there. I wanted to spend time with Bob. It was a Monday afternoon, I was just coming off a juice cleanse, and I wasn't looking to socialize."

The security camera in the elevator confirmed what Mohazzabi said. It showed the two men entering the elevator at 5:12 P.M. and going downstairs. On the ride down, Bob seemed happy to be with Mohazzabi, but also confused, getting off on the wrong floor before his friend pulled him back in.

Back at the One Hotel, Bob and Bo had a drink at the bar and debated getting dinner. There was a brand of tequila that Bob wanted him to try — Bo had a sip but didn't like it. Bo was conflicted about sending it back, since it had been Bob's recommendation, but Lee said not to worry about it. "Don't feel bad," said Bob. "Just send it back."

After their drinks, Bo wanted to show Bob his wireframe, and so the two men went up to Bob's room.

"What does that mean?" Talai interjected, asking what a wireframe was.

"I was using an app called Miro, a whiteboard app, to sketch out a business plan, what the product would be and what it would do. I made a technical sketch of what a user of this app would experience. That's what I was working on all weekend," said Mohazzabi.

"Spell that," said the court reporter, who was struggling to keep up with the fast pace at which Mohazzabi was talking.

Mohazzabi laughed. "M, I, R, O," he said with an exaggerated slowness, as if he were speaking to a child. It wasn't the first time, or the last, that Mohazzabi came off like an embodiment of the worst stereotypes about tech bros: juice cleanses; disingenuous praise for the police for "double-clicking" on something he said during an interview; and frustrations at the suggestion he was *pitching* Lee on his start-up rather than just talking about it. The Bob Lee I had come to know wasn't the sort of person who would inspire people to throw rocks at the Google bus. Bo kind of seemed like he was.

While Bo and Bob were talking about Bo's start-up idea (*not a pitch!*), Bob seemed distracted. He was making and receiving a lot of phone calls and texts — to Krista, to friends, and to many others. This was Bob in a familiar mode, craving company even in the presence of another person.

But then came a call that seemed different. When Bob put it on speakerphone, Bo could hear Khazar shouting in the background, but he didn't recognize the voice of the man. Bob told him it was her brother, Nima.

Nima was peppering Bob with questions: *What were you guys doing? What was going on with my sister? What did she take? What was going on? How about the girls getting naked? Who was that friend with you? What was his name?*

"I said, 'Bob, this is fucking crazy. Get off the phone,'" testified Mohazzabi.

Bob tried to mollify Nima, and when it seemed like he had calmed down, the call ended. They hung out in the room for a while longer, and then decided to go to The Battery for another drink. They got there around 10:00 P.M. Bob had a beer; Bo had two. They left around 11:30 P.M., going to the nearby apartment that Bo shared with his fiancée. When they arrived, she said hello to Bob but informed the men that she was going to bed — she had to work in the morning. Bo and Bob wanted to keep hanging out, and so they put on some music and poured themselves some club soda and water — because of the juice cleanse, Bo didn't have any alcohol in the place — and thought about what they wanted to do next.

Over their club sodas and waters, an idea emerged. Why not go to Miami together the next day? They looked up flights and found one leaving from SFO at 7:30 A.M. on April 4. Why not sleep on the plane and then Bob could show Bo around Miami that evening. As a backup, if they missed that flight, there was another in the afternoon. Bob had been having a great time in San

Francisco, but now it was time to go back to Florida. This would be his last night in the city.

"Bob's demeanor on this last night, was it different or abnormal?" asked Talai.

"No. He was Bob. There was nothing unusual," said Mohazzabi. Bob left around 12:30 A.M. Bo thought he was going back to the hotel to get some rest.

If Zangeneh's goal was to make Bo seem like an unreliable narrator, Bo had given him plenty of opportunities to do so.

For example, Bo had played down the drug use at Boivin's apartment, but when Zangeneh showed him the texts that Bob and Bo had sent to each other, the situation looked different.

Bo texted: "Are there any whippits 😊?"

Bob replied: "Dude a tank."

On the stand, an annoyed Mohazzabi said, "I don't remember him saying *dude*." Zangeneh handed him a printout. "The text does say dude," Mohazzabi conceded.

"You work in tech?" said the defense lawyer, moving on.

"I do," said Mohazzabi.

"You also work in the music industry?"

"What do you mean?" said Mohazzabi.

"You're a DJ?"

"What do you mean?"

"You don't know what a DJ is?" said Zangeneh, casting a bemused glance at the jury and moving on to a new topic before Bo could clarify. That was on purpose — once you've trapped a witness, you don't give them the opportunity to get out of it. Now we were watching the elevator video of Bo and Bob leaving Boivin's apartment. There was a moment where Bo pulled a plastic baggie out of his pocket. Zangeneh asked him what it was. Bo said he didn't remember. As Zangeneh pushed him, Bo continued to weave.

The bowl of white powder at Boivin's *might* have been cocaine. Bo wasn't sure. Bob *might* have suggested calling an escort at one point in the evening. Bo didn't know. The Battery wasn't an exclusive place, but it was "members only." Had Khazar and Bo dated in the past? "Mmm, I wouldn't say we were *dating*," said Mohazzabi.

Finally, Bo's time on the stand was done.

As Krista headed back to Marin to cheer at the last volleyball game of the season for one of the kids, the defense attorneys stood on the street in front of the Hall of Justice, debating where to go for lunch. Mohazzabi walked past them.

"What did you say your last name was?" he asked Zangeneh.

Zangeneh told him, and Bo chuckled.

"Not *zandan-eh*?" said Bo.

Zangeneh laughed genuinely. "In a different life," he said.

Mohazzabi left, and Zangeneh explained to the other attorneys that in Farsi *zandan* meant "prison."

23

My Brother Was Not the One Who Killed Bob

On October 20, Khazar Momeni silently walked across the street and entered the Hall of Justice wearing a $5,500 powder-blue Valentino Garavani dress with a lavallière at her neck, oversized sunglasses with orange lenses perched on her head, and holding a $1,000 Valentino clutch. Flanked by her mother and an attorney, a hangdog man wearing a wrinkled suit and carrying a battered JanSport backpack, she entered Judge Gordon's courtroom to take the stand in the murder trial of her brother. The courtroom was packed with observers, who watched in silence as Nima watched his sister. Her hair was all in place. Her makeup was perfect. Her poise was perfect.

"You came here with someone today," asked Reinstedt after she took the stand, pointing to the man in the wrinkled suit. "Is that your lawyer?"

"My lawyer has advised me to bring him," said Khazar in a halting, timid voice. "He's not my lawyer but he's been advised to guide me to the courtroom."

It was a puzzling start to what would become a strange series of days. Any hope that Khazar might fill in the gap at the center of this trial — the question of what exactly happened on the Main Street sidewalk when Nima and Bob were face-to-face — evaporated.

Reinstedt asked when she learned that her brother had killed her friend. Khazar looked stricken. She paused. The microphone in front of her picked up the sound of her deep inhales and exhales. Then she spoke.

"Um," she said, "a friend came to my house and let me know Bob had passed away."

"Slightly different question," said Reinstedt. "When did you learn it was your brother?

"My brother was not the one who killed Bob," said Khazar.

From the front of the gallery, her mother waved her arms at her daughter. Khazar didn't notice or didn't understand what Mahnaz was trying to communicate — that this was not the right answer. Nima admitted that he killed Bob. He was disputing the circumstances, not the death. A confused Reinstedt asked again, and a second time, Khazar denied what the defense had already agreed to — that her brother had killed Bob Lee. "I have not been following the case. I have been staying quiet," she said.

Reinstedt seemed as caught off guard as her mother. "Are you learning today, for the first time, that your brother in fact was the one who killed Bob, and the issue is self-defense?" he asked.

"My brother was not the one who killed Bob Lee," said Khazar, who looked as if she might collapse. "I do not know anything else about the case."

From there, Khazar attempted to explain what she could remember. But, she cautioned, "there are some [parts] I remember very well, and some that are not very clear." She had been partying, she barely slept, and she had been emotionally distraught. Under questioning, Khazar said that although she and her husband were paying for her brother's lawyers, she had not spoken to them except to arrange payments. She also said that she had not spoken at length to Sergeant Dittmer or the prosecutors, even though they had reached out to her, as recently as today, when Reinstedt, Talai, and Dittmer called her. In other words, this was the first time that most of us, including the lead police investigator and lawyers on both sides, were finally hearing what she had to say.

According to Khazar, she met Bob eight years prior, in 2017, at The Battery. They never had sex with each other, she said. They were friends and saw each other sporadically. Khazar didn't say it, but from the texts that Reinstedt showed her between her and Bob from late March and early April, she seemed to have been more invested in the relationship, whatever its actual contours were, than he was. Some texts she said she could remember. Others she said she could not.

On Wednesday, March 29, 2023, Bob texted her that he was in town and was staying at the One Hotel. He asked if she wanted to hang out. She was busy, she said, but she did want to see him, and they tried to connect over the next few days.

Khazar texted him at 7:39 P.M. on March 30 to see if he wanted to get together with her. "Doing anything tonight special man?" she wrote. Bob did not reply until two o'clock on the morning of March 31, when he wrote, "Hi, I fell asleep." They did manage to connect, and on the morning of April 1, Bob came over to her condo. Nima was there, which is where they met for the first time.

Bob met up with her again on the morning of April 3, bringing with him a tank of nitrous oxide. On his way over, he texted her: "Coming with a tank. Gonna cost you a blowjob."

"That weekend was extra," said Khazar when the prosecution read it to her. Krista laughed from the gallery.

"We were hanging out and talking," said Khazar. Bob arrived with his friend Jeremy Boivin, whom Khazar had never met. She shied away from talking about him by name, preferring to refer to Boivin as "the drug dealer."

Reinstedt tried his best to get her to clarify. She meant Boivin, right? "What was the context in which he was introduced to you?" he asked.

"I didn't know," said Khazar. "We don't get close to our drug dealers. We don't invite them upstairs. He was introduced as a friend."

"Did you hit it off?"

"I don't understand what you mean. He brought me a big tank of nitrous, and he had a liter of GHB with him. He was introduced as a friend, therefore I was nice to him."

Khazar explained that when the party broke up, Bob left to go conduct an interview for work. She and Jeremy continued to hang out. They drove to the beach, where they stayed for a while, and then returned to Boivin's apartment, where Boivin gave her cocaine, LSD, and the first shot of GHB she took that day. "He gave me a sweet little drink, a shot, and I drank it," she said. (Although GHB has a reputation as a drug given to unwilling victims, it is also taken voluntarily.)

Later in the day, Bob rejoined them. It wasn't a party in a real way. It was just a few people hanging out. Khazar had texted Aranza to come over, but she wasn't there yet when Bo showed up.

"The Bo guy was doing nitrous. He was being rude. He would stare at me and give me a smirk. It was awkward," she said.

"Were you friends?" asked Reinstedt.

"He's been a DJ since I was nineteen years old. I would see him around," she said. "He was being rude with his actions. He would consume drugs and stare at me while doing it. Give me a smirk. It was an awkward, awkward vibe."

On the way out, Bob tried to get Khazar to come with them. "He kept saying, *Get in the car, get in the car,*" said Khazar. But Khazar didn't want to leave, and so she blocked Bob on her phone.

By now, Khazar was beginning to feel the effects of the LSD. "All the colors were changing," she said. "I was becoming more vulnerable." Boivin brought out more GHB, which he put in shot glasses with fruit juice for the three of them to take. "I feel silly that I took them," Khazar said on the stand. In retrospect, she wondered what Jeremy had actually put in his own shot glass. She didn't see him mix the drugs, and when the girls reached for them, he said, "No, that's the wrong one, this one is yours." In total, Khazar had three hits of GHB — the one she had taken earlier, and then two more after Bob and Bo left. She continued to inhale nitrous and had some red wine from a bottle that Boivin opened for them.

"First I was feeling the acid. Things were colorful and pretty. From the third shot of GHB, I was going down. I couldn't really move. I would wake up and I couldn't move anything. I would open my eyes, then be out again," she said.

"Is it fair to say your memories are fuzzy?" asked Reinstedt. Momeni agreed. What she did remember was that she and Aranza were in Boivin's bedroom, watching music videos on his television. Then she passed out. When she woke up again, she was lying face down on the bed wearing a swimsuit that was not her own. She thought maybe they were planning to go downstairs to the Jacuzzi, but she wasn't sure. Jeremy entered the room wearing "tiny little red shorts." She couldn't remember the intervening time, but she had a flash of memory of Boivin pulling down her pants and slapping her ass, and another time grabbing it.

"I started crying. I've never cried like that before — from the bottom of my heart," said Khazar. "I started crying. I said to Jeremy, *Don't do anything to me. Let me go.*"

Khazar said at first Jeremy said no, but she found her phone and dropped a pin to show her location to her brother and her husband, telling them to come pick her up. Khazar said, "He was shaking me, saying, *You can't get me in trouble.*"

"You were scared of him?" asked Reinstedt?

"Yes, of course. He's a predator," replied Khazar.

When Nima and Dino arrived, Dino went to get Khazar's car while Nima went to collect his sister. The same elevator security camera that showed Bob and Bo leaving showed Boivin, Aranza, and Khazar, who appeared to be fixing her clothes, going down to meet him. Nima hustled his sister into his car — the white BMW — and drove her back to her condo.

"What was your brother's reaction?" asked Reinstedt.

"He was very calm and collected. He wanted to know what had happened. He asked if anyone sexually assaulted me. I told him that he slapped my ass and grabbed it," said Khazar. "And I told him the drugs he had given me."

"Did you tell him about any sexual assault from anyone beside Mr. Boivin?"

"No."

"Do you believe you were raped?" asked Reinstedt.

"I know I was sexually assaulted," said Khazar. "I don't know what else he did to me. He was shirtless, walking into the room when we were sleeping."

"So it's a possibility?"

"It could be."

It was during the car ride home that Khazar said she told Nima that Boivin had assaulted her while she was at his apartment. But Reinstedt seemed skeptical.

"Why did you invite Mr. Boivin to your apartment ten hours after you say he sexually assaulted you?" he asked at one point.

"Due to the hardship I had as a child, the abuse, I have a hard time believing when people hurt me, or sexually assault me," said

Khazar, speaking in a different, more formal diction than she used in the rest of her testimony. "I sometimes go back to my abuser. In this case, that is what happened."

"You continue to see Mr. Boivin up to this day?" asked Reinstedt.

"I — how is this? — I have seen him."

"He saw you on your birthday last month?"

"I do not recall."

"You have continued to have had a sexual relationship with Mr. Boivin?"

"I have not."

"No one actually sexually assaulted you, correct?" said Reinstedt, referring Momeni to texts she had sent her brother denying that a sexual assault had taken place.

"I was," said Momeni.

"But on the texts you told him, 'lol you dumb fuck bob never touched me no one did.' You are telling your brother no one touched you?" Reinstedt asked.

"I had explained to him when he picked me up from the drug dealer's house exactly what happened to me," said Khazar. "After that, I did not want to go down that route."

After he returned his sister to her condo on the forty-first floor of the Millennium Tower, Nima and Jeremy started texting. Boivin told Nima that he had left a water bottle at Khazar's place. Nima didn't think it was that big of a deal, but then Boivin explained that it wasn't full of water — it was full of GHB.

"When he came, my brother said first thing, 'I should have had six cops waiting for you,'" said Khazar. "Jeremy said, 'Let's go downstairs and fight.'"

Things settled down enough for Jeremy to grab his bottle, which he realized was empty. (They later figured out that Dino had found it and dumped the drugs down the sink.) Boivin stormed off. After Jeremy left, Nima stuck around Khazar's condo.

Khazar said from the stand that she wasn't sure how Bob ended up at the condo that night. At some point, she unblocked him, and they had been talking. "He was partying and wanted to join us," she said. "Either I invited him or he wanted to come over." Whatever the case, the prosecution showed texts from her to Bob around 12:30 A.M., asking him to bring over whippits.

She didn't remember if Bob did bring nitrous oxide, but Khazar did know that when Bob showed up at her door, she opened it for him. She said he put his arm around Nima's shoulder as the two men drank in her kitchen. Bob gave Nima a bump of ketamine, and the two men talked about what had happened.

"Nima questioned him about what drugs I had taken, what drugs were given to me by Jeremy at his house," said Khazar. She also remembered Bob showing Nima some pictures of a girl he was interested in. "They were going to the Gold Club," a strip club not far from Khazar's condo.

Finally, she told them it was time to go. As Bob left, he couldn't manage to put on his shoes, and so her brother got down on the floor to help him. That was the last time she saw Bob Lee.

Khazar Momeni was scheduled to continue her testimony on Monday, October 21. As we waited to be allowed into the courtroom, I asked Mahnaz, "How are you?"

"Life could always be worse," she said. "I could be living in Palestine."

On the stand, Khazar looked fragile and miserable, appearing as if she had barely rested all weekend. Reinstedt pointed her to a series of texts she sent Nima after Lee's death.

"Where did you drop him off?" she wrote to him in the texts. "Either I'll ask or the cops will. I want to know. I'll call the cops, since you called the cops too."

Confusingly, Khazar explained the texts as sibling bickering.

"He didn't answer," said Reinstedt. "Did you continue to ask him those questions?"

"I do not remember," she said.

"Did he ever tell you anything more about what happened that night?"

"No, he did not."

She told the two men she was going to bed, but that wasn't true, because at the same time they were leaving, she was texting with Boivin, telling him to come over. As soon as they left, she went down the elevator to go to a smoke shop, where she bought nitrous oxide and cigarettes. Nima called her at 2:40 A.M., but she didn't want to talk to him. "I remember he reached out to me," she said on the stand. "I was really — I was on my way to the smoke shop. I was trying to get off the phone. He wanted to see that I got to sleep. He said his night didn't turn out the way he wanted it to, and not to let Bob back in, because he was acting erratic."

"Did you question him about what that meant?" asked Reinstedt.

"I thought they had a disagreement of some kind. I didn't think anything more than that," said Momeni. "I was in the Uber and didn't want to tell him the truth, so I was trying to get off the phone really quick."

The prosecution showed the texts that Khazar and Jeremy sent to each other:

At 2:38 A.M., Boivin wrote to her with what was presumably a time estimate: "250 without tabk 315 with tank / you decide."

At 2:45 A.M., she wrote back: "Come now sorry that was

brother on the phone / Ripping me new one / He doesn't ever think I'm gonno talk to you again lol / He just doesn't want me to talk to Bob anymore." And then, because he had not written back to her fast enough, she added: "Are you dead?" At 2:57, Nima texted her, asking her to call him. Khazar said she could not remember if she did.

She and Boivin spent much of the next week together at her condo in the Millennium Tower, even after Dino walked in on them in bed together. Khazar said that while they were together, Boivin degraded her.

"When the drug dealer Jeremy Boivin arrived at my house, he brought a tank and other drugs," she said. "He blew smoke in my face, and he would record me almost dying. He had a fetish for that. I was completely gone." As she spoke, her voice, already tremulous, was shaking harder than before.

Despite the degradation she claimed, Jeremy and Khazar continued to have a relationship after that, which she described as violent and abusive: "He threatened to kill me. I was scared. There were a few incidents where I grabbed the phone to call 911, and he physically assaulted me. He wouldn't allow me to call the cops. My mom showed up to his house and he would run away. He would blackmail me, he said that he would put out videos and pictures of me. The cops have asked me about this, and I say that I'm scared. I can't say a single word about this."

Khazar said that one day eight months earlier, her mother contacted the police about Boivin after "he hit my head against the bed, choked me, and slapped me. But I wouldn't admit it to the police officers. They told me to speak up but I told them I was scared."

"The police responded to his apartment?" asked Reinstedt.

"Yes, many times," she said.

"We talked about this last week, but you didn't mention these things last week?"

"I was scared, but I decided to tell the truth and hope everybody will understand."

"He came to your birthday party?"

"I didn't have a party. I was sitting on the couch crying all day long. He's a drug dealer. He came over to drop off some stuff."

"You continued to contact him?"

"I put myself in that horrible situation many more times as well. I ended up in really, really bad places."

Khazar found out that Bob was dead on Wednesday, April 5. A friend told her. Nima hired a lawyer soon after that, and her private investigator told them to turn over all their phones to him; the Momenis then all bought new ones. "Your testimony was that you were shocked by your brother's arrest on April 13," asked Reinstedt. "Why was everyone in your family getting new phones three days before he was arrested?"

"We were advised to do so," said Momeni.

"What was your understanding of why you were giving up your phone?"

"For everyone's protection."

"Why were you giving up your phone?" he repeated.

At this point, the rumpled lawyer who had followed Momeni in on the first day of her testimony stood up from where he was sitting in the gallery. "I object, Your Honor," he said. Judge Gordon's affect turned stern. "Mr. Lee," she said, revealing that the judge knew who he was, even if we did not, "you do not get to object." He quickly sat down.

Returning to his questions, Reinstedt showed Momeni texts that she had sent Mohazzabi after she learned about Bob's death.

"Omg bo"

"Bo"

"My heart aches"

"Did I hear the correct news?"

"Whyyyyyyyy"

"I'm literally heartbroken. I fucking loved bob. This hurts."

"Moo r your cute I'm so sorry."

"Love *"

"💔"

Bo responded: ":(so sad."

Khazar sent one final message: "Love you baby I'm so so so sorry my heart aches."

Zangeneh began his cross-examination the next morning, October 22.

He led her through all the texts that Bob and Khazar had exchanged in the days leading up to his death:

The first came at 7:39 P.M. on March 29. Bob told her he was in town.

"omg omg," she wrote back. "Come see me cutie / You're right next to me"

Bob asked if she was home. She said she was. He wrote back saying he wanted to have a "chill night" but that she should "hit me up if you want to hang later."

"Ok love," Khazar wrote back.

"Doing anything tonight special man?" she wrote at 7:49 P.M. on March 30. At two o'clock the next morning, Bob wrote back, "Hi, I fell asleep." She liked his message at 7:11 A.M., presumably when she woke up.

On Friday, March 31, Bob told her he was going to Public Works, a nightclub in the Mission. "Maybe call you after," he added. From then until well after 4:00 A.M. the following day, Khazar texted Bob, trying to get him to come over.

"Mine?" she wrote at 12:46 A.M.

"Mine?" she wrote again at 3:31 A.M.

Half an hour later, Bob told her he was with a friend named Mica.

"Who's Mica?" she asked.

Bob ignored her until 4:40 A.M. on Saturday, when she texted him again, "Wanna come over?"

"Yeah"

"Who are you with?"

"It's just me"

"Perf," she texted, and then texted "coke."

"A bit," he wrote.

"Did you take this to mean he had a bit of cocaine?" asked Zangeneh.

"He always does," Momeni answered. Bob arrived at her place a little after 5:00 A.M. They were together for around two hours. By 7:00 A.M. they had parted, with Bob leaving for a party at the Twitter headquarters.

"What drugs was he taking at your apartment?" asked Zangeneh.

"Cocaine and ketamine," said Momeni.

"When he arrived did he appear under the influence?"

"Definitely under the influence."

"How so?"

"He was all over the place. Aggressive."

Around 8:30 A.M., Bob was still at the Twitter party and was texting Khazar to see if she wanted to join him there. "You should cum," he wrote. "Bring your girlfriend." Khazar wrote that Bob should come to her place instead. "No cum here," he wrote back. She didn't go to the Twitter building.

They stopped texting for a while after that, but in the early morning hours of Monday, April 3, they picked up the text thread again. They made plans to get together, and Bob texted that he was "coming with a tank" of nitrous oxide. "Gonna cost you a blowjob," he added.

"Now, you indicated Mr. Boivin touched you during your inebriated state without your consent?" asked Zangeneh, continuing his cross-examination.

"Yes," said Momeni.

"Believe me, I'm not here to minimize or question that, but I will ask, you were in no condition to give consent?"

"Correct," she said.

"Just to be clear," he continued, "you didn't tell your brother that Bob Lee gave you GHB?"

"No."

"Touched you against your will?"

"No."

"Woke up near him in a compromising position?"

"No."

At 10:30 P.M. on April 4 — almost twenty hours after the incident under the Bay Bridge — Khazar received a text from her brother, which Zangeneh showed her on the stand: "That was a really low point you took us to all today," Nima wrote. "Hope you can make better decisions and find some better goals and priorities in life and thinking about your place in the world and your impact on the world and the people around you."

She told Zangeneh that it was in reference to Dino finding her in bed with Boivin.

Nima then sent a message that read, "I'll help start the case against these guys but you fucked up and all of us over and over and will have to work your way out of this yourself."

"I don't remember it very well," said Khazar. From April 4 through April 13, the day her brother was arrested, she was using drugs heavily. When the police searched her condo, they found thirty canisters of whippits, as well as other narcotics. Khazar said that since then, her contact with her family had been limited. She also said that she had gone to rehab, completing a thirty-day program recently. (Khazar had been arrested twice in the time since Nima's arrest for driving under the influence, once in the North Bay and once in San Francisco.)

"I don't like bringing this up, but we have to," said Zangeneh, pulling up a text that Khazar sent to Nima on the afternoon of April 5.

"Bob never touched me," she wrote. "No one did. Your dad did who you kissed his ass and begged to get his approval."

Khazar was in tears as she read the text.

"This wasn't the first time you had dealt with this kind of situation?" asked Zangeneh.

"Yes," said Khazar, sobbing.

"You were assaulted by your father?"

"Yes."

As Zangeneh was finishing up his cross-examination, he asked Khazar if she had "received any messages from Mr. Lee's family that intimidated you?"

"Yes," said Khazar.

"Do these messages have any bearing on your desire to speak with law enforcement?"

"Yes," she said.

In his redirect, Reinstedt asked Khazar about the rumpled

man who had tried to object on her behalf. "He wasn't my lawyer," she said. They spoke at cross purposes for a while; his questions seemed to be getting nowhere. The judge cut in. "Who is he to you?" she asked.

"He was advised to bring me to the courthouse. I didn't know who he was," said Khazar.

"Are you aware he came into court in advance yesterday to talk to the judge on your behalf?" asked Reinstedt.

"No."

Reinstedt wanted to know why it seemed like when he was asking questions, Khazar seemed not to remember a great many things. But when the defense was asking her questions, he said, "your answers, hundreds of times, was yes?"

"I don't know," she said.

"We had conversations about whether you continued to see Jeremy Boivin socially. You said no. Does your answer stand?" asked Reinstedt.

"He sells drugs, so I see him day and night."

"Do you hang out?"

"Sometimes."

"How frequently?"

"I don't know. As I told you, I put myself in this horrible situation, trying to get control of it. I put myself in this situation with this person who hurt me."

"When I asked you if you had hung out with him socially, your answer was no. Now you say you saw him on multiple occasions. When — if ever — did that stop?"

"I haven't talked to him in months."

"You said you have not seen him for a number of months, but he was at your birthday last month?"

"He dropped off drugs on my birthday."

"You said you went through a thirty-day sobriety program?"

"Yes."

"That was before he dropped off drugs on your birthday?"

"Correct."

The next morning, Reinstedt continued to press Khazar, asking her about the texts Krista had sent about her.

"Somebody from his family was trying to intimidate me and speak badly of me," said Khazar.

"They were talking about subpoenaing you so you could come here and talk and they called you a name?"

"They were intimidating and threatening me, as if I were running away from the cops. I was at my house. They have my address," said Khazar.

The court took its morning break a short time later. As always, the jury went out first, followed by the press, and then the lawyers.

As we were walking out, one of the reporters asked Krista what she thought of Khazar's testimony. "My husband was murdered," said Krista angrily. "She has no right to make herself a victim in this when our family was the one that got murdered. She can go fuck herself."

I was a few steps behind them, and after hearing Krista, I turned to Cohen to get his reaction.

"What did she say?" he asked me. He had been too far back to hear. I repeated what she said. His eyes bulged, and he walked off to talk to the other defense attorneys. A few minutes later, Cohen walked back to me. "Where was the jury when she said that?" he asked. I pointed down the hall. They were in front of her, pretty far away, I said. I didn't think they could have heard her, especially given how bad the acoustics were in the hallway. Cohen thanked me, and he and the other defense attorneys walked quickly back into the courtroom. If one of the jurors had heard what she said, it could be a serious problem. I cringed. I didn't want to be part of getting a juror dismissed or, worse, causing a mistrial.

For the rest of the morning, the judge and the attorneys for both sides met with the jurors one by one to see if they had heard anything. It was a tedious process, but finally, when we reassembled that afternoon, the judge continued as if nothing had happened. Rick and Oliver were still seated in their usual places in the gallery. Krista was nowhere to be seen. (She would return the next day, but after that she was much quieter in the hallway, mostly letting her former brother-in-law talk to the press instead of her.)

"The first day of your examination, the prosecutor questioned whether or not you were actually sexually assaulted because you were with that person again?" said Zangeneh.

"Yes," said Momeni.

"Isn't that the exact kind of rhetoric that dismayed you from coming forward?"

"Yes, that was one of the many reasons."

"He's doing that as a prosecutor, questioning whether you were sexually assaulted because you took narcotics?"

"It makes me feel judged," she said.

"You came here today because the government sent you a subpoena?" he asked.

"Correct," she said.

"A lot of things have come out about your personal life as a result?"

"Yes."

"Things that a normal person would rather not testify to in front of seventeen people and all these media outlets?"

"Correct."

"But you told the truth?"

"Yes."

The judge then asked Khazar some questions submitted by the jury, and that was that. Khazar Momeni's part in the trial was finished. As she was walking out, the general sales manager of the BMW dealership where Nima had tried to sell his car was walking in to be the next witness. "Can you not slam the door in my face?" she shouted.

24

The Video

The next few days of testimony were less emotional. The BMW sales manager testified about the car, the prosecution showed a series of surveillance videos, and the police testified about searching the various places. By chance, I ran into my editor, who was in the building for jury duty. One morning at the coffee shop, Zangeneh pulled me aside to show me some screenshots he had taken from Bo's Instagram page. Not only did he call himself a DJ in them, but there were also pictures of him performing. And there was one in particular that Zangeneh couldn't believe, showing Bo on the playa at Burning Man, looking dusty but blissful. Next to him was the disgraced music producer Puff Daddy. The caption read, "It's not a party until Diddy shows up."

On Monday, November 4, I expected the proceedings to remain in the doldrums. But then Sergeant David Goff took the stand. He was the police officer who had recorded the surveillance video of Nima in the parking lot.

Around 5:00 P.M. on April 5, having been assigned to the case, Goff went to 4053 Harlan Street in Emeryville — the Besler Building — to see if he could find the white BMW. All he saw there, however, was Momeni's blue Jeep parked across the street. Goff parked and walked around looking for the car, but he didn't find it. He returned the next morning but again did not see the car. He came back on April 7, and again there was no sign of it. Hoping that Momeni might lead him to the location of the car, Goff put a

GPS tracker on the Jeep. For the next few days, he tracked Nima's movements, and on Monday, April 10, he saw that the Jeep was being driven in South San Francisco, a small city next to the more famous one.

Goff drove there. He found the Jeep parked at Luigi's Sandwich Palace, a lunch joint in an industrial park. "I entered the sandwich shop and observed Mr. Momeni at the counter," said Goff, who surreptitiously took photos of Momeni ordering his lunch, which he showed to the jury. As Goff followed him, Momeni ate in his car and then drove to a parking lot in Burlingame, another small city nearby, where he stopped.

"It was a building that contained several offices and a parking lot," said Goff. "We were just off of the main thoroughfare, which was Bayshore Boulevard. There were a lot of cars there and I parked. There was no signage or anything saying it was a private lot. No gates, nobody standing there, and nothing blocking me from the lot."

Nima went into the office building. Goff waited for him to come back out. Around 1:27 P.M., he did, along with another man, whom Goff later learned was a private investigator who worked for Paula Canny, Momeni's first defense attorney. Goff videoed the two men talking in the parking lot as Momeni smoked a cigarette. "Part of the request from Dittmer was to obtain a surreptitious DNA sample," he explained. "Momeni was smoking a cigarette, and I wanted to document it, so that when he finished smoking it, I could have a chain of custody, and we could send it to the crime lab for DNA processing."

The cigarette ultimately didn't reveal any evidence, because after smoking it, Nima crushed the filter and tossed it into the wind. But the ten-minute-long video did reveal something else.

"So I saw Momeni and Hendley talking," said Goff on the

stand. "It appeared to be very intense. Six minutes into the video, I observed Momeni make three distinctive stabbing motions with his right hand toward the left torso of Hendley. They were distinct and elevated from low to medium to high. On the third I saw that his right hand had the palm facing down. It looked like he was simulating holding an edged weapon."

"After the three stabbing gestures, what happened next?" asked Talai.

"They continued to speak for a few minutes, at which point I observed Momeni make a throwing motion with his right hand — as if he threw something."

Talai asked to admit the video into evidence. "Over a prior objection," said Cohen. The judge nodded. Here, at last, the jury would see the video that the defense had worked so hard to keep from them — although, of course, the jury did not know about the defense's efforts.

Talai played it.

Momeni and the investigator were standing in a parking lot, smoking. Nima was wearing the same clothes he'd been photographed in at Luigi's Sandwich Palace: a black jacket, a scarf, and a black baseball cap. A few minutes into the conversation, Momeni swung his right arm. It was a long, full extension, with his elbow locked and his fist pointed down and closed. Momeni slashed three times in quick succession. They talked for some more time, and then Nima made a throwing motion.

"This was taken a week after the homicide?" asked Talai.

"Yes," said Goff, "approximately."

"Did you ever see him simulate a struggle with another person?"

Cohen objected. The judge said she would allow it but asked Goff not to speculate in his answer.

"No," he said.

"At any time did you see what would be consistent with Mr. Momeni struggling over an object?"

Cohen objected again. Judge Gordon said she would allow the question, but after that Talai should move on.

"No," said Goff, "I did not."

"As far as you know, did Mr. Momeni know you were there watching him?" asked Talai.

"No, I don't think he did," said Goff. "My job is to stay unseen. If he had seen me with my camcorder, it would have been obvious to me."

Cohen began his cross-examination, asking Goff to recount again his investigation, looking for inconsistencies or evasions.

"You said two interesting things about this," said Cohen. "First, you said you wanted to see if you could pick up the cigarette?"

"Yes," said Goff

"But you didn't go inspect the area to pick it up?"

"No," said Goff."

"You said you had no idea it was his attorney's office. So why did you stop filming when his attorney showed up?"

"There was no particular reason," said Goff.

"So you never got the cigarette and you turned it off when the attorney showed up?"

"At some point I turned it off."

"Not at some point, exactly when the attorney showed up."

"Well, he wasn't smoking a cigarette then," said Goff.

"There's a sign here that says, PRIVATE PROPERTY," said Cohen, showing Goff a picture. "It says, TENANT PARKING ONLY. You were parked here while you were filming?"

"Yes," said Goff, who explained that he was parked inside that lot while filming.

Talai redirected.

"You were asked about many different gestures," he said. "Did you ever see on April 10 a gesture where there is a motion forward, then the fist redirects back and toward the body?"

"No."

"Are you aware now that eighteen months later that this is their story — this is their theory?" he said, referring to the defense.

"No," said Goff.

Cohen objected at the same time as he answered.

"Strike the word *story*," said Judge Gordon.

"Are you aware that their *defense* —" said Talai, his voice dripping with derision.

"I object," said Cohen in outrage. "You can't say *defense* with air quotes. It's a legal defense!"

"We will skip over that," said Gordon, "since we already know that Sargeant Goff is unaware that this is his legal defense." Behind her, a ceiling panel was hanging down loosely, as if about to fall.

Sergeant Dittmer was the prosecution's final witness. He had been the lead investigator, and for much of his testimony, he carefully walked the prosecution through the material that was by now familiar. Dittmer, who had been sitting with the prosecutors throughout the long weeks of the trial, spoke with a kind of detached bemusement at the whole thing, as if he had just woken up from a nap. But he was thorough, and he explained his investigation clearly. I could see the jurors watching him intently.

On cross-examination, the defense tried to make it seem like Dittmer had tunnel vision during his investigation, that he had focused too quickly on Nima. Zangeneh made a joke about Dittmer noting in his report that Nima had Magnum condoms on him when he was arrested. "Pretty impressive," he said.

And then the people rested.

At that point, the jury left the room. They were done for the day, but the lawyers stayed. The defense made two motions — one for a mistrial and another for the judge to rule that Momeni was not guilty.

They based their first motion on something that Dittmer said during his testimony — "I don't think he's ever gotten bond." That could seem like a minor throwaway comment, but it implied that Momeni was currently being held in jail. The judge and the lawyers had been careful not to bring that up in front of the jury, for fear that it could taint their judgment. (That's why, for instance, Nima wore a business suit each day that he was in the presence of the jury rather than the jail-issued orange jumpsuit. And it's why the *Standard*'s photos of Momeni in jail were such a problem.) "We go to careful steps to ensure the jury is unaware that my client is in custody," said Zangeneh. "While Sergeant Dittmer is correct, he's never gotten bond, that's an inappropriate thing to say."

Judge Gordon denied the motion.

Zangeneh thanked her and moved on to his next motion, for the judge to find Nima not guilty. He claimed that the prosecution had not shown a chain of custody on the knife, showing evidence that it had been under observation in each step of its journey from the parking lot to the police laboratory. Because the chain of custody had not been established, he said, the DNA from the knife ought to be excluded — and without that, the prosecution had failed to meet its burden to prove its case. Furthermore, Brass, one of his other lawyers, added, the prosecution had not entered sufficient evidence about what had happened under the bridge to negate Momeni's claim of self-defense. "In this case, the video shows a great deal," he said, "but fails to show how it was that the attack took place, and Mr. Lee's fatal wounds resulted."

"There's more than enough to give this case to a jury," countered Talai. "We don't now stop talking about common sense, when a man dies yards away from this knife with red stuff on it, and their client's DNA is on the handle whom video shows was at the scene and fled the scene." As for the self-defense claim, he said he looked forward to cross-examining Momeni to talk about it.

The judge denied that motion as well.

25

Sending You Love and Power!

The defense's first witness was Dr. Greg Hampikian, a recently retired professor at Boise State University. Hampikian fit the part of an absentminded professor almost too well. His long white hair fell into his face, his shirt fit poorly, and his belt was far too big for his pants. But Hampikian was a well-known DNA expert. Among the cases he had worked on was the trial of American exchange student Amanda Knox — it was his DNA analysis that helped her go free.

"How many cases have you worked on?" asked Aron, the defense lawyer for whom Nima regularly pulled out the chair.

"Hundreds," said Hampikian. "I don't know. Lots."

"How many papers have you published?"

"More than a dozen, less than a hundred. I should know that, but I don't."

Under Aron's questioning, Hampikian suggested two errors in Check's analysis of the DNA in this case. First of all, he said that while twenty years ago it might have been the case that an analyst could collect either fingerprints or DNA evidence but not both, "I haven't seen that problem lately," because techniques had improved. He also pointed out a statistical footnote in Check's analysis that the prosecution had not shown the jury. "I would be misled without that note — you've got to warn me about these numbers," he said.

Fair enough, I thought, although I thought it telling that Aron did not seek clarification about what those numbers, if included, would have indicated.

Reinstedt asked some questions about the math, which didn't seem to me to clear anything up, and then moved on to asking about Hampikian's compensation (about $12,000, plus travel and hotel costs), and if he agreed with a quote that thanks to advances in DNA technology, "most labs are able to produce profiles from most people who have touched an object," which went against what Hampikian seemed to be getting at by focusing on the footnote.

"No, I don't know that," said Hampikian.

"Would it surprise you that you wrote that statement?" asked Reinstedt.

"That's embarrassing," said Hampikian.

"It's a *New York Times* article you wrote from 2018," he said.

"Okay, I must have said it," said Hampikian. "I'm more careful now than I was being at the time, because it's a courtroom."

After the lawyers were finished, the judge read questions for Hampikian from the jury. Clearly they had been as unsure about the statistical conversation as I was, because many of them asked about it. "If it was my lab, I'd say do it again," said Hampikian in response to one of them, which was as close to clarity we were going to get.

Aranza Villegas sat nervously as she waited in the hallway for Hampikian to finish his testimony. She was even more nervous when she was on the stand. It seemed clear that she wanted nothing to do with the Momenis or this case, even if she had once been friends with Khazar.

Although the lawyers thought she might have needed a translator, because Spanish was her first language, Villegas spoke clearly and directly. She testified that she had first met Khazar in Mexico through friends at a dinner, and after she moved to San Francisco, Khazar was her first friend here. They weren't that close, she said, although they enjoyed socializing together. She met Nima right around the same time.

Villegas told Zangeneh that she had run into Nima, Khazar, and Dino at a club in San Francisco on Sunday, April 2. She was with them for some part of the night, and then went home. On the afternoon of Monday, April 3, Khazar asked her if she wanted to go to the beach.

"Did you already have plans?" asked Zangeneh.

"Yes, I had therapy," said Villegas. When she finished, she called Khazar to see where she was. Momeni gave her an address on Mission Street and said something about getting food. Villegas assumed it was a restaurant, but when her Uber pulled up in front of a tall residential building, she realized Khazar had summoned her to someone's apartment. After riding the elevator up, she met Jeremy Boivin for the first time.

Boivin and Khazar offered her drugs — LSD, MDMA, and cocaine. She didn't want any, but she did take a slice of pizza, some water, and a smoothie that Boivin made her. Boivin then offered her something he called G, saying it was like ecstasy, but only lasted forty-five minutes. She agreed to take it, as did Khazar. Then the women took a second shot and a third. (Her accounting of the GHB shots differed from Khazar's.) Something strange happened when Boivin brought the third round — "he brought three cups in one hand. I tried to grab it and he said no and moved it. He said take this one," said Villegas.

The GHB hit her hard, and Villegas started to feel sick and dizzy. As Jeremy was talking about going down to the Jacuzzi, she passed out, as did Khazar. When she woke up, Khazar was

wearing a full-body swimsuit, which she might have gotten from
Jeremy. Villegas threw up and then felt better. "I felt perfect," she
said.

"That's great. It reminds me of college," said Zangeneh.

Khazar was crying and trying to contact her family on her
phone. Villegas grabbed her phone from her and talked to Nima.
"I told him everything was okay," she said. "From my perspective,
everything *was* okay." Nevertheless, Villegas sent him their location, and Dino and Nima came over to help Khazar.

"Did you see Jeremey Boivin do anything inappropriate to
Khazar?" asked Zangeneh.

"No," said Villegas. Nima and Dino got there, took Khazar
home, and Villegas left. Nobody had mentioned Bob Lee. That
would have been the end of her involvement, except, on April 6,
Nima contacted her, saying he wanted to sue Boivin.

Talai handled the cross-examination for the prosecution.
He began by asking Villegas if she had seen the defense lawyers
before. Yes, said Villegas, while she waited in the hallway at court.
What about other times? Yes, she said. In fact, she had met them
the year before. She pointed to Zangeneh and Cohen, saying that
they had talked in a park downtown.

"Oh, you did? Tell me more about that," said Talai. Villegas
said that after the police contacted her about Lee's death, she
reached out to Khazar, who told her to talk to Nima's defense
lawyers. She did, after which she spoke to Sergeant Dittmer. "I
said the truth," said Villegas. She had told him that Khazar was
"just all about money and partying" and that Nima was being
"overprotective."

"Nothing physically inappropriate. You told Nima everything
was okay?" Talai asked.

"Yes," said Villegas.

"You did not tell Nima that Jeremy was a bad guy and did something to his sister?"

"No."

"You would have told Sargeant Dittmer if you experienced something like that?"

"Yes."

"Or if you saw Khazar having her pants pulled down?"

"She needed to change, so he was helping her do that," said Villegas.

"Helping her put her clothes on?"

"When that was happening, it was when I was the most dizzy. I remember seeing that image — Jeremy taking her bathing suit off of her."

"Helping with the clothes?"

"Yes."

"You don't recall at any point, people begging to be let go?"

"No."

"That would be a false thing to say?"

"Yes."

Talai then showed Villegas the texts that Nima had sent her on April 6, including one in which he mentioned Bob, a point the defense had left out of its questioning of Villegas. "Just write down details of what happened that day," Nima wrote to her, "times and also anything else you know/remember about bob and Jeremy. I will not talk about any of this to my sister or her husband and you don't need to protect her cause she already told me about him getting her naked and stuff." (Later, Villegas would say that when she received this text, she didn't know who Bob was — she only learned his identity after Nima's arrest.)

"This text was before he was arrested for the murder of Bob?" asked Talai.

"Yes," said Villegas.

"You did not expect a jury to see this. He wants details about Bob and Jeremy?"

"Yes."

On the next day, April 7, Nima texted her asking if she wanted to get dinner. She declined, because she had to work that evening. That was the only contact they had until April 13, when Villegas texted Nima after learning he had been arrested. Talai displayed the text for the jury:

"Nima!! I just saw the nws! I'm so sorry this is happening. I know it was no you. I will ask for a lot of energy help. I send you strength and fair [dove emoji] everything is going to be ok! Sending you love and power! I will prairie for you every day. I will send you the most powerful energies."

When Talai was finished, Zangeneh asked Villegas if she would tell the jury what the defense lawyers told her in the park when they met.

"They said I should tell the truth."

The defense called a few expert witnesses to introduce certain pieces of evidence it thought were important for the jury to see. Among them was a toxicologist who submitted a report on Lee and a computer scientist who added Momeni's cell phone data. These witnesses' testimonies were straightforward.

Dr. John Marraccini's was not. The former chief medical examiner of Palm Beach County in Florida, Marraccini had performed some four thousand autopsies over the course of his career. The defense had asked him to examine the autopsy performed for the San Francisco medical examiner's office by Dr. Ellen Moffatt, as well as other medical records and evidence in the case. The defense also proposed a hypothesis about what had happened and asked for his opinion. He was asked: "Is the evidence you reviewed consistent with the defense proffer that Mr. Lee drew the knife, and that the wounds occurred after the knife was redirected?"

"Yes," said Marraccini.

As was standard, Reinstedt asked if and how much Marraccini was being paid. "Around $8,000. It depends whether or not I get off the stand today," the physician responded.

"You want me to take a little longer?" Reinstedt joked. Marraccini didn't laugh.

Reinstedt asked him how he had reached his conclusion. Wasn't it true that the defense had told him to assume Nima had acted in self-defense?

Marraccini said, "I was not present for all of the hypotheticals that were worked out. There was a self-defense expert retained by the defense. He and the defense were working through some things, and having done that, they came to me and said, 'Hey, would this work?' And I would say, 'No that wouldn't work.'"

Reinstedt and Marraccini talked more about the level of drugs found in Lee's system after he died. The questions were meticulous and took up the rest of the afternoon. At the end of the day, Judge Gordon told Marraccini he would have to come back tomorrow. Marraccini sighed heavily and rolled his eyes.

"That was a look," said the judge. "And I have seen a lot of looks."

26

The Defense Calls Nima Momeni

Earlier in the morning of Wednesday, November 13, I ran into Zangeneh buying coffee at Social Cafe. He looked tired.

"How are you feeling?" I asked. "Is this like running a marathon?"

"It feels like running from dragons and lions while being shot at with lasers," he said, laughing at how elaborate his metaphor was. Then he turned serious.

"I'll tell you what it's really like to defend someone against a charge of murder. It's like watching a movie with an audience, and you have to convince them while it's playing to root for the villain. But then, at the end, you find out he's secretly been the hero the whole time."

We returned to listen to Marraccini finish testifying.

"Did they put you up somewhere nice at least?" Reinstedt asked him.

"I'm in a good place," he said, going on to explain that he had been on a Zoom call with self-defense expert witness and former police officer Steven Pomatto in which they talked about how the wounds on Lee's body might have been made.

"Was that while you were still workshopping ideas about the defense proffer? Or had you settled on something?" asked Reinstedt.

"The defense's theory was always self-defense. The question was geometry and mechanics," replied Marraccini.

Sensing trouble, defense attorney Mike McMullen tried to clean up Marraccini's answers. "When we are talking about things being workshopped, the proffers were the theories the government could possibly present, isn't that right?"

"Yeah, to prepare for the theoretical approach the prosecution might make," said Marraccini.

"We never wavered on two things — that Mr. Lee was the aggressor and that Mr. Momeni was the defender?"

"Yes, that's the general background of this case."

But Reinstedt, taking another turn, pushed back. Mr. McMullen just asked you about the government theories. So it wasn't just about self-defense?

"Everything was discussed," said Marraccini brusquely. "Could Mr. Momeni have come up and just stabbed the guy? Let's not beat around the bush. Sure."

"The defense calls Nima Momeni," said Zangeneh. It was now 10:45 A.M. Marraccini had just stepped down, hurrying to the airport.

Nima stood up from the defense table and strutted to the stand. He poured a drink of water, sat down, and agreed to tell the truth, the whole truth, and nothing but the truth. Momeni spelled his name for the record. The judge explained the rules to him, and then turned it over to Zangeneh.

"Public speaking is not my forte," said Momeni. "I'm going through a range of emotions right now."

Although he sometimes mixed up his words, Nima's account was easy to follow. He explained that he lived in Emeryville but had grown up in Iran, where he had taken martial arts classes in school. His father had been a wrestler and taught him to wrestle at home. When he was a teenager, he, his mother, and his sister left their home country for the Bay Area.

"Why was your father not there?" asked Zangeneh.

"We had to escape him. He was very abusive, especially to my mom and sister."

The transition was hard, said Nima. His father was a dental surgeon who invested in the petrochemical industry, so Nima was used to a higher standard of living. Not only did he have to learn a new language, but he had to adjust to being poor in a new country as well. One hobby he threw himself into was martial arts — Nima said he had taken classes in krav maga, muay thai, and kung fu. As he was explaining, his voice grew too fast to follow.

"Can you slow down a little?" the judge asked kindly, handing him a framed sign she kept on her desk that said BREATHE IN AND OUT. Nima steadied himself and continued.

"I started working when I was fifteen, doing anything I could find," he said. "I washed dishes, I worked in construction, and I worked in a flower shop. It wasn't much, but I had to pay for myself." Today, he said, he owned a consulting firm with five employees that did tech support.

Zangeneh turned to the topic of Nima's sister. "What's your relationship with her like?" he asked.

"We've been through a lot. We escaped together," he said. "We are like best friends." But in the past few years, his sister's drug abuse had worsened. Ever since COVID, the frequency and amount of her use had increased. "She's unstable," he said. "She can be gone for days." As an example, Zangeneh showed Nima a text exchange between him and his sister from February 2023, in which he asked her to "call me when ur sober," and she wrote back "go fucking die."

"maybe u can help take some weight off all of our shoulders by spending less time posting reports and updates for social media apps," Nima wrote back, "and help the people that actually deserve it for a change. Did you get my message about the battery club?"

"I hate your fucking energy," she said, and then blocked his number.

"It's been a major problem every weekend," said Momeni. He and Khazar's husband would have to get involved until they could sober her up and calm her down. "Dino is amazing, he's like a brother," said Momeni.

"The jury has some questions about their relationship?" asked Zangeneh.

"It's an open marriage," Nima replied. "It's none of my business. They are grown people who can do whatever they want."

March 31, 2023, was a Friday. Nima worked for a half day in his home office in Emeryville before driving to Sacramento for a business meeting with a friend. They returned around midnight. On the way back, they made plans with Khazar, who was having a party at her condo on the forty-first floor of the Millennium Tower and wanted to introduce Nima to a friend of hers named Lis, who was from out of town. Nima arrived at one or one thirty in the morning, after having stopped to pick up drinks. When he arrived, it was just his sister and Lis. They had some drinks and did some cocaine. Nima said he didn't do much, because "I was trying to stay in shape while talking to Lis." It was now the morning of Saturday, April 1.

An hour or two later, his sister answered the door, and Bob Lee walked in. He was coming from a party and "was energized to finally meet me," said Nima. They hit it off, talking about festivals they liked to attend. Finally, Nima had enough and went home to get some sleep.

April 3 was a Monday. It was a full workday, said Nima, and he was in the Besler Building when his sister called him. "I was pretty sure she was partying," he explained. He was concerned at first, but after he talked to her friend Aranza, he calmed down. Nima did what he often did — called Dino and made a plan to take care of Khazar. Nima drove to the Millennium Tower and picked up his brother-in-law; the two men drove in Nima's white BMW to Boivin's apartment.

They parked downstairs, and Jeremy brought Aranza and Khazar to meet them. Nima had never met Jeremy before, but he seemed "super polite," Nima said. Dino went to get Khazar's car, and Nima drove her back in his. On the way, she called their mother.

Nima parked right in front of the Millennium Tower, in the valet area. "They all know me," he said, and left his car there as he took Khazar up to her condo. Dino "was a little tired of her," said Nima, and left to get ready for a scheduled surgery the next day. After he left, Nima said Khazar told him that Bo "was being a jerk to her" and that Boivin had given her too much GHB "and was fondling her."

"It didn't make sense," he said. "I didn't know what the situation was."

"Were you upset at Bo?" asked Zangeneh.

"No. He was a nobody."

"At Bob?"

"No. He wasn't even there."

It was then that Nima called Bob around 9:45 P.M., getting his number from his sister. He said Bob vouched for Boivin, saying he "wouldn't do anything. He's not that kind of person." They talked for five or six minutes and then got off the phone.

Zangeneh showed him texts that Nima and Bob exchanged that day, too. At 9:23 P.M., Nima wrote, "Bob this is Nima, will call u in a bit"

Bob wrote back: "hahahaha / I just texted Tina and told her to give you my #"

After the call, Nima wrote: "Thank u again for talking to me, good timing 🙏👌"

Around the same time, Nima said he was texting with Boivin, who wanted to come over to Khazar's to pick up his bottle of GHB. "Why do you even have so much GHB?" Nima said he asked him. "It's for business," said Boivin, who was flirting with Khazar, chatting and holding hands with her.

Nima decided that earlier his sister had just been emotional and trying to get attention. "Everything was cool," Nima said. Yes, he had mentioned the police to Boivin, but not to threaten him, only to say it was dangerous to carry around that much GHB. Eventually, Boivin left.

At 11:17 P.M., an hour and a half after they spoke, Bob texted Nima with an invitation to a strip club. "Gold Club? 😊😊😊," he wrote. Lee arrived at Khazar's apartment an hour later.

"Were you upset at Mr. Lee?" asked Zangeneh.

"No," said Momeni.

"Was he upset at you?"

"No."

"Was there any reason for animosity?"

"Not at all."

Bob came in, grabbed a drink, and did some lines with Nima and his sister. Nima said that in the course of hanging out, he drank two beers and did one line of coke. While they were chatting, Bob's roommate from Miami, DJ Dangerous Rose, called. He introduced them. "She was asking when he was coming back," said Nima. "He said it would be tomorrow."

Just before 2:00 A.M., Khazar texted Nima and Bob from her bedroom. She told them she was going to sleep and asked them to leave. "She was evicting us," said Nima. (He thought she was going to bed, but he later realized she had asked them to leave because Boivin was coming over.)

Zangeneh played the video from the elevator surveillance camera of the two men exiting. It was one fifty-eight on the morning of Tuesday, April 4. They went down to where Nima's BMW was parked and got in, Nima opening the door for Bob, who was carrying a beer.

"When you were leaving, were you arguing?" asked Zangeneh.

"No," said Momeni.

"Before you left, did you retrieve a three-and-a-half-inch-long Joseph Joseph paring knife?"

"No," said Momeni. "Absolutely not."

Nima said they sat in the car for a while, figuring out their strategy. Last call at San Francisco bars is 2:00 A.M., which is when the Gold Club closed, too. Some other strip clubs stayed open later than that, but they didn't serve drinks. It was a dilemma, and they debated what to do as Nima drove aimlessly around.

On Main Street, he said, there was a pothole. He hit it, the car bounced, and Bob spilled his beer. Nima said he pulled over to the first spot he could find and handed Bob a towel that was under the seat. As Bob was cleaning up, he found a tank of nitrous that Khazar had left behind when he picked her up earlier in the day. She had hidden it there so that her husband wouldn't find it. Bob took some hits, said Nima. "He was being silly, chatty," said Nima, "and was making weird noises." Then Nima said that Bob said he felt like he was going to puke, so Nima let him out of the car.

Outside, Nima said Bob steadied himself and, feeling better, suggested that they go back to his room at the One Hotel, where Bob had left a bag of cocaine.

"What was your mindset?" asked Zangeneh, inexorably leading Nima to the moment of the fatal confrontation. This would be Nima's chance to fill in the gap for the jury.

"After he spilled the drink," said Momeni, "I was annoyed. I was thinking of ending the night. He wanted to convince me to stay out more, so to try to get out of it I made a bad joke. I said, 'If it was my last night in town, I would hang out with my family instead of fucking around at the strip clubs.'"

"How did he take that?" asked the lawyer.

"Not good," said the defendant. "It set him off."

Nima said that Bob blew up. "He went from zero to one hundred just like that." Nima could see the tension in Bob's face. He knew that he had offended him. He tried to explain that it was just a bad joke, but "everything I said just made it worse."

Nima said that Bob started circling around him and got in Nima's face, cussing and yelling at him. Bob's back was to the fence, and Nima's back was to the street.

"It was so fast," said Nima, "I can't remember."

Nima said that Bob pushed his chest and accused him of saying that Bob was a bad parent. Then "he reached into his jacket for something and pulled his hand out."

"Did you recognize what it was?"

"It looked like a knife."

Nima said he was afraid for his life and grabbed Lee's hand to control the knife.

"Which hand?" asked Zangeneh.

"It was my left, his right."

"What did you do next?"

"I grabbed it, his left hand —" Nima sputtered. "Sorry, his right hand, and I tried to control it. He broke away."

Nima said that after Lee pulled his hand free, Bob took a swing at him with the knife. Zangeneh asked him to stand up to demonstrate. Nima rose.

"He took a swing," said Nima, sweeping his right arm at full extension horizontally. "I said, 'What the fuck? What is this?' And then, said Nima, Bob Lee walked away. Nima said he tried to follow him, but when he saw the knife on the ground, he doubled back, grabbed it, and threw it over the fence.

Zangeneh swung his arm. "Is this the exact thing you did?"

"I don't remember it exact," said Nima. "It was so fast."

The prosecution objected, and the judge cut in. "How much memory of the moment do you have?" she asked.

"The general movement."

She said she would allow the demonstration.

Nima stood in front of Zangeneh, his lawyer demonstrating what Nima said Bob did, and Nima demonstrating what he said he did. Zangeneh swung his arm. Nima grabbed it and pushed it twice into his lawyer's chest. Nima sat back down.

Nima said that after Bob walked away, he got back in his car and drove away. Maybe he was going too fast at first, he said, but after getting on the bridge he drove at a normal speed. He said that from his car, he called Khazar.

"This is kind of important," said Zangeneh. "What did you tell her?"

"I told her Bob went crazy," said Nima.

When Nima got home, he said he looked up Jeremy and Bob online, to see if either man had a criminal record.

"With Boivin," said Zangeneh. "What did you find?"

"He's a rapist," said Nima.

The prosecution objected, and the judge told the jury to disregard what Nima had said.

Zangeneh tried again. "You said you researched Jeremy Boivin. Did you find something?"

"Yes, a criminal history involving GHB," said Momeni. "There were many counts of sexual assault. It was horrible. It made me rethink the whole thing." Nima said he found a sealed record of criminal charges against Lee as well.

After the sun rose on April 4, Dino found Khazar in bed with Boivin. "He was furious," said Nima, who heard what happened because he was on the phone with Khazar at the time. "I've never seen him so mad."

Nima said he found out that Bob was dead on the morning of Wednesday, April 5. "I was in complete shock," he said. "I'm heartbroken. He may have attacked me, but he didn't deserve that." Fearing that things were spinning out of control, Nima hired an attorney, Paula Canny, and drove his BMW to his mother's place in Mill Valley, where he stayed for the next couple of days.

Nima was at Canny's office most of the day on April 9 and again on April 10, when Sergeant Goff secretly videotaped him talking to the private investigator in the parking lot.

"Now, what you demonstrate in this video," asked Zangeneh. "Who are you demonstrating as?"

"Bob," said Nima.

Zangeneh asked a few more questions and then brought his examination to a close. Had he convinced the jury that Nima was secretly the hero the whole time? It remained to be seen.

"How do you feel?" asked Zangeneh.

"I feel awful for him and his family. I don't think anybody deserves that. I don't know why this had to happen."

"We tender the witness," said Zangeneh, and he sat down.

Talai rose immediately. "You knew in April that Mr. Lee was a prominent, and beloved, and respected man in the community?"

"Of course, I felt the same way about him," said Momeni.

"Your story is that this prominent, beloved, respected man wanted to kill you over a dumb joke?" said Talai, his voice disdainful.

"That was the situation," said Momeni.

"Over a dumb joke?" said Talai, slowly enunciating each word. One part of his strategy appeared to be to try to bait Momeni into displaying anger, which Talai did by repeatedly needling him.

"I don't know why he took off like that," said Momeni. "It doesn't make sense."

"It doesn't make sense — I agree with you."

Tala questioned Momeni for hours.

"When you were at the Millennium Tower, you said the two of you were laughing?"

"Yes."

"No bad jokes?"

"No, he was doing most of the talking."

"This was the one and only bad joke, the one under the Bay Bridge?"

"Correct," said Momeni. "He took it personal. He took it to heart."

"He did take it to heart," said Talai. Zangeneh erupted in objection, and the judge pulled both lawyers aside for a sidebar.

When he returned, Talai asked Nima to go over the events of the night again. Nima said that they were driving around aimlessly, trying to figure out where to go. So why, Talai asked, did Nima later text his sister that he didn't know what Bob "ended up doing at the bar or strip club?"

Nima seemed unsure how to answer.

"You've read all of these texts, yes?"

"It's been a while," said Momeni.

"You studied them?"

"I've looked at them."

"All the videos?"

"I'm sure you have, too."

"*You*," said Talai, pushing back against Nima's attempt to take control of the cross-examination. "You have looked at all the videos, right?"

Nima said he had.

"All the evidence?" asked Talai.

"No," said Momeni.

"You're on trial for murder and you have not reviewed all of the evidence?"

"Have you?" asked a frustrated Momeni.

"I have, and I'm not being paid $20,000," said Talai, referring to the amount that the defense had paid its expert witnesses. This produced another loud objection from Zangeneh and an intercession from Judge Gordon

After she finished, Talai asked Nima: "You were present when Dr. Marraccini testified, right? He said in response to Mr. Reinstedt, there were a variety of hypotheticals we workshopped with the defense attorneys to come up with one that matched the physical evidence." When he used the word *workshopped*, Talai used his hands to make air quotes. Momeni was offended.

"The expert was approved by you guys, there's no need for air quotes," he said sharply. Judge Gordon interceded yet again. Zangeneh asked for a sidebar. The judge denied it.

"Now, later on, Dr. Marraccini said, 'I'm going to tell a defense attorney, what you are telling me is not going to work. And then they work through it again, and I say yeah, that would work. Yeah sure.' Do you recall him saying this?"

"Not exactly that, but I heard a version of it," said Momeni.

"Were you involved in this process?"

"I already answered that," said Momeni. "No."

Talai moved on to a new topic, asking Momeni if he knew on April 5 that Bob Lee was dead. Momeni said that was right. *So he just happened to stop driving the BMW on that same day? Why did you stop driving it?*

"I have multiple cars. The car involved in a mur —" He caught himself. "— a person I had just seen had died. I am seeking counsel. There's work. Dealing with cars is not something I'm not trying to work on." He said that he left the car in a carport at his mother's apartment.

"Knowing you were on Main Street, knowing Bob Lee was dead, and that you drove him there in a white BMW, that had nothing to do with leaving your car at your mom's house?" asked Talai.

"No," said Momeni, who explained that he had left the car at his mother's because of a problem with raising and lowering one of its windows.

Later, Talai walked Momeni through the text messages that he and his sister had exchanged.

"Ten hours after the incident with Bob, your sister texts you, 'You're fucking psychotic.' You're saying that has nothing to do with her other text to Bob about Nima coming down way hard on you?"

"I have no idea," said Momeni.

"Your sister texted you that you were being fucking psychotic on the same day you killed a man?"

Zangeneh objected: The text was from the day after. Talai rephrased his question.

"Does she call you a psycho regularly?"

"You should see her in person," said Nima, drawing laughter from the gallery.

"She said, 'No bitch blow messed up your kind and makes you act lunatic.' *Kind.* Does that mean 'mind'?"

"I'm not sure."

"You're not comfortable telling us she probably means mind?" said Talai.

"I don't know what she's thinking when she's fucked up," said Momeni.

Talai read the next text, in which she said the Bob thing hit hard. Nima said he wasn't sure what she meant. But didn't he write back that Bob ended up at the bar or strip club? "Do you now have a better understanding?" said Talai.

"I don't know. I think you are trying to confuse people," said Momeni.

"I am reading them chronologically," said Talai, who turned to his counterpart on the defense, who was flipping through pages. "Are you keeping up with me, Mr. Zangeneh?"

"My whole life, I'm trying to keep up with you," said Zangeneh, sighing. Momeni looked exhausted.

The next morning, Nima sat and faced Talai again, who began by asking him again about his BMW.

"Where was it?"

"Right there in the carport," said Momeni.

"That had nothing to do with it being used in a murder?" said the prosecutor.

"No, my door was open. You had my cell phone number. Why didn't you —"

Talai cut him off. "We're a minute into this and you are asking me questions. Is that what you were doing with Bob?"

"You are changing the facts," protested Momeni.

"Bo said you were asking Bob question after question after question. You asked me a question within a minute today. Is that coincidence?" asked Talai fiercely.

"Wouldn't you?" Nima shot back.

"You want answers from me in the same way you wanted answers about what happened at Jeremy Boivin's?"

"No sir," said Nima. "I was asking basic questions. *Who is this guy? Is he safe?*"

Momeni said that Bob put his mind at ease. Aranza said the same thing — his sister had wanted the drugs. Nothing had happened sexually. Talai asked some questions about Nima's jacket. He said he didn't know where it was, although he guessed it might be at his mother's. Then Talai asked when he knew Bob was dead. April 5, said Momeni.

"Were you concerned about the police coming after you?" asked Talai.

"No. I thought maybe he had been in an altercation with some-body else," said Momeni. Talai seemed shocked by the answer.

"You thought Bob Lee died because of some other situation that had nothing to do with you?" he asked indignantly.

"Yes," said Momeni, his voice rising to a whine. "He walked away. He was fine."

"Every single article regarding Bob Lee's death said he died on Main Street. Are you surprised to hear that?" said Talai.

"I was, yes."

"You're telling us maybe he died from something other than this crazy incident involving a knife with you?"

"He walked away. He ignored me. He was on his phone."

"These articles all said he was stabbed. You thought it was possible that this guy with the knife happened to die on the same block, but someone else stabbed him with another knife?"

"There were a range of things going through my mind," said Momeni.

Watching from the gallery, I was trying just to listen and not make up my mind. But what Nima was saying seemed preposterous. Did he really expect the jury to believe that on April 5, he — the last person to see Bob Lee alive — had thought that someone else killed him? Did he really expect us to believe he knew no more about Lee's death than Elon Musk or the hosts of the *All-In* podcast did?

Talai was showing Nima more texts from April 5. In them, his sister was asking about Bob. "Where did you drop him off?" she texted. "Either I'll ask or the cops will."

"I have a question to ask," said Momeni. "Would you mind putting the full thread on the screen?"

Talai bristled. "I ask the questions," he said sternly. "You answer the questions. Maybe it's different from how you practiced it, but I'm going to ask the questions." Momeni went silent. Talai showed the next text, in which Nima wrote to Khazar, "I talked to the attorney today about your overdose and attempted rape case. You need to take some tests. LMK when you want to deal with that."

If Nima's version of events was true, Talai asked, why did he not simply tell her what had happened instead of changing the subject? "Why didn't you text her back, *Bob went crazy. He attacked me?*" he asked.

"I'm sorry my communication style does not — my attorney had advised me —" said Momeni.

"You had an attorney on April 5?"

"They had advised me to not talk about the case."

"You were already advised not to tell the truth?"

"I had already told her. There was no point in talking about it over and over," said Momeni. Talai sparred with Momeni for a while longer, with the prosecutor trying to get Nima to say more about what the siblings had said on the phone call between the two of them just after 2:30 A.M. on April 4. Nima was evasive. Finally, Talai returned to the question of whether Momeni's sister had been sexually assaulted. Unlike Reinstedt — who, when he was examining Khazar, asked questions that seemed to indicate he did not believe her about being assaulted — Talai's questions seemed to indicate that he *did* believe her. Either it was a clever strategy by the prosecution to throw Nima off balance, or something had changed their minds in the last few weeks.

"Is it fair to think that if someone thought their sister was date-raped with drugs, that someone would be very angry?" he asked.

"Yeah, I was putting together a legal case against the guy," said Momeni.

"What have you done with it? A case that went nowhere?"

"I couldn't pursue it. I had to deal with this."

"You would agree that if someone thinks their little sister was given drugs and raped, they would be very, very, very angry?"

"Depends on the situation," said Momeni.

"There are circumstances where a brother might not be? Tell me them."

"She knew what she was taking," said Momeni.

"Can I tell you — it is never a woman's fault. Are you saying it is a woman's fault?" asked Talai. Zangeneh objected. The judge sustained it. Talai moved on. It seemed as if whatever the prosecutors really thought had taken place, it was enough for them to try to show that Nima thought his sister had been sexually assaulted. Talai returned to the confrontation on the sidewalk.

"He wanted to kill you over a bad joke?" said Talai.

"He got angry and pulled out a knife. I defended myself."

"You said, 'If it was my last night in San Francisco, I would have spent it with my family, not fucking around in strip clubs.' And that made him try to kill you?"

"Yes," said Momeni.

Over and over, Talai pressed Momeni. *Tell us the joke.* I told it to you already. *What did Bob do?* He was circling and yelling. *Where did Bob pull this knife from in your story?* It's not a story. *How many times did you practice this story before coming here? How many times did you practice that demonstration?* I don't know, not many. *Did you think Bob had just been killed at random?* I don't know. *Someone else stabbed him at random?* I don't know. *At random?* I don't know. *Someone jumped out of the bushes?* Possibly. *Did you know you were on cameras?* Of course. *Why didn't you tell anyone about it after?* I don't know. *Did you think Jeremy raped your sister?* No, she invited him over. *Did you know Bob's sealed arrest was just for a DUI?* No. *Do you even know what you are talking about? Do you? Do you? Do you?*

27

In What Circumstances Will You Lie?

That afternoon, Brass called to the stand Steven Pomatto, hoping to bolster what Marraccini had already told the jury — that Momeni was acting in self-defense.

Pomatto reviewed his career as a police officer. In his twenty-three years with the San Francisco Police Department, he had worked as a boots-on-the-ground cop, as a violent crimes investigator, as an internal affairs officer, and finally as an instructor at the police academy, where he taught self-defense.

"Have you ever been an expert witness for a defense before?" asked Brass.

"No," said Pomatto. This would be his first time in the role. In April 2024, a mutual friend had introduced the two men, and Pomatto agreed to help Brass with the case. He said he looked at the evidence that Brass sent him.

"What is odd about the shape of those wounds?" asked Brass.

"If you are face-to-face with someone in a fight, those are very odd places for wounds," said Pomatto. As he went on to explain, the best possible explanation he could come up with was what Nima said had happened — Bob pulled a knife on him and he defended himself.

"Is it a reasonable interpretation that someone could land those wounds?" asked Brass, meaning whether or not Nima could have made them.

"It's possible," said Pomatto.

"Do you think it's more reasonable these wounds happened while the knife was in Mr. Lee's hands?"

"Yes."

At this point, Pomatto and Brass demonstrated. Pomatto stood in front of the jury. He took a pen out of his hip pocket. Brass grabbed Pomatto's wrist. They struggled, and the pen grazed Pomatto's hip. Then Pomatto pulled his hand free and swung it horizontally at Brass, who grabbed the arm and redirected it back to Pomatto. Brass pushed the pen across Pomatto's chest once and then another time. Then they sat down. The demonstration looked just like Nima had said the stabbing happened.

"In what circumstances will you lie?" Talai asked Pomatto on cross-examination.

"I would tell my daughter that Santa Claus exists," said Pomatto.

"In your capacity as a police officer?"

"I don't think I ever have."

Talai was clearly going somewhere. These were not standard questions. Pomatto began smiling, perhaps nervously.

"Is this funny?" snapped Talai.

"No," said Pomatto.

"You told people you were a Navy SEAL?"

"No sir."

"That never happened?"

"It's a complete misunderstanding. I can explain it to you," said Pomatto. Talai did not give him a chance, moving on to questions about the scenario that Pomatto had described.

"No reasonable scenario in which Mr. Momeni was the attacker?" asked Talai, his tone icy.

Pomatto paused for a long time. "I'm trying to think of the knife being in the hand of the deceased," he finally said. "There's a possible scenario in which he pulled the knife out and turned it in an awkward manner. But then you would have an awkward time explaining the hip." Pomatto held up his pen and twisted his wrist.

"You got paid thousands of dollars to say this?" asked Talai. (Pomatto said he was paid $9,500 for his work on the case.)

"Yes," said Pomatto.

Talai quoted what Marraccini had said, reading his words from the transcript: "Obviously you work with individuals who were creating a defense. I was not there for all of them, because he and the defense were working through some things. Having done that, they came to me and said, 'Could this work?'"

"He's referencing a Zoom call we had," said Pomatto. "We were thinking about different scenarios that might have happened, and eliminating various ones."

"Dr. Moffatt and Dr. Marraccini both said the wounds cannot tell you exactly how it happened. They wouldn't say one scenario was more reasonable than another. How is it that you are saying one is more reasonable than another?" asked Talai. Pomatto sputtered out an answer: *Anything was possible.*

The next morning, Brass returned to questioning his witness, asking him to explain why Talai had accused him of lying the previous day.

What Pomatto said was this: In his third year on the police force, he applied to work on the SFPD's specialist team, which includes units like the SWAT team and the bomb squad. When he was asked what his qualifications were, he said that he had served in the special forces when he was in the navy before joining the police department. But the SFPD said it could not verify his credentials, and he was passed over.

"I was very upset," said Pomatto. Two years later, a consultant the department hired to do some maritime training mentioned that he had worked with Pomatto in the navy, confirming his service record. Pomatto reapplied and was accepted. "I said I was in navy special operations for seven years," said Pomatto. "I was a navy explosives disposal specialist and a diver after that. There was a miscommunication about being in special warfare, which is the SEALs, and special operations, which is explosives and the divers." Pomatto chalked it up to a cultural difference — unlike many of the tight-knit members of the department, he had not grown up in San Francisco. "There's a culture I did not fit into," he said, "not being from the city." He wanted to be humble, but it hadn't worked. Nevertheless, Pomatto was never disciplined, nor was he put on the Brady List, a roster kept by the prosecutor's office of police officers it refused to call to testify because they were known to have lied.

But Talai would not accept Pomatto's answer. "Now, you've characterized this as a misunderstanding with one person," asked the prosecutor tersely. "Who is Brian Hu?"

"He was a captain."

"If he was to come into court and say you told him you were a Navy SEAL, would he be inaccurate?"

"I don't think I've ever told Brian Hu I was a Navy SEAL."

"SEAL — the world *SEAL* — he would be incorrect?"

"I don't recall ever telling him that," said Pomatto.

As his testimony drew to a close, Brass asked Pomatto for the details of his service record one last time.

"I spent nine years as a senior explosives ordnance technician. I'm very proud of what I did," said Pomatto. "I would put an EOD tech side by side with a SEAL. I worked with SEALs. I can verify my service. I can verify my class status. I can show you nine hundred individuals on my phone I worked with. I worked with SEALs during the Gulf War in 1993. I find it disrespectful to question my service. I was commended for valor in the Gulf War."

"I thought you said you liked to be humble?" asked Talai.

"Until now," said Pomatto.

The prosecution called four rebuttal witnesses. Three of them were friends of Bob Lee's, each of whom testified that they had never seen him act violently while he was on drugs. The final one was Brian Hu.

Hu entered wearing his police dress uniform, with his shoulders thrown back and his chest forward. He was currently the commanding officer of the Taraval police station — a senior member of the force. For nineteen years, he had been on the police specialist team. He had also been in the army, and was currently in the National Guard. In his life, he had been deployed four times to the wars in Afghanistan and Iraq, and "throughout my career, I worked with Navy SEALs," he added.

In 2004, Hu was an instructor on the specialist team, which was where he met Pomatto. "He was one of fifteen students," said Hu. "He introduced himself as someone with navy military experience."

"What did he tell you?" asked Talai.

"He told me he was a Navy SEAL," said Hu, who said that he followed up by asking if Pomatto had the SEAL trident, an insignia worn by its members. "He said yes, and gave me his SEAL class number. He said he had the trident."

Hu said that he quickly grew suspicious. "My job is to do physical fitness. Throughout the two-week course, Pomatto was number nine. In our department we had people who had served as Rangers and Green Berets. Those individuals score super, super high. The fact is he claimed to be a SEAL, but he was not at the level he claimed to be." Hu overheard Pomatto telling other people he had been a SEAL and so brought his concerns to a superior officer. Pomatto left the training program.

Two years later, Hu had been promoted, and remembered Pomatto asking him how it would look if he reapplied. Hu asked his superiors, who said it was okay for Pomatto to try again. That time, he went through the training course and succeeded.

"Am I missing anything?" asked Brass. "Is there a document? A piece of paper? A memo that you have given the district attorney's office? Do you have a single document that Pomatto wrote saying he was a SEAL?"

"No," said Hu.

"You know that Steven Pomatto was chosen for internal affairs?"

"I didn't," said Hu. "Our department is so large, you can't keep track of every assignment." The last time Hu saw him, Pomatto was working at the police academy.

"How many times has somebody lied about or embellished their military résumé?"

"He's the only one. He didn't just lie to me. He told a lot of people in that course."

"Your testimony is that a police officer lied to you about something serious and you created no documentation, and you have no firsthand knowledge if there was any way for anyone to find out?"

"If my sergeant wanted a memorandum, I would have written one."

"The first time you have testified about that twenty-year-old lie is today?"

"Yes."

"And you never documented it?"

"Yes."

28

It's the Knife!

As the judge read her legal instructions to the jury, it struck me that Bob Lee probably would have liked to watch the trial. It certainly would have been strange, given the subject matter, but I think he would have understood the process very easily.

"The defendant is not guilty if he acted in lawful self-defense," Judge Gordon was saying. "The defendant acted in lawful self-defense if he believed he was in danger of immediate death or great bodily harm, defended themselves, and acted proportionately."

There had been a lot of statements like that — it took her more than an hour to read through them. I was struck by their form — if/then statements. If something, then something. If something else, then something else. This is the basic logic that computers use, too, the logic that Bob was so good at using. This trial — the judge, the witnesses, the jury, the evidence, all of it — was like a big computer. The prosecution was trying to make its program run successfully and return a guilty outcome; the defense was hoping to introduce enough errors to make it fail. Now we were waiting to see what the output would be.

Reinstedt gave the closing arguments. He looked weary but determined to push through to the end. With his head bowed down and his hands collapsed in front of him, he listened to the recording of Lee's 911 call one last time.

"Help," we heard Bob say. "Help. Help. He stabbed me. Help me, please!"

"One person called 911, pleading for help, saying someone stabbed me," Reinstedt said. "Not that there was a struggle. Not in passive voice. *Somebody stabbed me.* Telling us with his last words what happened that night, and begging for help over and over. The other person did not call 911. He did not contact the police. He did not —"

The defense objected. There was a sidebar conversation, and then Reinstedt continued what he had been saying.

"— A year and a half later, after he had an opportunity to review all of the evidence arrayed against him, he told you a carefully crafted story to work around that evidence. But one person was stabbed on the night of April 4. Not one time, through a lucky redirection, and not twice, with some struggle for the knife. Three separate times. Deep, clean wounds. Clear punctures.

"One person was a passenger. He took him there, knowing that it was about as isolated as it gets in a city like San Francisco. It had easy access to the freeway for him to flee back to the East Bay.

"One person had no conceivable reason to carry a knife. Not one. No reason why he would have that. No reason beyond this fabulous bad joke to have any animosity.

"The other person had every reason and opportunity. He knew where his sister kept her knives. He learned his little sister had been given date-rape drugs and sexually assaulted. If that's not a motive, I don't know what is.

"One person received text messages telling him he was a classy man and thanking him for handling it with class. The other person received texts calling him fucking psychotic. A lunatic. An animal. His own sister telling him, 'You scare me.'

"One person left DNA only on the blade of the knife, from the blood that streaked it when he was stabbed. The other person left his DNA on the handle.

"One person is dead.

"The other person sits in this courtroom."

The prosecution had charged Momeni with murder in the first degree. To find him guilty of murder, the jury would have to find beyond a reasonable doubt that Momeni had killed Lee with malice aforethought without lawful excuse or justification. To find him guilty of the first degree, it would also have to find beyond a reasonable doubt that the malice was willful, deliberate, and premeditated.

It had been a long trial, Reinstedt said, but in the end, it was a simple story. Nima Momeni was super protective of his sister. In the morning, Bob came over to her apartment with Jeremy Boivin. They partied and then separated. That afternoon, they got back together at Boivin's apartment, where Bo Mohazzabi joined them. Reinstedt showed video of the men in the elevator, joking around with each other. "Bob and Bo are goofing around. They are friends who haven't seen each other for quite some time."

Krista was sobbing, and pulled her children close to her. Silently, several rows behind her, District Attorney Brooke Jenkins was sitting, wearing her formal green uniform. It was the first time she had been here during the whole trial.

Whatever actually happened to her, Khazar told her brother that she had been sexually assaulted. "We know from her testimony that she told him in no uncertain terms that she had been sexually assaulted. He was upset — understandably. The defendant noted, when he spoke to Mr. Talai, that his sister's trauma was the most concerning thing for him at that moment. That's one of the few things he said that was true."

Nima went into a flurry of activity. He called and texted his mother, Aranza Villegas, Jeremy Boivin, and Bob Lee. When Bo overheard that call, it bothered him. "He told Bob this person is crazy," said Reinstedt.

Reinstedt finally added a piece to the picture that had been bothering me the whole time. If Nima was going to kill anyone, why didn't he kill Boivin? "Bob introduced Jeremy to her. He was the catalyst. And then he vouched for Jeremy. That made Nima think that maybe Bob could have been involved."

Nima knew where his sister kept her knives, said Reinstedt, repeating himself. He would often cook for her, after all. It was a pretty clear inference where the knife had come from. And if Momeni had in fact taken it from her kitchen, that would be evidence of premeditation.

Reinstedt played the video recording of Lee collapsing in front of the Portside building. As we watched Bob fall to the ground, Krista and the children left the courtroom in tears. Nima impassively watched the next video, of the police responding to Bob on the ground. It was impossible to know what the defendant was feeling.

Reinstedt walked the jury through the police investigation, how they roped off the scene and found the knife. How they recovered the video evidence. He talked about what the medical examiner had found — three stab wounds and no evidence of a struggle. He talked about the texts that Khazar sent her brother: "No bitch blow [messes] up your [mind] and makes you act lunatic." "The Bob thing hit hard." "Nima you're fucking psychotic at times." "You scare me." "You're an animal 24/7." And he talked about the DNA — Nima's was on the handle and Bob's was on the blade.

"The defense's own expert said: 'Well, I mean everything was discussed. Let's not beat around the bush. Did Mr. Momeni come up and stab the guy? Sure.' Their own expert said the wounds were consistent," said Reinstedt. Nima had fled the scene, lied to his sister about what happened, and tried to hide the evidence, ditching the car at his mother's and later attempting to sell it. Then there was the video of Nima in the parking lot, making three slashing motions. "In that video, he is reenacting what happened," said Reinstedt, dismissing the defense's claims. "One, two, three stabs. Not so coincidentally, the same number of wounds that Bob suffered."

It looked like Nima was as guilty as could be. What defense could he possibly have? "So he has to hire experts," said Reinstedt. "And Dr. Marraccini gave up the goods. They workshopped ideas to come with something that could possibly match up to the wounds and the other evidence. They are insulting your intelligence, because Dr. Marraccini told you how the sausage is made. He explained that this defense was made up. He did not have a defense, but a series of defenses workshopped to match the evidence. Even the defendant admitted the demonstration was rehearsed."

Reinstedt reviewed the rest of the evidence before summing up his points.

"The DNA is not easily controvertible," he said. "Only one person wielded the knife. It was Mr. Momeni. All of the evidence makes this clear. There is only one reasonable conclusion about what happened that night. I'm not going to pretend like Pomatto or Marraccini that I can tell you the blow-by-blow of how it happened. But all of the evidence, together, paints a very clear picture, one that is pretty simple. This defendant brought a knife under the Bay Bridge, brought Bob under the Bay Bridge, and stabbed him there. So we are going to ask you to find Mr. Momeni guilty of murder."

The next day was Zangeneh's turn. Krista was back in the gallery, watching. Jenkins was gone. For a while he spoke about Pomatto, saying that his testimony showed how important this case was for the government. They had hung one of their own out to dry, he said. "Every case that Sergeant Pomatto testified, every case he touched, there will be defense attorneys running to this court-house trying to reopen them. Because the prosecution has with-held information. People convicted of assault, rape, pedophilia — "

Talai objected and was overruled.

"That's how much this case matters to them. The DA was here yesterday —"

Another objection. Again, overruled.

"It's so important for them that they were willing to out a dedicated, twenty-year police officer. I don't know if this police department sweeps liars under the rug when it hurts them, but boy do they bring them out when it helps them," said Zangeneh, moving on to his main point.

"The government's whole case rests on motive. Motive is everything, even though it's not necessary to prove motive. Because if my client doesn't have a motive, it doesn't add up," he said. McMullen was working the slide deck, cuing up videos and images as Zangeneh was talking. But there seemed to be some confusion between the two men, and they paused to work it out before Zangeneh continued.

He continued. Why would Nima have a motive to kill Bob? Aranza said Jeremy was the only person there. And why would Nima have taken the knife from his sister's kitchen drawer? By the way, he added, why had the prosecution never produced the knife itself? All they had ever done was shown pictures of it. The jury wouldn't be allowed to see it, to touch, to examine it for themselves.

The judge cut in, saying that in this jurisdiction, no jurors were ever allowed to touch knives or other dangerous objects, even if they had been entered into evidence.

Zangeneh thanked her for the clarification, then turned to other questions. Why had Boivin never been called? "Boivin was unequivocally the centerpiece of motive," he said. "Jeremy Boivin did not get called. I will tell you this. Jeremy Boivin has another open case against him. Jeremy Boivin has a lawyer. And I will tell you, defense attorneys cannot offer immunity."

The prosecution objected, and the judge sustained it. Zangeneh began to talk about Bo Mohazzabi. As he did, he pulled a small plastic baggie out of his pocket. The judge saw it and was horrified. "What is that, Mr. Zangeneh?" she asked. He whipped around and put up his hands.

"It's just sugar, Your Honor. Just sugar," he said and poured it into his coffee. (It came from the Cuban coffee shop.) He took a sip and said that Mohazzabi was unreliable. "You remember he said he didn't know the bowl was cocaine? When I said were you intoxicated, he said define intoxicated. I said you're a DJ? He said what do you mean by DJ? It's the first two letters on his Instagram! He didn't want to budge," said the defense lawyer.

"So where does this take us? Jeremy Boivin, the guy accused of giving her GHB, of sexually assaulting her, who might be the target of a vendetta, goes to her place. Nima is there. Nothing bad happens. He's not beat up or bruised. They were flirting — that's obvious. Dino finds them in their marital bed the next day. She's still on drugs, messed up, she says she's getting better, but even Bo said that Khazar had a reputation for being bipolar, exaggerated, a princess. She is definitely hot and cold, but most people would not be friendly to him if he touched her against her will. But she was. This motive that these guys have made up is

suffocating. It is sinking faster than a sinking ship. It's not there."
Zangeneh pointed to the text messages in which Bob was asking
Nima about going to the Gold Club.

"Do you see the shift that's going on here? That motive is sinking. Now. Does Nima get pissed off again? Of course. They had
a confrontation on Main Street. Nima gets attacked. He calls his
sister after. She texted JB that my brother called me, yelled at me,
and doesn't want me to be friends with Bob. Nima goes home
and Googles Jeremy Boivin. What does he find? Sexual assault
charges that include drugging someone with GHB. Maybe this
slick guy did want to rape my sister? What do I know about Bob?
He has a sealed case. If I haven't convinced you, then I haven't,
but let's get real. There's no motive here. There's no motive.
To think this beat-up old knife was used as a murder weapon
because Jeremy had touched his sister's ass? That's a motivation
for murder? Think of how crazy that sounds. Imagine you hear
this on a news show. Unless this guy is a serial killer, imagine how
crazy it sounds. To kill the friend of someone who touched his
sister's butt? That's crazy, but that's what they are saying."

Zangeneh reviewed the rest of the evidence from the point
of view of the defense. Nothing the prosecution had said made
sense, he said. If Nima wanted to kill Bob, why would he drive
him to Main Street of all places? *Main Street?* What could be less
out-of-the way than that? (In the end, Zangeneh was good, but
he wasn't from here: San Francisco's Main Street was, in fact, one
of the more out-of-the-way streets in the city.)

From his suit pocket, he produced a piece of cardboard cut to
look like a knife. "We bought the same exact knife and we traced
it and cut it," he explained. "I'd implore you to make a mock cardboard knife, too. When you hold this, your hand is not just on
the handle, it will be on the blade. The blade and the handle.

One would expect your DNA would be both on the blade and the handle. But it's not. And you have to ask yourself, 'In a kitchen drawer full of knives, does this look like the murder weapon? This is a paper clip. It's not much bigger than a paper clip. Maybe two paper clips.' Things have to add up. The weapon doesn't make sense."

As he finished talking, Zangeneh continued to hold the mock cardboard knife in his hand. He reviewed the video Goff had taken, the texts, the other witnesses, and so on. Then it was time to finish. "I'm almost done," he said as McMullen clicked ahead in the presentation.

"That isn't right," said Zangeneh, turning to look at what was on the screen. It was a dimly lit still from a video of Bo and Bob standing outside the Battery Club. "Mike, can you — wait, hold on." Zangeneh peered more closely at the image. "Well, what is this? This is a video outside of the Battery Club at ten at night. This is surveillance video the government has had since early April of 2023.

"Play it," he said to McMullen as he narrated it. Bo pulled out a baggie — maybe the green one that we had seen him holding in the elevator on the way down from Boivin's. "Here's Bo about to snort it," said Zangeneh. "And then he gives the bag to Bob. Bob puts something into the bag, then takes it to his nose, there, and then evens it out with the other. Did you see that? Can we go back?"

McMullen rewound slightly. Bob was holding something about the size of a pen in his hand, using it to bring the coke up to his nose to snort. Zangeneh thrust his hand, which was still holding the mock cardboard knife, toward the screen. Every muscle in his body was tensed, and his limbs were fully extended, as if he were a ballet dancer performing a difficult routine or Michael Jordan flying through the air to dunk a basketball.

"That's the knife!" shouted Zangeneh.

"Holy hell, it is the knife," said the juror wearing the black HYPOCRITES T-shirt.

Krista laughed loudly. As she did, Zangeneh pirouetted and shouted at her: "Miss Lee, this isn't funny!" Talai sprang to his feet and shouted, "I don't think counsel should be speaking to her during this!"

"I don't think she should be laughing," Zangeneh shouted back.

The judge shouted at both of them to control themselves.

"That's the knife," said Zangeneh, once he had composed himself again. "That's the knife in Bob's hand outside The Battery at 10:00 P.M. It's been there the entire time."

The jury had never seen this video before. Certainly you couldn't introduce new evidence in closing arguments? But that wasn't what Zangeneh was doing. In fact, this was one of the surveillance videos that had been introduced by stipulation at the very beginning of the trial. It had been in evidence the whole time. It was just that nobody had yet brought it up.

"They are going to say I am making up a crazy story. I just want you to remember what I said," said Zangeneh.

Zangeneh was right about that. On a break from the trial, Krista summoned the microphones to say that Zangeneh had made up a crazy story. "Bob never did coke off a knife," she said. "He always did it off a collar stay" — those disposable plastic inserts that men sometimes use in dress shirts. Krista was clearly frustrated that she wouldn't be able to make that claim to the jury.

By law, the prosecution would have one more chance to speak. This time it was Talai's turn.

"Mr. Zangeneh in his closing took an hour and a half to say 'my client,'" he began. "He said it one time during the first hour and a half. He doesn't want to speak about his client or his testimony. He talked about a Green Beret. He talked about me. He's trying to distract you, throw garbage against the wall and hope some of it sticks. His client is on trial for murder and he doesn't want to talk about him.

"He wants you to think we're hiding the ball, and he's lying to you. Anyone could bring in evidence. That's a fact. And you know it. He's trying to distract you with things that are not true," he said.

"Even if you have eighteen months and all the money and the workshopping, the truth will come out. What they have done here is not just kill Bob. I want to be clear about what has happened over the last couple months. The defendant says Bob was the aggressor. Bob was the bad guy. Bob had the knife. He didn't just kill this man, he is now trying to kill a legacy of a man who his friends said while he was under the influence was a sweet, gentle, loving man who tried to defuse conflicts. He is not here to defend himself — because the defendant killed him. There is no evidence that Bob was angry, upset, or annoyed, other than the man whose DNA is on the handle and admitted he lies, other than a still put up by the defense who lied to you about the knife. I told you at the beginning you were sitting in here with a murderer. You now know that. You have been walking in here four days a week and coming in at nine thirty and sitting here with a murderer. Nima Momeni is a murderer. If that makes you uncomfortable, it should. What should be uncomfortable is being stabbed and left to die. Being the only person who called 911 and begged for help. That is uncomfortable. And then having this father, this man's legacy, attempted to be killed. I also said we would ask you to convict the defendant, but not based on a word out of my mouth. Because of the evidence, the testimony, the witnesses, the science, and your common sense. Bob Lee will always be a man who died at forty-three, senselessly, far too young. But he does not need to be a man who died without justice. Help is what he begged for. He was dying and crying for help while the defendant drove away. He was dying while his defendant wanted to go on with his life. As the judge said, you have the last word. Help. Help Bob by following the law and using your common sense. Do not let him get away with murder."

The jury began its deliberations.

29

We'll Still Be Here

Across the street from the Hall of Justice is the Question Mark Bar. The day that the judge gave the case to the jury, I was sitting there eating a Caesar salad in the back. Its owner, Jeremy Paz, had told me that he was trying to broaden its reputation as a hangout for cops and prosecutors. I wasn't sure having his German shepherd live there and decorating the place with cop paraphernalia was quite doing the trick, but there was no question that Paz was well connected. Not only was he friends with Tony Brass, but he had also been friends with Bob Lee. They met, he explained, when Paz was working the door at a nightclub. Bob was a good guy, he said, always friendly and happy to talk. He dressed like a suburban dad, but he was a fun person to be around.

Small town, I thought.

"It took me months to realize how rich he was," said Paz.

At the table next to me, a well-dressed Black woman wearing a cowboy hat was drinking Champagne. The waitress came by, and she loudly asked her to put on something by the singer Sade.

"I don't think I'm allowed to change the music," she said.

Paz overheard and cut in: "You're allowed to change the music for her."

And so, as "The Sweetest Taboo" was playing, I asked her what her name was. She introduced herself as Salahaquekyah Chandler. I felt like I had met her before, somehow, and asked what she was celebrating.

"My son was killed in a quadruple homicide ten years ago," she said. "It took ten years, but they've finally convicted the killer. I've been to every hearing for the last ten years."

It was then that I recognized her.

Ten years ago, Chandler's son and three other young Black men had been sitting in a stolen Honda double-parked on the street in the Western Addition when eighteen shots hit the car. Two guns were found in the car, and police said the crime was part of a gang feud. But Chandler had always maintained that her son was in the wrong place at the wrong time. According to her, he had just gotten a paycheck from his job at a restaurant and asked his friends to give him a ride to cash it.

I had just started as a journalist when the shooting happened, and along with a large group of reporters, I went to a commemoration for the four men at a community center. I remembered some ministers speaking. The police chief vowed to make an arrest. London Breed, then a supervisor, eventually to become mayor, was there, too. Addressing the press, one of the mothers confronted us for not caring about Black San Franciscans. "At the end of this night, you're going to go home," she said, "and we'll still be here and we'll never see you again."

I remember that at the march that followed, another one of the mothers was wearing a Batman costume to honor her son, and her grief was so overwhelming that she was keening, a sound that I had never heard before and have never heard since. There was a lawyer running after her, trying to press his card into her hand, saying he would sue someone for her, but she didn't even notice him, so loud were her cries.

I also remembered that I never went back.

And here, ten years later, was Chandler. She had, of course, been here the whole time. There were no reporters covering the trial of her son's alleged killer. There were certainly no books being written about it. "When people hear the word *gang*," she said, "they stop paying attention."

I didn't know what to say to her, so I asked her what she wanted people to know. Especially white people like me.

"I want people to know that there is no democracy in this country for Black women — or for our children. And it's killing us," she said. Then the waitress came with another bottle of Champagne for her — on the house, she said, just like the last one.

30

Guilty

Days passed as we waited. The deliberations continued without a sign of progress. Outside the courthouse, a strange man held up a hand-lettered sign reading JUSTICE FOR BOB LEE. I went to talk to him along with another reporter covering the case, but when we reached him, he began spouting conspiracy theories, accused my colleague of secretly working for the defense, and made fun of my name. So I avoided him after that.

At 1:55 P.M. on Thursday, the jury left for its afternoon break.

Cohen had been called out of town for another trial. Brass was looking restless, and as Aron idly looked for Chinese restaurants, Zangeneh showed off his watch and told us a story about being mugged in Puerto Rico years ago. He had been carjacked, and after he got free, some cartel members he knew found the man who did it. They showed him to Zangeneh and asked what he wanted them to do.

"I told them to give him a job," he said. "He's doing good. We're still Facebook friends, actually."

From what we could see, it seemed that the jurors were frustrated. As they took a break, most of them clustered in the back of the hallway. But Juror Number One — the one with the shirt reading HYPOCRITES — sat on a bench by himself, far away from them, holding his head in his hands. His face was red. The jury was due back at two ten. As that time approached, Brass joined Zangeneh and Aron inside the locked courtroom. He threw up his hands as he entered. "I don't know what's going on," he said. "I was called in." Two ten, the time they were supposed to go back to deliberations, came and went. The two men were still outside; the rest stayed in the hallway. Juror One looked like he was crying — or praying. The minutes passed — two fifteen, two twenty, two twenty-five. My old yoga studio sent me a spam email with the subject line "REMEMBER TO BREATHE." Two thirty. Two forty. Juror Seven took selfies in front of the courtroom. Two forty-five.

At two forty-eight, the jury was called back to their room, a few minutes passed, and then the prosecutors and the defense left the courtroom. "We're staying close," said Zangeneh. My fellow reporters and other court-watchers resumed waiting, our vigil interrupted only briefly by the pro-Palestinian protestors who left their own trial, chanting.

Late in the afternoon, the jurors went home. The judge ordered them to come back to try to break their deadlock on Monday afternoon.

The verdict was delivered on Tuesday morning.

Nima Momeni was found guilty of murder in the second degree.

As Nima was being led away, the Lee family promised they would be filing a civil suit and his lawyers vowed an appeal.

"We're just thankful that Bob's kids will never have to walk the streets with his killer," said Oliver.

In February, Jeremy Boivin appeared on an episode of NBC's *Dateline* about the case, making his first public comments since the verdict. He claimed that Khazar and he had a physical relationship following Lee's death and that although he had touched

Khazar casually on her buttocks during the party at his apartment, not only were Khazar's allegations against him "baseless and really unfounded" but also that after her testimony she called him to apologize. For her part, Khazar Momeni maintained her public silence.

31

Last Night in San Francisco

On May 5, 2023, Krista hosted a memorial service for Bob Lee on the top floor of the Ferry Building at the San Francisco waterfront, not far from where he was killed. More than five hundred people showed up. Matthew O'Connor, Bob's friend from his days at Square, told me that he was struck by how many different kinds of people attended. Entrepreneurs. People Bob knew only from hanging with them at Burning Man. Party friends. "I would be standing next to someone talking about rubbing crystals together and then the next person over there would be this super nerd who could only talk about obscure databases."

As the night wore on, Krista found herself in the bathroom with Lee's girlfriends and exes. They were trading stories about him, loving stories, the kinds that made them laugh and cry as they held on to the memory of the man they all had loved. One of them looked Krista in the eyes and smiled.

"You realize it was always you, right?"

"What?" said Krista.

"He loved you the most."

Many parties were held in Lee's commemoration. He would have liked that. He was celebrated in San Francisco, at Burning Man, and in St. Louis. Each of these gatherings gave people who knew him a chance to share memories and impressions and to talk about the moment they each found out he had been taken away from them. Everyone was there — except Jack Dorsey, who never reached out to Bob's family at all. Harper Reed tried to text him after Bob died, but it turned out that Jack had changed his number, and so Harper ended up randomly texting with a stranger about Bob.

When Kevin Bourrillion, who'd earned an industry award with Bob for creating the Guice code at Google, learned that Lee was dead, it felt surreal. "If you told me this was going to happen to somebody I knew, Bob would have been the last person on my list," he said. He woke up one morning and looked at his computer. A friend forwarded him a link and asked, "Did you see this?" Bourrillion clicked and saw the headline. All he could do was stare. His friend had been taken away from him. Suddenly. Unexpectedly.

"It was sad to me that most of the world saw a San Francisco financial executive with a partying lifestyle. They have a very different impression of who he really was," he said. "He would be as likely to be programming at two in the morning as he would be at a bar. I know Bob had drugs in his system. I'm sure that will color some people's perceptions. But he was just as murdered either way."

Jesse Wilson, another Google programmer, felt that not only had his friend died but also that a way of life had passed by — a sense of optimism and boundlessness that had at one time suffused the industry in which they worked. Maybe it was gone. Maybe he was just getting older. Wilson wasn't sure how to feel. The world wasn't so exciting anymore. The phones that he and Lee helped build didn't feel quite like tools for exploring strange new worlds like *Star Trek* had promised. He knew what people used them for — wasting their lives playing Candy Crush, scrolling on Instagram, and spreading rumors and lies about his friend's death. And the company they worked for seemed very different from what it once had been.

"We went from something artistic, driven by creativity, to something that is more industrial," said Wilson. "Like if you are Google, and it's 2004, the only reason you exist is that a few very smart people got together in the right place. If you are Google in 2023, you exist to put ten million into the machine and make twenty million come out."

"When he bought his house in Mill Valley, it was the last time I saw him," O'Connor said. "I went to go see it. He had this little waterfall behind the house, and we went up there. He wanted to change. He wanted to settle and to be close to his family. He wanted to change, to do less drugs. He wanted to turn over a new leaf."

Occasionally, Lee would message O'Connor to tell him that he hadn't done any drugs recently. *My mind is so clear*, he would say. *I feel so productive.*

O'Connor shook his head. He wished that Lee had the chance to make the change he was talking about — to really make it. Lee was an addict, there was no other way for O'Connor to say it. "But he was functional. He had a handle on it."

One summer day, I was standing about ten miles east of St. Louis, across the Mississippi River in Illinois, on top of an enormous grass-covered earthen mound, the silent, eerie remnant of what was once a great city called Cahokia. Before the European invasion, this was the capital of a Mississippian society that stretched from the Great Lakes to the great river's basin.

In the distance, I could see the tops of the towers of downtown St. Louis, the markers of the technological civilization that the descendants of those Europeans — and many others — have built.

I can almost see where Lee grew up, but not quite. I was on a road trip, and I had always wanted to see the ruins. I couldn't tell you why.

At the height of its population, forty thousand people lived here. That may sound small, but in fact, it wasn't until 1780 that another city on the North American continent would have more inhabitants. Its people built enormous pyramids out of the soil, which are the most visible remnants today of their existence. But the world they built has disappeared. The name we use for this place was not even the city's name — Cahokia is the designation given by French explorers in the 1600s.

The people who lived here worshipped gods, ones they saw in the stars. They traded copper, shells, and tools. They farmed. They played sports. They fought battles and signed peace treaties. They raised their families. They worked and they died, here at the center of the world. The city "offered much to its inhabitants and neighbors," wrote one archaeologist in a book I read about it. "Peace, religion, food, friends, allies, order, and security."

Once, this was the greatest city in North America. Now it was just grass, dirt, and a few hills. There weren't even ten cars in the parking lot when I was there. It felt like a graveyard. It felt like nowhere.

Bob Lee and Nima Momeni lived in what, for a brief moment, may have been the most important city in the world. I lived there, too. They each had a part — one larger and one smaller — in the most important story of our lives, a revolution that rivals the domestication of wheat or the invention of the steam engine. One was rich; the other struggled to succeed. One was lauded; the other ignored.

And then one night, one of them stabbed the other.

So much about it had been misreported, mischaracterized,

misunderstood: Lee's death was no statement on public safety in the city. It was no indictment of liberalism and urban governance. It had nothing to do with homeless people or mental illness. It was not a story about some secret sex cult. It was not an honor killing, nor did it have to do with some ancient religion. It was not an indictment of our godlessness. It was not some referendum on urban decay.

The jury found that Lee's murder was a brutal crime committed by an angry man who had, he told the court, been abused by someone else. So had his sister. One short moment, three swings of the knife. That was all it was. And although it is possible to construct explanations from the outside in, only two men really knew what happened, and one of them was dead.

Nima Momeni is now in prison. There will be appeals and civil lawsuits. That's it. We're done. Another story will replace theirs. Several already have. That *Law & Order* episode has already been forgotten. Elon Musk has tweeted about countless things between then and now. Maybe the San Francisco tour guides will work Bob and Nima into their patter, alongside all the other criminals, victims, magnates, and outcasts who make up the grimy history of this port town.

Someday, San Francisco, a city whose inhabitants are given to considering it the center of the world, is going to disappear, too. There will be nothing but graveyards and hills. Maybe some trace of our culture will be detectable by the archaeologists of the future. They'll come to see how power, money, and prestige flowed into the city. They'll ponder over the religious rites at Burning Man. They'll archive our music and dissect our newspapers. They'll think, *How could these people act like this was going to last forever?*

Even our buildings will crumble. They'll fall into the ocean or onto the ground. We can't hold out against the earthquakes

forever. Maybe a few massive structures will survive in some form.
Could the Millennium Tower ironically be one of them? The Bay
Bridge? Maybe someday, many years from now, somebody will
climb up to the top of a ruin and watch the sun rise over the hills
and think about the people who once lived here and try to come
up with a story about it all.

Many people loved Bob Lee. Only a few knew him well.

"There might be a movie about him," said Krista. The direc-
tor Gus Van Sant was supposed to fly up to meet with her soon.
"I doubt that I'll ever watch it. When I see myself in the news,
they get things wrong, and I feel like I should call them and tell
them. But I get over it quickly. Because that news article was just
something somebody read over their morning coffee. They don't
remember the details. The public is always going to make up their
own narrative."